into the
heart
U 2

THUNDER'S MOUTH PRESS

U2: INTO THE HEART – THE STORIES BEHIND EVERY SONG

Text copyright © 1997, 2001 and 2005 by Niall Stokes
Book design copyright © 1997, 2001 and 2005 by Carlton
Books Limited

Published by Thunder's Mouth Press
An Imprint of Avalon Publishing Group Incorporated
245 West 17th St., 11th Floor
New York, NY 10011-5300

Published in Great Britain by Carlton Books Limited,
20 Mortimer Street, London, W1T 3JW

Library of Congress Cataloging-in-Publication Data
available.

ISBN 1 56025 765 2

8 7 6 5 4 3 2 1

Research: Olaf Tyaransen
Design: Vicky Harvey, Andy Jones, Adam Wright
Editors: Kate Swainson, Ian Cranna, Penny Simpson
Picture Research: Charlotte Bush, Faye Parish
Production: Garry Lewis

Distributed by Publishers Group West
Printed in Dubai

author's acknowledgements

A lot has been written about U2, some of it very good. Researching this book, the insights to be gleaned from John Waters' 'Race of Angels - The Genesis of U2', Bill Flanagan's 'U2 At The End Of The World' and Brian Eno's 'A Year With Swollen Appendices' were particularly valuable. I owe all three writers a vote of thanks. Carter Alan's 'U2 Wide Awake In America' and Dave Bowler and Bryan Dray's 'U2: A Conspiracy of Hope' cover a lot of ground and were also very useful sources of reference and information. Where covering ground is concerned, however, it would be impossible to equal Pimm Jal de la Parra's exhaustive 'U2 Live: A Concert Documentary' - a remarkable labour of love!

Other sources of reference included: Pete Williams and Steve Turner's 'U2: Rattle And Hum'; 'U2: The Rolling Stone Files' edited by Elysa Gartner; 'The Penguin Book of Rock 'n Roll Writing', edited by Clinton Heylin; 'The Unforgettable Fire' by Eamon Dunphy; 'Faraway, So Close', by B.P. Fallon; 'The Greenpeace Book of The Nuclear Age', edited by John May; 'Cultural Icon's' by James Patza and numerous editions of *Propoganda* , the U2 fan magazine and U2 *Collectormania*. I don't think I have taken any undue liberties with any of this material but if I have - sorry! Inevitably, I plundered the *Hot Press* files and in particular the material gathered in 'The U2 File' and 'U2: Three Chords and The Truth', both of which I had the - dubious! - pleasure of editing all those years ago. (Editing is always a dubious pleasure). Finally, in terms of critical writing about U2, there is nothing out there to match Bill Graham's superb 'The Complete Guide To The Music of U2'. I have to admit that its existence made my job difficult because so much Bill wrote hit the bullseye. It meant that I had to take a very different approach. What you are about to read is the result. I hope that you enjoy it.

It's over twenty years since I first met Bono, Adam, Larry and The Edge and they have never been less than utterly courteous and genuinely helpful and supportive in all our many encounters over that frightingly long period. This book might have happened without their co-operation but I certainly wouldn't want to have read it! I would also like to offer a special thanks to Olaf Tyaransen who undertook so much of the preparatory hard labour for me. Others who helped enormously in different ways were, Ali Hewson (for loaning me her husband!), Gavin Friday, Ossie Kilkenny, Anne-Louise Kelly, Candida Bottaci, Paul McGuinness and everyone at Principle Management, Joe O'Herlihy, Steve Iredale, Flood, David Herbert, Ian Jones, Neil Storey, Guggi, Dermot Stokes, Neil McCormick, Colm Henry, Steve Lillywhite, Howie B, Saoirse (of the hair-raising coffee) and Ian Cranna. At *Hot Press*, Liam Mackey carried me over the hump and Mette Borgstrom and Chris Hackney were wonderful - thanks a million to them, to Paula Nolan, Miranda Moriarty, Maureen Buggy and all of the *Hot Press* crew. As McPhisto might say, 'I'm baaaaaack'. My commissioning editor Lorraine Dickey was a model of composure throughout what must have been a difficult ride (stay calm, Lorraine).
Revising and updating a book like this, there's always more that you'd like to add or change. But you just have to get on with it. Very special thanks are due on this occasion to Neil McCormick, Peter Murphy and Olaf Tyaransen, whose interviews with Bono, published in Hot Press, provided vital insights and quotes. (Olaf's book *The Story of O* is brilliant – get a hold of a copy.) Also, salutations to Daniel Lanois, Caroline Sprinkler, Sheila Roche, Holly Peters and Edge. To Chris Hughes and Sheila Convery at *Hot Press*. And finally to Penny Simpson at Carlton. Thanks for your patience.

And finally, the biggest thanks of all to Mairin Sheehy, Duan Stokes and Rowan Stokes without whom it wouldn't have been worth doing. I love you.

Niall Stokes

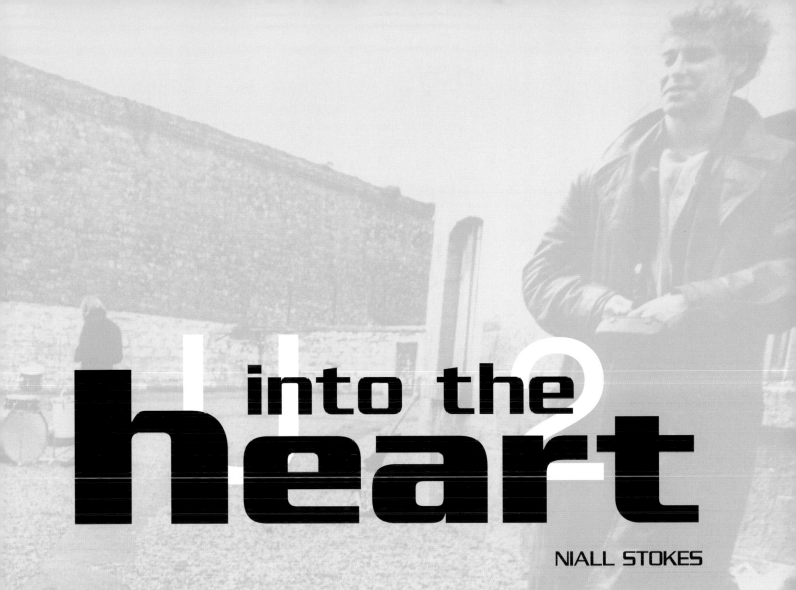

into the
U2
heart

NIALL STOKES

THUNDER'S
MOUTH
PRESS

contents

'Into the Heart' is dedicated to Bill Graham 1951-1996.

"a book is a mysterious object, I said, and once it floats around the world, anything can happen. All kinds of mischief can be caused, and there's not a damned thing you can do about it. For better or worse, it's completely out of your control."

Paul Auster,
Leviathan, 1992

introduction

Would the remaining passengers for Zoo Airlines flight U2 please board immediately...

As with books, so with songs...

Writing a book about the stories behind U2's songs, it seemed necessary to live, sleep and eat the music. It becomes a kind of obsession. You keep looking for extra clues, something you might have missed. And so you keep listening harder. Some songs begin to grow, the more you listen. Others fade. You go through phases. But some just keep on growing till you know you're never going to get them out of your head. Ever. *"Take my hand,"* you sing, *"you know I'll be there*

if you can, I'll cross the sky for your love." And people look at you. You hadn't even realised you were singing.

It's one of the standard questions nearly every cub rock reporter asks, with all solemnity, as if it's never been asked before: how do you write your songs? But it's an interesting question all the same, and one that even experienced songwriters like to hear being answered. Because every writer experiences some insecurity, some paranoia, some sense that there's a trick that they might just be missing. And usually they're right. U2 have a lot of tricks, but even they wouldn't claim to know them all.

Bono calls it songwriting by accident and it describes the process pretty well. But however the songs are written, more often than not over the past 25-plus years, the end results have been glorious.

U2 have developed in every imaginable way, but especially in their songwriting. *Boy* was a brilliant, original, energetic and ambitious debut album, which had its share of insights, but no one could claim that the lyrics were its strongest suit. Travelling, within six years, from there to the maturity of *The Joshua Tree* – an album on which Bono firmly established his credentials as one of rock's finest lyricists – was quite clearly an extraordinary achievement.

But even then, in an industry where so many artists who consider themselves to have arrived are content to rest on their laurels, U2 refused to allow themselves to stagnate. With each subsequent album, Adam, Larry, Bono and The Edge have consistently broken new ground.

Achtung Baby, released in 1991, was U2's second acknowledged masterpiece, and won a whole new audience for them; conspicuously, many of them had previously disliked the band. Without diminishing the spirituality or the desire for transcendence at the heart of the band's creative impulse, it also introduced a new phase for them aesthetically and intellectually. Broadly speaking, *The Joshua Tree* and *Rattle and Hum* had been direct, emotional and heartfelt. In contrast, *Achtung Baby* was oblique, coded and elusive, and the follow-up *Zooropa* continued in the same vein. Both were more consciously cutting-edge in their musical settings, and unashamedly technology driven.

There were reasons for this shift other than the ever-present desire to make great records. It had to do with the fact that, with *The Joshua Tree,* U2 became one of the most successful rock groups of all time. And with that success came a whole lot of baggage, in terms of the attitude of both fans and the media to the group. Suddenly U2 found that they were a target for the tabloids. *Rattle and Hum* was widely panned. And, in some quarters, their commitment in itself became a

cause of ridicule. Against that backdrop, on the surface at least, *Achtung Baby* reflected a strategy to conceal rather than reveal. It was a deliberate attempt to step out of the mainstream, to challenge audiences and to confound critics.

With *Achtung Baby,* with the *Zoo TV* tour that followed it, and with *Zooropa* itself, U2 became more playful and experimental. The group's sense of humour was discernible in their music for the first time. And the pleasure principle was also newly in evidence, in the increasing emphasis on dance rhythms, on the culture of the night, and on the erotic. Sometimes misunderstood, *Pop* continued in the same vein. But for *All That You Can't Leave Behind* and *How To Dismantle An Atomic Bomb*, the band released themselves again from the need to run everything through the hip-ometer – and made music that was no less hip at all as a result. Indeed, with the hugely impressive *How To Dismantle An Atomic Bomb*, they have brilliantly returned to their roots, renewing themselves magnificently – and with enormous commercial success – as a result.

They say that in love there are no rules. Nor should there be in rock 'n' roll. One of the great things about U2, is their attitude that nothing is sacred in the pursuit of excellence.

It's a fine theory until you attempt to put it into practice; that's where the sheer grinding

Bono takes flight.

hard work comes in. But since they first blazed a trail into our hearts towards the end of the 70s, U2 have put in more of that than almost any other band on planet Earth, and they have the songs to prove it.

And the scars.

Mick Stokes

boy

it was always going to be called *Boy*. "The album cover has been in the back of my mind for two years," Bono explained, just after its release. "There is a feel to it. Holding the cover and listening to the album is perfect."

The title was decided on long before this band began to record. It wasn't a concept album, but there was a strong linking thread running through the songs. U2 were still in their teens when they signed to Island, and *Boy* reflected it unashamedly.

"The songs are autobiographical," Bono stated. In an explosive burst of adolescent energy, they embraced the teenage themes of confusion, longing, faith, anger, loss and burgeoning love in a nakedly emotional way. At the heart of the record was the frantic search for an identity in which all of the band were themselves still immersed.

Having played most of the songs for over two years, U2 probably believed that they knew them thoroughly. It still wasn't an easy album to make. A lot of tough, disciplined work went into getting the rhythm section tight, and Bono had to confront in earnest for the first time the need to finish definitively the band's songs.

Under Steve Lillywhite's sympathetic direction, *Boy* emerged bright and shiny, all glistening treble, shimmering guitar, exuberant drumming, breathless vocals and urgent bass. It was a lyrical, romantic, spiritual odyssey, which resonated with one particularly marvellous, distinctive quality. Above all, *Boy* was an honest record.

(Island ILPS 9646)

Produced by **Steve Lillywhite.**

Recorded at **Windmill Lane Studios, Dublin.**

Released **20 October 1980.**

Iris Hewson died on 10 September, 1974, following a brain haemorrhage. It was a terrible twist of fate, coming as it did just after her own father's funeral at the Military Cemetery in Blackhorse Avenue, Dublin. Bono was 14 at the time, and the experience devastated him. Even now – over 20 years on – he admits that he finds it difficult to remember what his mother looked like. It is impossible to imagine what he might have become if she had lived.

i will follow

What we can say is that he was plunged into a period of emotional turmoil, that he began running in 1974 and that he has scarcely stopped since – and that this restlessness has been a powerful motivating force in his work. Bono remembers his adolescence as a time of psychological violence and 'I Will Follow' captures some of the drama of that era, the four walls coming down on top of the song's narrator in an image that captures well the suburban claustrophobia that was returned to, almost obsessively, throughout the first album. But there is something else going on here: a sense of terror and confusion which runs deeper than the common crises of identity from which teenagers suffer.

His friends on Cedarwood Road remember Bono as a kind of stray after his mother died. He'd turn up at Gavin Friday's house one night, and Derek Rowen's the next, just in time for tea. "He was calling around as much to be with my mother as he was to be with me, I have no doubt about that," Gavin recalls now. They fed him and minded him, but he had to return all the same, as twilight fell, to a house inhabited only by men – his father Bob, his brother Norman and himself.

In the past, Bono has talked about the song being a sketch about the unconditional love a mother has for a child, but it is clearly more than that. There is a palpable yearning in the lyrics that has much more to do with what a child feels when his mother walks – or is taken – away from him, and the suicidal urge to follow. *"A boy tries hard to be a man/His mother takes him by the hand,"* Bono sings and immediately you know that this is not the stuff of which teenage pop is normally wrought. Opening *Boy*, 'I Will Follow' was a perfectly appropriate statement of intent, signalling that this was an album about teenage confusion

and rites of passage, but also – and perhaps more crucially – that there was a restless spirit at work which could never be satisfied with conventional or clichéd answers to the important questions that provide the base metal from which great art is ultimately cast. Looking back now, with the benefit of both hindsight and experience, it's a song of which Bono clearly remains proud.

"I think it's coming from a very dark place," he says. "Pop music at its best seems to have a duality. Whenever it's one thing or the other it's flat, but if it has two opposing ideas, pulling in different directions, it achieves a different kind of power. 'I Will Follow' has both anger, *real* anger, and an enormous sense of yearning."

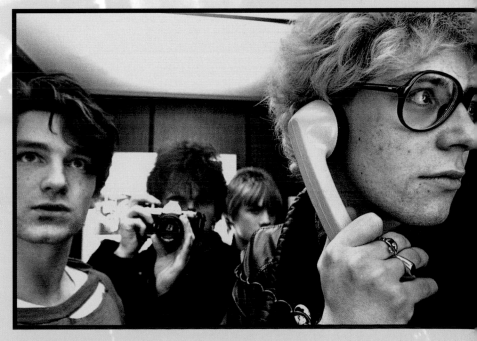

"Is that Dial-A-Pizza?" – portrait of a hungry young band.

The band's performance was suitably urgent, marking the track down as one that would inevitably be released as a single to coincide with the launch of the album. In particular, The Edge careens in on the kind of treble high that became his trademark. At the time a limited guitar player in conventional terms, he was an original stylist even then. "I knew more what I didn't want to sound like than what I wanted to sound like early on," he reflected later. "In some ways that's why my playing is so minimal. Play as few notes as you can, but find those notes that do the most work. It became a whole way of working. If I could play one

Bono: "That's me by the sea."

note for a whole song I would. 'I Will Follow' is almost that."

It is, as a result, concentrated and hugely powerful. "Most of the early rehearsals were just rows," Bono recalls. "It was just one long argument. I remember picking up Edge's guitar and playing the two-stringed chord for 'I Will Follow' to show the others the aggression I wanted. It was his riff but I wanted it to have an edge to it."

There is a hallucinogenic quality to the lyrics – *"Your eyes make a circle/I see you when I go in there,"* Bono sings in the bridge, rifling the memory bank and desperately trying to make sense out of feelings of separation and loss. 'I Will Follow', finally, is the love song it set out to be. But it is as much about a boy's confused love for his mother as it is about a mother's unconditional love for her child.

The journey had begun. U2 were going in two different directions at once.

"The subtext," Bono says, looking at the lyric sheet, "is everything. Isn't it?" He can't resist a wry chuckle, looking at the rough type from the inner sleeve of *Boy*. "Those lyrics are wrong," he says looking at the text of one track. "That's wrong," he repeats, scrawling the correct lyric to another. 'Twilight', he leaves untouched.

twilight

the song first surfaced on the B-side of their second single 'Another Day', released through CBS in Ireland. Legend has it that it was recorded in just five minutes and suffered as a consequence. But on *Boy* it comes through strongly, a small epic that's loaded with sexual ambiguities. No one in Ireland thought of the song as dealing with homosexuality, or the confusion of sexual identity that so many adolescents feel to one degree or another. And yet it's there in the lyrics, once you come at them from a certain angle. In Dublin parlance of the '70s, "the old man" was the commonly used term for your father. But in Britain and the USA, where gays had begun to express their identity in much more overt ways, this song seemed to have been written for them. Bono sings: *"The old man tried to walk me home, I thought he should have known."* Who he was and what he should have known is never explicitly stated.

"It was curious," Adam Clayton reflects. "But we picked up a strong network of gay fans on the strength of *Boy*. We didn't have a clue what was going on. These guys used to turn up at our gigs, dressed in leather gear, with leather gloves on and so on, and we used to think of them as rich punks."

"Then we did an interview with this guy Adam Block,"

The edge briefly contemplates a solo career.

> "'Twilight' is a song about the grey area of adolescence, that twilight zone where the boy that was confronts the man to be in the shadows. It is also about the confusion, pain and occasional exhilaration that results from that confrontation."
> – BONO

Bono continues, "who was gay, and he was saying that he'd always thought of us as a gay band. And I was like, 'wow! you must be joking!' He made the point that within the gay community, people were excited about the fact that we were the first band to deal with sex outside machismo. Rock 'n' roll was always written from the point of view of men – or at least of boys pretending to be men – but we were doing something different. And so he told me to go back and read the lyrics."

Bono is reading the lyrics again now, reciting them in short snatches. "That's amazing," he says, shaking his head in apparent disbelief. "That is about being approached by a guy. I was actually approached, but then everyone is. But it's so explicit, from the point of view of gays hearing it for the first time, I mean. Where's that verse that Adam Block quoted to me: *"I'm running in the rain/I'm caught in a late night play/It's all and everything/I'm soaking through the skin."* I never had any homosexual experiences myself but I guess people close to me had a hard time about things like that. But it is quite funny when you look at the lyrics. It's incredible."

'Twilight' is a song about the grey area of adolescence, that twilight zone where the boy that was confronts the man to be in the shadows. It is also about the confusion, pain and occasional exhilaration that results from that confrontation. And it is sufficiently ambiguous that it speaks to everyone, of whatever sexual proclivity, about the experience. No mean feat.

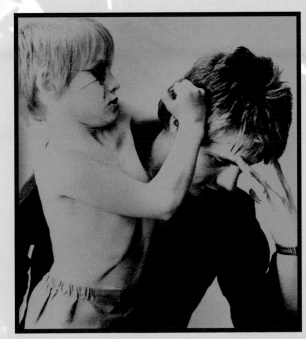

The boy can't help it: Peter Rowen bops Larry.

History records that at least a million people attended this gig: U2 at one of their legendary Dandelion Market shows in Dublin, 1978.

When U2 formed in Mount Temple Comprehensive School on the north side of Dublin, Bono had already started the relationship with Ali Stewart that would result in marriage. But the path of true love didn't always run smoothly.

an cat dubh/
into the heart

they split for a short time and Bono – as ever, restless and hungry for experience – had a short fling with another schoolmate.

"That one's about sex, definitely about sex," Gavin Friday says, without the slightest hesitation. "But I think you should ask him why 'An Cat Dubh'? Irish wasn't his thing. If that had been me, fine, because I was Fionán and that Irish thing was there in the background, but not in Bono's case. So why not just call it 'The Black Cat'? Where sex was concerned, Bono was very precocious as a teenager.

He was a lot more knowledgeable than the rest of us in Lypton Village."

"It's definitely about sex, that," Bono agrees. "I think the title is in Irish because the girl it was about was a sort of 'as Gaeilge' type of person. What happened was that Ali and myself had split up for a minute and I just ran off with somebody and felt guilty about it.

"The image is of a cat and a bird. The cat kills the bird and shakes it – you know the way they do, they play with the dead prey – and then sleeps beside it. That's where the image comes from. It's like someone has taken you, thrown you around the place and then you sleep beside them. I think for the sake of the song I switched things around, but in reality I think I was the cat. I was the one who did the dirty. That lyric should read *'and when she is done/she sleeps beside the one'*."

In fact 'An Cat Dubh' was as important for its muted, evocative instrumental passages as for its – again – sexually ambiguous text. The lyrics may have been improvised, as Bono told Neil McCormick of *Hot Press* during 1981, but the music felt as if it had been thought through. The restraint in the instrumental passage leading from 'An Cat Dubh' into 'Into the Heart' is especially impressive, a performance from The Edge that anticipated the unique genius he would bring to contemporary rock guitar-playing.

"We spent all our time on the music," Bono reflects now, "and on working out improvisations. We got hooked on guitar sounds, on bass lines, on drums. And then when we were doing that, we'd maybe seize a few minutes and I'd write the song down. Even though a lot of these songs were played live before we recorded them, I never learned the lyrics. Playing the Dandelion Market – or wherever – the lyrics would be changed. I think we can blame Iggy Pop for that. We'd read that he improvised his lyrics on the microphone and if it was good enough for Iggy, it was good enough for us. So it wasn't like I had worked out the lyrics and then had time to think about them. They were always changing."

The segue from 'An Cat Dubh' into 'Into the Heart' had more to do with the exigencies of performance than with theme. The sequence worked on stage, and therefore it made sense to do it that way on record. It remains a piece of shimmering, quiet beauty. The dynamics are beautifully controlled by producer Steve Lillywhite and the clear, ringing guitar has a haunting, ethereal quality. The lyrics of 'Into the Heart' betray the weakness that could inhabit songs that were being made up as the band went along. No doubt the intention is to mourn lost innocence and what the late Bill Graham of *Hot Press* called the destruction of the secret garden of youth – and that effect is evoked musically with great tenderness and feeling. But it wouldn't have taken much in the way of craft to hone lyrics that seem curiously self-contradictory on paper to a stage where they had a level of internal coherence. Craft would come later.

"It's really a non-lyric period, in one sense," Bono reflects now. "Nobody talked about lyrics back then. It wasn't really on the agenda. I think it was only really after *Unforgettable Fire* that we started saying – or that I started saying – hold on a second, give me a bit of space here, to think about these things, to thrash these things out."

For now, to a very large extent, it was down to where the group's collective instinct would take them. On balance they weren't doing badly.

U23 was U2's debut recording salvo. Released on CBS Ireland, it came in 7-inch and – almost unique in Ireland at that time – 12-inch formats. Jackie Hayden, then marketing manager of CBS, enlisted the assistance of Ian Wilson, the producer of the Dave Fanning Rock Show on 2FM, the pop channel attached to the State broadcaster, RTE. Listeners to Dave's show were invited to help pick the record's A-side from 'Out of Control', 'Stories for Boys' and 'Boy Girl', by voting for their favourite. They opted for the first, which went on to become one of U2's best-known anthems.

out of control

Compared to the original version, the *Boy* re-interpretation had an even greater power and clarity. In the neo-punk era "oh-oh-ohs" and "oh-e-oh-e-ohs" were commonplace and the band indulged themselves here, but it scarcely diminished the energy and sense of compulsion which marked this song as something special from the start. It had been written on Bono's 18th birthday.

"'Out of Control' is about waking up on your 18th birthday and realizing you're 18 years old and that the two most important decisions in your life have nothing to do with you – being born and dying," Bono told me in 1979, before the release of *Boy*. "The song is written from the child's point of view and it's about a vicious circle. He becomes a delinquent but the psychologist says 'It's in his childhood'. No matter what he does, it can't be because he wants to – it's always because of what went before, and

"Is this a record?" – The Edge and Bono examine their first waxing

13

boy

there's no decision in anything. Then again, that's [a] slightly spiritual [theme] – the question, what is happening if you've no freedom?"

Remembering now in tranquillity, Bono places the song in the context of his own psychological traumas at the time. He recalls flipping out in school at the age of 16, turning over chairs and tables, and not knowing himself what switch had gone on – or off – to cause the explosion. It was a feeling that recurred: he was haunted by the sense that the whole crazy business of human life, and human reproduction in particular, was out of control. The song was an attempt to come to grips in an adolescent but nonetheless urgent way with the reality of existential angst as it gnaws away at the heart's core.

Nowadays he isn't inclined to take it too seriously. "That one was translated by the Japanese," he says. "It went out with the album and the Japanese version of the opening lines translated back into English as *'Monday morning/Knitting years of gold,'* which is a hell of a lot better than *'Monday morning/Eighteen years of dawning'*" [laughs].

But for an 18-year-old those feelings were utterly real, and the sense of impending disaster which accompanied any notion that you might simply replay the same old suburban

> "'Out of Control' is about waking up on your 18th birthday and realizing you're 18 years old and that the two most important decisions in your life have nothing to do with you – being born and dying."
>
> – BONO

Ever the innovator, Larry attempts to play the drums with his elbows.

> "It was a feeling that recurred: he was haunted by the sense that the whole crazy business of human life, and human reproduction in particular, was out of control. The song was an attempt to come to grips in an adolescent but nonetheless urgent way with the reality of existential angst."

dramas enacted by your parents was impossible to shake off.

"My father had lived through the '50s Depression," Bono reflects, "and as a result he taught us not to expect too much in case we might feel let down. His attitude was: don't do anything that seems like you're aiming higher than your allotted station. All my mates were intent on going to college and on doing things. I'd always been bright in school – I never did a tap but I'd done well and the last thing I wanted was to stay stuck in any kind of rut.

"Joining the band was my emancipation from all this. At that age, it was my ticket to freedom. It was my way of attempting to change the circumstances of the world I was living in."

Again, the musical arrangement is significant. From Larry Mullen's thumping drum entry, the song powers along with the expected urgency. But where other bands of the era might have gone for overkill in a tortured guitar solo, U2 instead dissolve the focus to let Adam Clayton's quietly insistent bass line through. There's a languor to the instrumental break which suggests that U2 will refuse to go for the obvious.

"We knew what sort of material we wanted," The Edge told *Hot Press* at the time, "so if you want a particular idea, you start picking instruments and amps and effects and what have you. When you start doing that, you start to develop a sound. Then, when you have a sound, you find certain things work better on that and you get into a certain vocabulary of music. And before you know what's happening, you're on the way to a style, a sound and to musicianship."

'Out of Control' was an important stepping stone along the way.

'Stories for Boys' was one of the band's earliest songs. A highlight of their live set, it was chosen for *U23*. At the time, Bono explained it in relatively conventional terms. "All the songs point to one thing – getting people to think for themselves," he

told *Hot Press* in an interview around the time of the release of *U23*. "There's also a reaction against heavy advertising and television images and things like that. I remember seeing heroes on television – people like James Bond and so on – and thinking, 'I'm not very good looking – I'm not going to get things like that,' and being unhappy about it. We feel that we're qualified to comment on things like that because we are teenagers."

but there were other things that they might have been qualified to comment on, too. The band's manager, Paul McGuinness, was always convinced that it was a song about masturbation. Gays too identified with it, reading a homo-erotic slant into the lines: *"Sometimes when a hero takes me/Sometimes I don't let go/Oh oh oh/Stories for boys."* In fact the line about the hero had been varied between choruses in an early version of the song. *Sometimes I can't let go.* And in a cryptic note on the lyric sheet he added: "Pop stars, bionic men, soon to be featured in verse 3 yet unknown." But you couldn't blame gays for taking the song as their own, all the same.

"This was it. For the gays in our audience, this was definitely a love song to a man," Bono smiles. "I thought of 'Stories for Boys' as just simple escapism. And it's not really. We were very conscious on one level but there was a whole subconscious thing going on too. There really is a sense in which the songs write themselves."

This was particularly the case with U2. Bono has often spoken about the feeling that he is merely a conduit, the vehicle by which ideas, emotions and feelings, are delivered into the public realm. It's a perspective on his own work that relates particularly to those early years. Now, he wonders if he and the band really knew what they were saying. "I never write lyrics until the last minute because they're constantly building as we work out the song. They build subconsciously, because I found that I can write exactly what I *want* to write subconsciously, better than sitting down and trying. When the song is complete – when the idea is right – I then assemble the lyrics."

It's a very particular approach to the aesthetics of songwriting and sometimes, doubtless, it works. But at this early stage there was often a feeling that in fact the words to U2's songs were, somewhat ironically, themselves out of control.

Or maybe that was appropriate, after all.

stories for boys

boy

U2 grew up on Dublin's north side. Along the complicated shoreline of the county, a series of beaches run from Dollymount strand out to Sutton beach, on to Howth and then back into the Portmarnock inlet.

the ocean

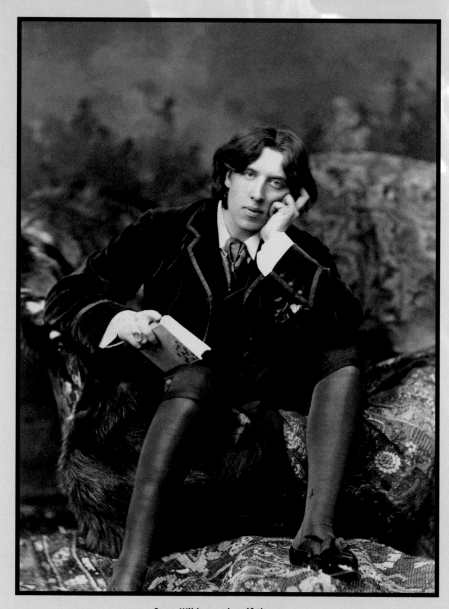

Oscar Wilde wonders if there might be any royalties in 'The Ocean'.

Out further there's Portrane, Skerries and Rush – they were small towns, their economies built around the summer holidays, weekend breaks and day-trips that people from the north of the city used to take there. These places loomed large in the collective imagination of city-dwellers. They were places of mystery and escape; for children, they provided an opportunity for the spirit to run free, the imagination to take flight, borne up by the comforting sound of the sea lapping up on the gradual shoreline.

Bono's family, on his mother's side, had bought a former train carriage, located on a farmer's land, close to the sea in Rush. All of the family would go there at weekends and revel in the lure of the sea.

It was an idyllic time that was destined to come to an abrupt end. The farmer who owned the field died and his son took over. He told the family that there was no contract entitling them to keep their holiday home on his land and that he wanted the carriage removed. When it didn't happen, he had the site levelled, destroying the carriage in the process. They took him to court and won, but Rush didn't hold the same appeal any more and they moved their holidaying to a caravan in Skerries. The Irish Sea was common to both places.

Dubliners are familiar with the sea, so there was no giant leap of the imagination required for Bono to picture himself wandering – lonely as a cloud, as it were – at its edge, the ocean splashing the soles of his shoes and washing his feet. "'The Ocean' is just a complete teenage thought," Bono told his former classmate Neil McCormick, in a *Hot Press* interview in 1981. "It is the thought of every teenager. It is the thought of everybody in a band who thinks he can change the world. There is another verse which got left out on the record, it's on the sleeve: '*When I looked around/The world couldn't be found/Just me by the sea*', which is the resignation that no matter what you do, people are going to go their own way."

The most crucial line, however, is in the first verse: "*A picture in grey, Dorian Gray/Just me by the sea/AND I FELT LIKE A STAR.*" On one level, this is just teenage narcissism and self-indulgence. Musically, it achieves an appropriately lyrical and poetic quality – but Bono's response now is one of amusement. "That takes some fucking neck," he says. "That's great. That's quite funny. On the record it doesn't sound funny, but we used to open the show with that. We used to walk out and go straight into that. In a way it was so audacious. And it's nicely ironic. It's quite smart and a great opening gambit for a show. *'I thought the world could go far/If they listened to what I said.'* So many people feel that, but so few say it. That's great."

The Dorian Gray reference is to Oscar Wilde's character of the same name. Gavin Friday remembers it as something that would have been on the Leaving Certificate syllabus at the time."I'd certainly read Oscar Wilde," Bono recalls. "I'd read Joyce but not Beckett. I'd read other Irish writers, as well as people like Baudelaire and other French things, because I thought they were arty or whatever."

There was a poet on the premises. He was searching for a voice.

> "It was an idyllic time that was destined to come to an abrupt end."

The Edge had already begun to fashion a distinctive guitar style. There was very little of the blues in his playing. You'd never hear him plucking out a 12-bar walking rhythm on the bass strings. He seldom played solos. And he didn't torture his young musician's fingers by attempting to b-e-n-d the notes. Instead he used open strings to create a drone-like effect.

a day without me

Tom Verlaine: a seminal guitar influence on The Edge.

there was a lot of treble in his playing, arpeggios and harmonics touched and left to hang. And against that cushion he'd play melody lines, often of crystalline purity. If he was already advancing along this alternative track, there's no doubt that getting hold of an echo unit confirmed his direction as a guitarist.

Bono remembers a developing interest in atmospherics within the band, referring to David Bowie's *Low* and to Joy Division among the influences that were coming on-stream at the time. From Tom Verlaine of Television, The Edge had learned that less is more, and had begun to develop an awareness of the architecture of sound: songs could be *built*. It was, as he later told John Waters, about judgement and your brain rather than your fingers. It was about ideas. Gavin Friday identifies The Jam, The Associates and The Skids as having made a huge impact on the way U2 saw themselves.

Bono claims that he acquired the Memory Man echo unit for The Edge, believing that it would take the band into another musical realm. The guitarist admits that it was Bono's idea. He remembers borrowing money from a friend and getting a really cheap unit. With it as inspiration, they wrote

> "I was fascinated by the thought: would it make any difference if you did commit suicide?"
> – BONO

17

'11 O'Clock Tick Tock' and 'A Day Without Me'. Originally intended as an enhancement, it became an integral part of The Edge's guitar sound. 'A Day Without Me' resonates with its cheap but highly effective technological magic.

It was the first track that U2 recorded with Steve Lillywhite as producer. Released as a single in advance of

The late Ian Curtis of Joy Division

Boy, it confirmed for both Lillywhite and the band that they could work together. As singles go, this was a song with a big theme – or series of themes – which were only sketchily executed. A guy Bono knew – "he was an acquaintance of a friend of mine, Sean d'Angelo" – had tried to commit suicide. "In fact I went up to the hospital with Sean to see this guy and they tried to keep Sean in! He went to find a bathroom

and he was gone for half an hour. When he came back he had this strange look in his eye. He'd been walking around the pharmacy, looking for a toilet, when they stopped him. They thought he *looked* like an inmate. They were asking: 'Where are you going?' And he was telling them that he was just visiting. And they were taking him by the arm and saying 'Everything is going to be alright. Just come this way.' It was very funny. He had a hard job trying to convince them that he was just in to see his mate."

The suicide attempt played on Bono's imagination and emerged in 'A Day Without M'", with the protagonist looking back at the world he has "left behind" from the perspective of the grave – or more likely a vantage point somewhere above the graveyard, as he watches the funeral and takes note of those who haven't shown up. "I was fascinated by the thought: would it make any difference if you did commit suicide?" Bono recalls.

Typically, that is just an undercurrent. The song also touches on the theme of insanity, and on the collapse of the self, reflecting another common teenage insecurity. But Bono also sees it in continuity from 'The Ocean'.

Most teenagers wallow in the feeling that the world has reserved a special kind of misery for them. They want to run, and to keep on running. But in the midst of all that self-pity, the feeling that they are special inspires some with a belief that, given half a chance, they can do almost anything. This was true of Bono. But it was also true of the whole band, who never had any doubt about the fact that they were going to become huge. As early as 1981, Bono was comparing U2 to The Beatles and the Stones, as if they – rather than Echo & The Bunnymen – were U2's true peers. He's inclined to view 'A Day Without Me' against that kind of backdrop.

"'*I started a landslide in my ego*'," he quotes. "That's a great opening line. A lot of this stuff is awful but that's really ballsy. I think this is about our own megalomania, actually [*laughs*]. There was never any doubt in our minds, certainly in my mind, that the band had something special, and that we were going to go all the way. That was it. And so this is – this was writing about the future success of the band. It's so embarrassing [*laughs*]. It's actually writing about this as a given. And saying 'good luck' to everyone else! Against the background of what was going on in and around Ballymun, I think the band gave me a sense of 'we're off'. That's how it felt."

And that's how it was.

Happiness is always somewhere else. The tragic hero of teenage artifice is frequently forlorn and disillusioned. There was very little in the way of joy on *Boy*, if you looked at the lyrics. And yet in many ways it was a very "up" record: the joy was in the making, in the musicianship, in the mission. It was in Larry Mullen pounding the drums.

another time another place

Amazing pictorial confirmation that The Edge actually has two heads!

It was in Adam finding the confidence to launch into a melodic bass run to fill the space between The Edge's angular, ringing guitar slashes. It was in Bono unleashing the demons inside, posing and pogoing around the stage, leaping into the crowd and being – sometimes literally – carried away. The joy was in the group's sense of abandonment – of the conventions and restrictions implicit in being four suburban Dublin boys in the bleak '70s.

'Another Time, Another Place' is one of those wistful, evocative titles which sounds like it came first, though Bono has no memory of the Bryan Ferry album of that name. "At that stage, because so little attention was paid to lyrics, most of the songs did begin with the titles. Usually, we'd work on the music first, in fact we still do. And then, as the music begins to feel a certain way, the first thing we do is to find a title that captures the feel of the music, and then you work back from that."

You can argue that 'Another Time, Another Place' is merely self-indulgent, romantic stuff. It sounds seriously under-worked. But there is in it – as there is throughout *Boy* – an admirable sensitivity to the plight of children, lost in the suburban jungle. Here, simply, because they're here, because they're here, because they're here...

"I actually think it's about sex in Dublin as a teenager," another acquaintance from the era suggests. "It's about finding a place where you can be with your girlfriend, which was a real problem at that time."

'Another Time, Another Place' certainly prefigures a theme that would dominate U2's later music. *"In my sleep I discover the one,"* Bono asserts, but it is never clear whether he means the Loved One or the Supreme Being – or both. Possibly he didn't know, although the promise *"I'll be with you now/We lie on a cloud"* certainly suggests some sort of romantic intent, Ali working her muse on him already.

"There is in it – as there is throughout Boy – an admirable sensitivity to the plight of children, lost in the suburban jungle."

19

A quick glance at the lyrics and you'd scarcely get any sense of what 'The Electric Co.' was about. Within Lypton Village, a defining emphasis was on developing a private language that only insiders could understand. There was a desperate desire to communicate – but only to those you thought would be capable of understanding. Some of that wilful obscurantism may have spilled over into Bono's lyrics.

the
electric co.

St Brendan's Psychiatric
Hospital, Grangegorman,
Dublin.

Within the village set, people may have known that 'The Electric Co.' was a reference to Electro Convulsive Therapy, but the lyrics only hint at the deep sense of disturbance that the song in its entirety explores.

Gavin Friday remembers it as a common feature of the neighbourhood. He pictures women walking the suburban streets in mid-afternoon in their nightdresses. "It'd be a case of 'oh there goes Mrs So-and-so again.' And a couple of days later you'd hear that she was back in hospital. And everyone would be whispering that she'd got 'the treatment'. They'd whack her with an electric shock and she'd be back a few weeks later and she'd be stable then, for a while. There were a few women like that. Nowadays they'd just give them Valium or Prozac, but they were big into ECT at the time."

When Sean de Angelo's friend tried to kill himself, he went about it in a spectacular way, with a chainsaw. He ended up in St Brendan's psychiatric hospital, notorious in Dublin lore simply as Grangegorman, or "the 'Gorman". It was a bleak, miserable, foul institution in which those with long-term psychiatric problems were effectively incarcerated. Electric shock treatment was frequently used there and so the prospects for Sean de Angelo's friend were pretty bleak. "It was very sad," Bono recalls. "But that was the background to the song."

It was as a musical set-piece, however, that 'The Electric Co.' exploded with the power of its concealed intent. 'The Electric Co.' burned with anger at the injustice of it all – beginning with the reality of mental disturbance and insanity itself, but more particularly raging against the hubris of doctors who took on themselves the power to mess with people's brains. "ECT is nothing more than witchcraft," Bono commented bitterly at the time.

"'Electric Co.' was about anger," he says now. "It used to be an incredible release on stage. This idea that rock 'n' roll is a kind of revenge – on society, and on the people you perceive as having done you down – is really true. When you're on stage, and going all out, certain songs do become vehicles or vectors for that. For me 'The Electric Co.' was a licence to get in touch with that desire. I've jumped off balconies, I've whacked people, I've been whacked doing that song live. There's a bit of an Alex, the main character from Anthony Burgess's *A Clockwork Orange*, in there. But essentially it was an angry, cathartic experience every time we performed it."

William Golding's *Lord of the Flies* was an important text around Lypton Village. Part of the driving force behind that community within a community involved the rejection of adulthood and the mind-numbing convention that seemed to accompany it. The purity and innocence of childhood seemed far more attractive than a life of never-ending compromise.

and so Bono, Gavin, Guggi and the other inhabitants of this imaginary place resolved to live like children, and to behave with a child-like honesty. "We got into this *Lord of the Flies* idea of not growing up," Bono told John Waters, later. "We said, 'we won't grow up. We'll stay as we are . . . nine!' Ahem, I guess we succeeded there! It was a little bit gauche and a little bit all over the place, but that's where it was coming from."

That belief in the purity of a child's-eye view of the world is important in understanding the entire ethos of *Boy*. It underscored the band's reliance on instinct in the way the lyrics were written. And it explains, in part at least, the nakedness of some of U2's emotional pleading.

The title 'Shadows and Tall Trees' was taken from the fourth chapter of *Lord of the Flies*. "When I came up with the title, I remember thinking, 'Wow! I can do this!' Again it was like a moment of realization," Bono recalls. It was an early

U2 song, the only one from their original demo session, recorded with Barry Devlin of Horslips as producer, which made it onto *Boy*. A ballad, it feels as if more attention was paid to the lyrics than on most of the tracks on the album. "Yeah," Bono laughs. "Look at that: '*Is life like a tightrope/Hanging on my ceiling?*'. Ouch! I guess I would have considered that to be quite writerly at the time. But then there are other parts of it that are quite beautiful. '*Do you feel in me, anything redeeming/Any worthwhile feeling?*' – which I guess if you were listening to it as a song or at a concert would have to bring something out. It would have to hit you on an emotional level."

The shadows and tall trees of the title were a reference to the atmosphere around the pylons that towered over Cedarwood Road and environs. "I remember thinking about that comparison between *Lord of the Flies* and where we were in Cedarwood, between Ballymun and Finglas. It was a quiet little street in one sense but my memory of it, growing up, is of being stuck between cowboys and indians, rumbles between the top end of the street and the bottom end of the street, between bootboys and skinheads, and so

shadows and tall trees

on. That's the way it was. And I remember thinking the shadows and tall trees are different here – but it's the same story, isn't it? It's all about war. We're all stuck on this island of suburbia and we're turning on each other."

The Mrs Brown, whose washing turns up in the third verse, was in fact Mrs Byrne, Iris Hewson's best friend and near neighbour on Cedarwood Road. Inevitably, the Byrne kids recognized the fact that their dirty laundry was being washed – or watched! – by Bono in public. "They were happy enough about that," he laughs. And why wouldn't they be, with immortality? Of a sort.

Bono takes a corner.

boy

Left: The Lord of the Fly? Author William Golding

portland, Oregon. 22 March, 1981. Four Irish boys, wide-eyed and trusting, trying to throw their arms around the world. Three girls sashay backstage after the show. Hey, these must be groupies.

The Irish boys are happy just to talk. And they do for 10 minutes, 20 minutes, half-an-hour. "Oops," the girls say, "time to go." And they're gone. They seemed pretty cool, didn't they? Very cool. "Has anyone seen my case?" Bono asks. Shit. My case is gone.

Three smart Portland girls opening the door to their apartment, carrying a case. Inside are $300 and a bunch of hand-written scrawls. Lyrics. Bono's lyrics. For the new record. All gone.

Four Irish boys searching high and low. For the lyrics. Gone. Three years to write *Boy*. Now, 12 months' worth of hard labour stolen – with only 12 weeks left to write the follow-up. Nervous breakdown time.

Things were fraught. Bono, Larry, The Edge heavily into Shalom Christianity. Adam isolated and confused. Touring taking its toll. The band almost falling apart. Bono up against it. Improvising lyrics in desperation. Steve Lillywhite driving him. "You can write a song in five minutes. Do your job."

Thought of calling the album *Scarlet* (the colour of Bono's face when he discovered the lyrics had been nicked?) Decided instead on *October*. A big theme hinting at our own insignificance.

Or it was the month the album would be released in.

(Island ILPS 9680)

Produced by **Steve Lillywhite.**

Recorded at **Windmill Lane Studios, Dublin.**

Released **October 1981.**

Paul McGuinness may privately have raged about the possibility that the involvement of Bono, Edge and Larry in the Shalom group might derail a band which he instinctively knew could otherwise become enormously successful.

gloria

h e may have schemed with Adam about how to create the kind of momentum that would sweep the others along, and in the process bury the doubts that were assailing them about being involved in rock 'n' roll at all. But Paul always respected the fundamental impulse behind the trio's immersion in the Shalom experiment.

'His attitude was always very cool," Bono recalls. "He'd say: 'Look I don't share your views but I do believe it's the most important question, and I do respect the fact that you're trying to come to terms with it.' The only thing that he found in his own religion that he could relate to was the music, and so he gave us an album of Gregorian chants to listen to."

The opening lines of the opening verse of the opening song on *October* crystallize the central dilemma with which the band, and especially Bono, were forced to grapple throughout the album: *"I try to sing this song/I, I try to stand up but I can't find my feet/I try, I try to speak up/But only in you I'm complete."* The song reflects a desperate desire to find a voice, a language, a way of expressing at once the faith – the certainty – that was at the heart of their conversion, and the terrible confusion it had plunged them into about their roles, both individually and collectively, as musicians and members of a rock 'n' roll band. Looking back now, Bono feels that he may have been too embarrassed about the ideas that were beginning to flood his work as a lyricist to write them down. Instead he improvised, with the result that – almost immediately – he is stuttering, only barely achieving any kind of coherence.

On 'Gloria' he succeeds. From listening to Paul McGuinness' Gregorian chant album, the idea emerged of doing the chorus in Latin. In the context of the prevailing nihilism of punk, and the dandyism of the new romantic movement which was emerging in London at the time, this was an extraordinarily audacious gesture. Gavin Friday remembers Bono asking Gary Jermyn – a mutual friend who had gone to study in Trinity College in Dublin – to do the

initial translation. "Bono wanted to make sure that the Latin made sense," Gavin recalls. "I couldn't help him because I never did Latin in school but Gary did, and so he was dragged in to do it." The final draft was completed, according to Bono, by Albert Bradshaw, a teacher in Mount Temple, who had taught medieval and renaissance music there.

Whether Mr Bradshaw would have been aware of the song's more heathen antecedents is uncertain. As an Irish band, U2 were certainly conscious of Van Morrison – they had done a cover version of 'Here Comes the Night' on their second gig – and his sexual paean to 'Gloria'. However, on *Horses*, an album that Bono had fallen in love with at a party and which hugely influenced U2, Patti Smith had done a magnificently potent, erotic, lesbian version of Them's garage band classic. There's no doubt that its impulse is felt here. "It is a love song," Bono says. "In a sense it's an attempt to write about a woman in a spiritual sense and about God in a sexual sense. But there certainly is a strong sexual pulse in there."

Even now the exultant choral climax makes Bono smile. "What happens when you improvise is that these things come out," he says. "I let them come out. But the meaning often doesn't become clear until much later."

"You could hear the desperation and confusion in some of the lyrics," The Edge told Bill Flanagan. "'Gloria' is really a lyric about not being able to express what's going on, not being able to put it down, not knowing where we are."

Not being able to express what's going on? Perhaps. But – in this instance at least – doing it very well, all the same.

> "You could hear the desperation and confusion in some of the lyrics."
>
> – THE EDGE

Patti Smith: another glorious 'Gloria'.

i fall down

The meaning of a song often doesn't become clear until later. Looking back, it's one of Bono's dominant feelings about U2's early work. But it can happen too that a song develops a set of associations that cloud and obscure whatever the original intent may have been.

> "It got to the stage where Pod couldn't talk to me because I was a heathen. An atheist."
>
> – GAVIN FRIDAY

Country Life: The Virgin Prunes go native.

24

The new meaning takes over and colonizes the song, to the extent that even the person who wrote it forgets the source of the initial creative impulse.

"A really funny thing happened during the October tour of America," Bono recalls. "We were playing the Ritz in New York and this girl slipped onto the stage. It was towards the end of the set and I used to do this thing even then of dancing with someone from the audience. So we were dancing and she says, 'It's me. It's Julie.' And I said, 'Oh great. It's nice to meet you.' It was one of those things. I met her afterwards. She's a daughter of a wealthy lawyer in New York, who kind of spun out and ended up coming back here to Ireland and getting involved in the Shalom group. She ended up in a relationship with Pod, who was in our road crew at the time."

"I think that John in 'I Fall Down' was actually Pod, who was originally the drummer with the Virgin Prunes," Gavin Friday recalls. "He was one of the staunchest Christians going. I don't know – there was a weird breakdown there. It got to the stage where Pod couldn't talk to me because I was a heathen. An atheist. There was a period of about a year and a half when myself, Guggi and Bono didn't see eye to eye over various things. People used to run when they saw me and I was saying, 'I'm not going to sacrifice animals on stage.' And so Pod left the Prunes and went to work with U2 on their American tour, as their main roadie."

Gavin himself had been involved in the Shalom group. "That didn't last long," he laughs. "At the meetings we were having, I was pushed into a corner. It was a case of 'Let's change the name to The Deuteronomy Prunes, Gavin. Let's stop wearing eyeliner,' and so on. So I just said no, no, no. I knew I didn't want to buy into all this. But after he'd left the Prunes, Pod fell in love with Julie, who is also mentioned in the song. I think Pod was almost like a religious prayer-master in the group at the time. And so when he got together with Julie, she became another ringleader of the Shalom group, along with Pod."

The song is experimental in a number of ways. Whether the influence of new-wave song-stylists like Elvis Costello, Joe Jackson and Squeeze was subconsciously seeping through is a matter for conjecture, but the introduction of the Julie and John characters frees the band from the tyranny of the direct declarations of emotional intensity that Bono was prone to. The result is a more relaxed, conversational approach, in the verses, which gives greater substance to the biblical metaphor of the fall in the chorus (and the title). The Edge's shimmering piano, tightly worked backing vocals and a superbly judged Steve Lillywhite production mark this as one of the band's most fully realized early cuts, a complete pop etching that must be a strong contender for any future comprehensive *Best of U2*.

Bono wouldn't go so far as to suggest that 'I Fall Down' was written about Julie before he met her. "I don't really know," he says. "That's what she thinks. And who's to say?"

It could, of course, merely be a case of life imitating art. But if so, surely Bono would know who he originally had in mind when he created the Julie character in the song. "There was really no one that I can think of," he says. "I have no recollection about where the idea for the song came from."

Anger is an energy, John Lydon declared in his PIL manifestation, and he should know. That same energy was the essential driving force behind British punk rock, a movement which Lydon effectively spearheaded, in the guise of Johnny Rotten, lead singer with The Sex Pistols. Punk was crucial to U2's formation.

bawling, screaming, yowling, howling, angry, selfish, confrontational, adolescent, indulgent, insolent, sneering, shocking, aggressive – depending on where you were coming from, punk could be any of these things or all of them at once, but it was driven by one core principle: you had to make an impression. "Bono was the first punk in school," a former classmate recalls. "He turned up one day with a new haircut, tight purple straights, a '60s jacket and a chain leading from his nose to his ear. He wanted to freak everyone out and he succeeded. People were both horrified and fascinated."

Bono acknowledges the anger, the resentment, even the hatred that gripped him as a teenager. But he never felt easy with those emotions. Naturally reflective, he couldn't strike out without agonizing about the rights and wrongs of what had been done to him – and, more characteristically, of what he'd done. He was inherently suspicious of self-

i threw a brick through a window

John Lydon: punk up the volume!

"Bono was the first punk in school," a former classmate recalls. "He turned up one day with a new haircut, tight purple straights, a '60s jacket and a chain leading from his nose to his ear."

styled rock 'n' roll rebels – of the attitudes they adopted and the poses they struck. "The old cliché of rock 'n' roll rebellion is a joke at this stage," he said around the time of the release of Boy. "It's so conservative you could actually write a rulebook on how to behave as a rock 'n' roll rebel. Whereas I think rebellion starts within your heart. I think going out and getting pissed and dying your hair red is not necessarily any indication of menace at all."

Thematically, 'I Threw a Brick Through a Window' would have sat comfortably on Boy. Musically it was more spacious than most tracks on the band's debut with a hint

25

that U2 – or possibly Steve Lillywhite – had been listening to some of their label, Island's, extensive reggae catalogue. Adam Clayton's bass and Larry Mullen's drums are both afforded opportunities to take the spotlight but – as is so often the case throughout *October* – it is The Edge who shines. But lyrically, 'I Threw a Brick Through a Window' returns to suburban claustrophobia, and the desperate desire to find a way out of the domestic horrors

Bono reflects on progress so far.

> ## "It was, like, suddenly we were weirdos."
> – GAVIN FRIDAY

involved. In some ways, that sense may have been heightened by the band's experiences of touring.

"Bono was always crashing, bikes, cars – everything broke down on him, he'd always be losing things," Gavin Friday recalls. "We were walking around the neighbourhood and suddenly it was like: 'they're on drugs', and 'Paul Hewson's gone mad on a motorbike.' A motorbike!!! And it was, like, suddenly we were weirdos. Now that we were in bands, we were no longer lovely boys. We were brats.

"On one occasion Bono was going to a party with Alison and he decided to splash out on a bottle of wine. It was mega to be able to afford a bottle of wine in those days! There was this couple up the road called Mr and Mrs Corless, and Bono was driving this crock of a car – and whatever he did he crashed into Mr and Mrs Corless' gate and the whole fucking post fell into the garden. The wine spilt all over the car and the Gardaí thought he'd been drinking. And there were all these fucking neighbours, all these two-faced Catholics, standing in judgement. And it was, like, 'I have to get out of this fucking kip.' So there was this sort of brick through the window of that Gay Byrne world, that was closing in on us all. And the feeling was: 'Sorry, Cedarwood has to go.'"

"*I walk up to a window to see myself/And my reflection, when I thought about it/My direction, going nowhere, going nowhere,*" Bono sings. But there is more to this than meets the eye. There is anger and confusion here, for certain, but it is as much about what's going on in the mind and the heart as it is about the restrictions of suburbia. It's as much about the senseless violence that erupts between men confined together in a small space, and the guilt and torment that follows. "There was a row in the house," Bono recalls. "The three of us who were left – my father, my brother and myself – didn't get along very well at the time. And whatever happened, I remember throwing a carving knife at my brother and it sticking in the door. I missed – but that's what 'I Threw a Brick Through a Window' was about.

"Or that's how I remember it, anyway."

One of the girls eventually blew it by going to the headmaster's office and asking him to announce over the intercom that the school now belonged to Jesus. It was a measure of how intense the collective feeling had become.

"That was the first wave, in '76, if you like," Bono remembers, "and there was a kind of an echo of it around about 1981 or '82. Charismatic things started happening. That was when we became involved in the Shalom group. We were studying the Scriptures and it was amazing. When everyone else was figuring out how to get served and how to score, we were all completely wrapped up in this."

'Rejoice' is a celebration of that spiritual involvement. It is also quite explicitly a rejection of the pretentions of bands – like The Clash – who were coming on at the time as if punk rock were the key to the revolution.

The Edge has commented that some of Bono's best lyric writing is done under pressure, on the mike, but that theory isn't borne out here. You can sense the bluster, feel the desperation. *"And what am I to do?"* he asks. *"Just tell me what am I supposed to say."* Improvised on the spot, the line almost certainly sparked a silent cynical rejoinder from Steve Lillywhite, who was finding Bono's apparent lack of preparation enormously trying. But the singer succeeded in coming up with some memorable lines even under pressure. "Only last week I had some American come up to me and say, 'I can't change the world/But I can change the world in me.' So naive!" he reflects. "But there was something real happening all the same. At that point we were so removed from the culture. Rock 'n' roll – that was just the day job. We used to get together every single night, meeting in people's houses, reading, studying Scriptures. The band was what we did during the day."

The Edge remembers *October* as an album that suffered because of the lack of time U2 had to prepare it. He has a point, especially given that it was his superb, propulsive guitar-playing that rescued 'Rejoice'. But, overall, there was less to celebrate here than Bono felt at the time.

Left: Look what Bono's got up his sleeve – his arm!

rejoice

Bono talks about an extraordinary renewal that took place in 1976. Amazing things happened in Mount Temple, with nearly half the school undergoing some kind of religious experience. One of the teachers had quite an effect on a lot of people. She was always on about the Scriptures, the thing took hold, and during a period of about two months there was an eruption of spiritual fervour.

october

fire

I remember Bono taking me out to his car, parked outside Windmill Lane studios in Dublin, and playing me the band's new single. The implicit distinction was important in itself. At that stage, U2 were still thinking about putting stuff together that would crack the charts, and during a break in their American tour, they'd stopped off at Chris Blackwell's studios in Nassau, in the Bahamas, to increase their chances.

On an initial listen I was struck by the glistening guitar power, the suggestion of sabres rattling and the sun glinting off them. It was a small triumph at least: released in June 1981, in advance of *October*, it provided the band with their first British chart success.

With its roots in the Book of Revelations and the circumstances of the second coming, it is apocalyptic in tone. But if you weren't already aware of the band's interest in religion, there was nothing that explicitly signalled the underlying biblical frame of reference. At a push, 'Fire' could have been about some imagined nuclear-fuelled Armageddon. However it was read at the time, Bono dismisses it now as nonsense. "As I recall, 'Fire' was our attempt at a single. God knows where our heads were at," he laughs. "There was something good about it – I just can't remember what it was."

He isn't entirely serious when he attributes the song's failure to the fact that they were recording, for the first time, in the lap of luxury. "That was an amazing trip," he says. "It was our first time going to the Caribbean and it just blew us all away. There is that thing when you're in a baby band, where you feel that you're on holidays all the time, and you can't believe that you haven't been found out. So when you're in a place like Nassau, you don't really want to go in and work, do you? And you realize why all these great groups make crap records when they go to record there! It's because they just don't feel like working when they're in the Bahamas."

The whole debacle had its lighter side – in retrospect. "You know the story about *Top of the Pops* and 'Fire'?" asks Bono. "It was our first time on *Top of the Pops* and the record company were really thrilled because we were going to have a hit single. We went on and the single went *down* because we were so bad. The miming was all over the shop and it was operatic in a way that TV will never understand. I was dressed in this black military kind of sleeping bag shirt, with a bad haircut."

Calling, calling...

The Grim Reaper turns up hoping for a spot in the 'Fire' video.

When Bono went to see Ridley Scott's chilling futuristic thriller *Bladerunner*, he was impressed. Visually the film was stunning and its claustrophobic, nightmare vision of the future seemed enormously impressive. But there was a flaw. Something jarred. At first he couldn't figure out what it was. Then, gradually, it dawned on him. It was the music. "I am a fan of Vangelis, who wrote it," he reflected at the time, "but I was thinking that in the '90s people won't be listening to electronic music. Who wants electronic music in an electronic age?"

bono felt that a significant shift was about to take place in music, in painting, in architecture – that modernism was about to be rejected, because in the era that *Bladerunner* represented, it was not technology that would be needed most in art and in music but those instruments that restored people's humanity. On Bruce Springsteen's magnificent, low-fi *Nebraska*, he identified a fragile quality to the music that had to do with the tones and textures of the acoustic guitar and the harmonica. Released a year earlier, 'Tomorrow' had explored the same terrain, utilizing the timelessness and the power of Vinnie Kilduff's uileann pipes as its signature.

tomorrow

The choice of an instrument that was intimately associated with Irish traditional music was no accident. In what was undoubtedly a reaction to touring, and in particular to the band's initial experience of the rigours of American roadwork, Bono talked about waking up suddenly and realizing that he was Irish. It was a feeling that the whole band shared. Adam Clayton always liked the song's lilting Irishness. The Edge, similarly, singles it out as one of

Scene from Ridley Scott's *Bladerunner.*

his favourite U2 tracks of the time. It isn't just the plaintive quality of the music, however, or even Bono's superbly soulful vocal performance. The more attention you pay to the lyrics, the more poignant they become. There was a time when Bono used to talk about 'Tomorrow' as a song about what was happening in Northern Ireland at the beginning of the '80s. In an atmosphere of deepening sectarian conflict and savagery, a knock on the door increasingly became a sinister invitation to accept a bullet in the head. No one knew for certain what was waiting for them when they opened the door, opened the door . . .

Presumably, these images of violence and fear were crowding together in Bono's imagination. But he's been revisiting the song recently, and is in no doubt now about what had really been troubling him so deeply back then. He may not have wanted to admit it to himself at the time, but 'Tomorrow' is a song about the death of his mother – no more and no less. *"Won't you come back tomorrow/Won't you be back tomorrow/Can I sleep tonight?"* he pleads, and the sense of desolation and loss is palpable. "There are things that have to be worked out, that are going to come out," he says. "They'll find holes. It's still amazing to me that I could have convinced myself that this was about anything else. It's amazing that you can be so completely out of touch with yourself and with feelings you're trying to express."

An Edge power chord has unforeseen consequences.

The *October* recording of 'Tomorrow' is marred by a somewhat clumsy attempt at folk rock, as the band clatter in more than half-way through, and there's a messianic piece of proselytizing tagged on at the end of the lyrics that stands as one of the most catastrophic misjudgements in all of Bono's occasionally wild flights of improvisation. All has been rectified, however, on a new recording of the song, featuring Bono and Adam, on Donal Lunny's 1996 album, *Common Ground*. Meanwhile, in their own right, throughout the '90s, U2 have been grappling with the demons unleashed by the electronic revolution. I guess you can't expect to be right about everything.

Bono was always ready with a theory. "U2 music is not urban music," he said in 1980. "It's more to do with hills, rivers and mountains – and so it actually suits us being in a space, rather than being contained in a club."

october

He might have been talking about 'Tomorrow' or the first half of it at least. But even more accurately, he could have been describing the context that gave rise to the immensely troubled and still deeply moving title track of album number two, 'October'.

Clearly this was one of The Edge's most brilliant moments of inspiration to date. The guitarist remembers it as a song that could have gone places, but Bono was bereft of further lyrical inspiration and they didn't have the time necessary to squeeze out whatever sparks might have been flickering. They decided to put it out as it was. His memory does the controlled power and beauty of the finished track a grave injustice. U2 happily admit that songs frequently come together by accident: this was an example of that process at its happiest.

Not that that is such an appropriate metaphor in the context. In fact, 'October' is suffused with an other-worldly sadness and resignation that undoubtedly taps into the tangled emotions that were driving the band just then, and that risked driving them apart. On the run-up to recording 'October', Bono, The Edge and Larry were living out in Portrane, beside the beach on the north coast of Dublin, with the Shalom group. Bono was baptised in the sea in Portrane, and they were living in a caravan in a field there. They were praying a lot and fasting. The Edge describes it as an incredibly intense time spiritually, during which he wrestled at length with his conscience about whether or not, as a Christian, he could continue to play in a rock 'n' roll band.

The three Christian members of the band had been under a lot of pressure from other members of the Shalom group to quit, that they had to choose one way or the other. It was on the beach in Portrane that The Edge broke the news to Bono that he might be leaving the band. If The Edge was going, Bono decided that he would too – that they'd break up the band. The Edge asked for two weeks, to give him time to go away and consider his position. When he came back he had decided that being a Christian in a rock 'n' roll band involved a contradiction alright – but one he could live with.

"'October' . . . it's an image," Bono told a Dutch television interviewer, Kees Baar, in 1981. "We've been through the '60s, a time when things were in full bloom. We had fridges and cars, we sent people to the Moon and everybody thought how great mankind was. And now, as we go through the '70s and '80s, it's a colder time of the year. It's after the harvest. The trees are stripped bare. You can see things and we finally realize that maybe we weren't so smart after all, now that there's millions of unemployed people, now that we've used the technology we've been blessed with to build bombs for war machines, to build rockets, whatever. So 'October' is an ominous word, but it's also quite lyrical."

As extrapolations, go it makes some kind of sense. The title came first: it was what Bono wanted to call the album. The Edge hadn't played the piano in years but he had a real feel for it and he began to pick out this pure melody, underpinned with simple chords. The group wanted him to find what they called ice notes: clear, shimmering, crystalline things that would be hard but beautiful. 'October' was the result, and while Bono may have seen it as a grand statement about eternal verities, its nakedness in fact said as much about the crises the band had been going through, both personal and creative.

'October' captures U2 in a moment of supreme vulnerability, and is all the more compelling as a result. There may indeed have been a bigger, more complete song there to be written. But sometimes, as U2 would find again and again, these things are best left to find a life of their own. And a meaning.

> "The three Christian members of the band had been under a lot of pressure from other members of the Shalom group to quit."

Take one, take two... take three! U2 recording their video at Kilmainham Jail, Dublin.

october

There is an underlying tone of defiance that runs throughout *October*. U2's debut album had been made in a spirit of optimism. The culmination of almost four years of apprenticeship, *Boy* harboured a surfeit of brightness and bounce: you got the feeling that U2 were ready to take on the world.

with a shout

but touring the album had been a draining and disillusioning experience. The more they got to know about the music industry, the greater the extent to which U2 were repelled by the cynicism and corruption of it. Their idealism had taken a battering, hearing stories about how bands they'd respected and been inspired by, ostensibly politically motivated outfits like The Clash and The Jam, treated their road crew, and seeing the inner workings of the record business for the first time. In a

sense, they went into the recording of *October* with the attitude that if people didn't like it, it just might be better for everyone concerned. Rejection would make it easier to walk away.

It's hard to conceive of anything that could have been so terminally unhip as Bono exhorting the great unwashed to make tracks for Jerusalem, but that's precisely what he did on 'With a Shout'. "We don't want to be the band that talks about God," he had said during 1980, but the crucifixion imagery was unmistakable. You could interpret it as a logical conclusion of Bono, Larry and The Edge's belief in what they thought of as the spirit that moves all things. Equally, you might dismiss it as an effective abdication of the responsibility he had, both to the band and to their audiences. Or it may have been simply an unhappy by-product of a combination of unfortunate circumstances. Whatever the cause, there is no mistaking the spirit of abandon with which Bono met the challenge of constructing the lyrics. On the one hand there was trust: I will rely on Him for inspiration. On the other there was doubt: No matter what I do, it is all irrelevant, trivial, meaningless, tainted. And finally, there was perhaps a core of self-belief: Fuck them. Why should we hide what we feel? Why should we disguise who we are?

There's a note of apocalyptic triumphalism in 'With a Shout' that's highlighted by the addition of trumpets, courtesy of Some Kind of Wonderful, a local Dublin-based soul band of the era. Bono had been reading the Psalms of David at the time.

> "The Psalms are amazing about music. They're all about bang that drum, whack that cymbal and, you know, dead bones rising up." - **BONO**

"Yeah, there's triumphalism there," Bono reflects. "But in an odd way the walls of Jerusalem, or the walls of Jericho, were a great image for punk music, and the idea that went with it, that music could shake the foundations. The Psalms are amazing about music. They're all about bang that drum, whack that cymbal and, you know, dead bones rising up. Music as a wake-up call for the spirit – I think that was what we were driving at."

You could say that it was a brave failure. The imagery would be revisited, much more effectively, later.

Some Kind of Wonderful: they didn't lack bottle!

In the early days, David Bowie had been a significant influence on the band. "Half of my Bowie collection was robbed by Bono, who'd never buy anything," Gavin Friday recalls. "He used to bum them and I'd get them back, wrecked, with jam on them and all sorts of shit."

you could see it in some of Bono's stage moves: there was a self-conscious theatrical Bowie-esque side to the band in their pre-*Boy* days, that disappeared for a long time, resurfacing only with Zoo TV. It's curious then that Bono doesn't recall seeing Nicolas Roeg's *The Man Who Fell to Earth*, in which Bowie made his screen debut. That film was based on a Robert Heinlein novel; Heinlein also wrote *Stranger in a Strange Land*, which gave Bono the title for one of *October*'s most effective lyrics. Touring was a time for reading. Books were consumed on the tour bus and in hotel rooms. Some images, ideas, titles, lingered. The experience could also provide its own moments of inspiration.

"You have to remember that the only travel we did as kids was to go over to Wales on these camping holidays," another friend recalls. "Bono used to go over to Wales to see some girl he knew from camping when he was ten.

"I remember we all went over and knocked on her hall door and she was going out with another guy and it was like 'Fuck off!' And we were left camping on this site and it was the middle of winter so we thought, 'Let's walk around town in our underpants.' And we had airguns and we were all arrested – they thought we were the IRA or something. That was kind of a big adventure for us. None of us had seen the world. We were very sheltered."

So when U2 began to tour, it was an eye-opener. Perhaps if Bono hadn't lost his satchel of lyrics, there'd have been more postcards from a tour bus on *October*. In the event, 'Stranger in a Strange Land' seems like an exception, not just in its theme but in the confident simplicity of its lyrical style.

"We were going to Berlin," Bono recalls. "We were all in the back of the van in our sleeping bags and we had to travel through the corridor between East Germany and West Berlin. And we were stopped by this border guard. The song was just a little portrait of him. He was our own age, with short hair, in a uniform and his life was pretty grim and he was seeing these guys in a rock 'n' roll band passing through. I had a feeling that he realized how much we had in common, and yet it was all over so quickly."

The song had a quality that was relatively scarce on *October*: empathy: *"We asked him to smile for a photograph/We waited around to see if we could make him laugh/The soldier asked for a cigarette/His smiling face I can't forget."* Clearly, it was written rather than improvised. "That's quite a good lyric," Bono says, looking at the song afresh. "There aren't many like that. It's terse, simple, well-executed. That wasn't made up on the spot." It's been speculated that the soldier could as easily have been a British Army squaddie in Northern Ireland but at most that's an undercurrent.

'Stranger in a Strange Land': British soldier in Northern Ireland.

stranger in a strange land

october

scarlet

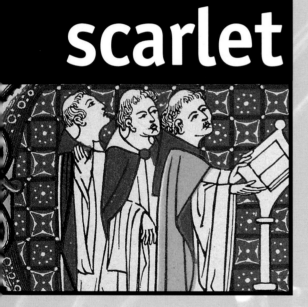

There had been a lot of pressure on the band to use their music in the cause of Christianity, of Jesus, of Shalom. People within the tightly knit group thought that U2 should use the platform they'd won to proselytize. "I remember thinking: does God need salesmen?" Bono recalls. "Do we really have to reduce this to pulpit-thumping? By this stage I'd been to America and I'd seen the state of the Evangelicals and the fundamentalists, and of religious broadcasting in America – the preachers with their hands reaching out of the television trying to steal your money. People would say, 'Are you embarrassed? Are you ashamed?' I'm not ashamed. I'm just not going to go around and flog it like a second-hand car salesman."

Adam pulls the strings.

and so, 'Scarlet' takes a minimalist line. It may originally have been an instrumental piece for which Bono failed to come up with a lyric, but it stands the test of time all the better for its simplicity. The Edge is at the piano again, Adam Clayton contributes a resonant, melodic bass part and Larry plays the role of percussionist with admirable restraint. The influence of Paul McGuinness' album of Gregorian chant is discernible in the straight choral lines of Bono's delivery. And there is something healing rather than triumphalist about the effect when he sings the one word over and over: "Rejoice".

A prelude to '40', it identified a vein that would yield further, greater riches later.

The album could have ended with 'Scarlet', but for some reason that no one can quite figure out now, they felt that it needed an end-piece. Patti Smith used to make her records by writing her titles first, sketching out the word-frame and then creating the music with those suggestions in mind. Or so U2 had read.

an ambience was created, the music took shape and then the lyrics were written and improvised on the mike, coming together by a kind of process of trial and error. She may have had an end-piece on *Horses* and the band wanted to follow suit. Or it might just have been that someone had thought that it was a good title for a final track – and once the title had been invented, they had to deliver the "song".

"I think after the album came out we thought 'uuuh'," Bono shrugs. *October* has its moments of sheer beauty. For an album that was frequently dismissed, parts of it stand up surprisingly well. But even when it fails, it tells us much about the confused and perilous state of mind U2 were in at the time. Arguably, 'Is That All?' says more about that theme than any other track precisely because it says so little. They should have known better.

U2: stars and bars.

A good title it may indeed have been, but the end result is a mess. The guitar riff is lifted from 'The Cry', an earlier song that was often incorporated into 'The Electric Co.' but never made it onto disc. Otherwise 'Is That All?' was written in the studio, and it shows. Larry's cracking snare and superb drumming notwithstanding, it is confused and incoherent, but unintentionally revealing nonetheless. *"Is that all that you want from me?"* Bono pleads, in a giveaway line that seems to acknowledge his own feelings of creative frustration and failure.

is that all?

war

For all its ringing assertions of faith, *October* had been conceived in an atmosphere of doubt. The involvement of Bono, Larry and The Edge in Shalom Christianity had temporarily undermined U2's conviction about their mission as a rock 'n' roll band. The album was recorded under a cloud, in a rush. It had moments of sweet inspiration but it felt unfinished.

(Island ILPS 9733)

Produced by **Steve Lillywhite.**

Recorded at **Windmill Lane Studios, Dublin.**

Released **March 1983.**

The trio were under increasing pressure from within the Shalom group – about how they should dress, what they should look like, the way they should sound. They resented being crowded, dictated to. It was time to move on. Looking around, they didn't like the nihilism into which punk had descended. The New Romantics were as irrelevant, peddling pop of the most self-regarding and vacuous variety. Meanwhile the real world seemed to be permanently in the grip of one kind of crisis or another. Everything was out of kilter.

As U2 toured *October* through '81 and '82 they became hardened by roadwork. Adam and Larry's playing was tighter, tougher, more aggressive. The Edge's too. They had regained their confidence as a rock 'n' roll band. Bono was driven by a need to bring all the pieces together. Now was the time to declare war on everything that was cynical, phoney, defeatist and limiting. Their third album would be a document of the times. There could be no shirking. Personally, politically and musically, U2 would declare their independence. Loud, angry and demanding, the *War* album and tour would see U2 triumph.

The events which formed the backdrop to one of U2's most explicitly political songs are etched indelibly into the text of Ireland's troubled colonial history. The counter-intelligence unit of the original Irish Republican Army, under Michael Collins, identified 14 British undercover agents who had been responsible for the systematic killing of members of Sinn Féin over the previous months. On 21 November, 1921, they broke into their houses early in the morning and assassinated them in their beds.

in retaliation, armed forces – in the form of the Regular Royal Irish Constabulary and the notorious Black and Tans, a ruthless auxiliary police force used to crush nationalist opposition in an era of widespread political upheaval in Ireland – went into the headquarters of the Gaelic Athletic Association in Croke Park. There, in a calculated act of indiscriminate brutality, they opened fire on the crowd attending a football match.

In all, 12 people – men and women – were shot dead and 60 others were wounded. Hundreds were trampled and injured in the ensuing stampede. That day became known as Bloody Sunday.

That horrific double-incident, intensified in its impact on the collective psyche of the Irish people by the fact that the Croke Park massacre was witnessed first-hand by so many, was echoed in Derry in 1972. In an infamous attack which is still the subject of controversy and political recriminations, the elite Paratroop Regiment of the British Army opened fire during a civil rights demonstration and killed 14 unarmed people, their bodies lain low on the streets of their home town. Another 14 were badly wounded. The images of that day remain unforgettable. In particular, footage of the man who would become Catholic Bishop of Derry, Edward Daly, holding his handkerchief aloft as an improvised white flag, as he crawls on his hands and knees towards the lifeless silhouette of one of the victims of the slaughter, serves as an emblem of the innocence and vulnerability of those who had been slaughtered. Those two events formed the immediate political backdrop to the opening song on *War*...

"I can't believe the news today."
It was an introductory line which crystallized the prevailing response, especially among younger Irish people who had not been suckled on the politics of sectarianism, to the series of outrages that devastated the Northern landscape, and the people of Northern Ireland, throughout the '70s and early '80s. To a large extent those who lived in Dublin had been immune. But, in an increasingly politicized band, Bono had come around to the view that neither he nor they could ever simply wash their hands of the violence in the North, or of the injustices which had spawned it. "It was only when I realized that the troubles hadn't affected me that they began to affect me," Bono reflected at the time. "The bombs may not go off in Dublin but they're made here."

'Sunday Bloody Sunday' was not a partisan statement. Live, it was always prefaced with a disclaimer. "This is not a rebel song," Bono would declare. By that he meant that, the deep resonances of what had happened on Bloody Sunday notwithstanding, it was not to be taken as supporting the Republican cause. It was, rather, an emotional response to what, from any perspective, was a horrifying political reality. "What I was trying to say in the song is: there it is, in close-up," Bono explained. "I'm sick

sunday

bloody

sunday

A member of the 'Black and Tans', Ireland, 1920s.

war

of it. How long must it go on? It's a statement. It's not even saying there's an answer."

The important thing, as U2 have emphasized again and again over the years, was at least to ask the right questions. It was The Edge's idea to explore the theme, and to link what was happening in Northern Ireland back to the original Christian blood sacrifice and subsequent resurrection on Easter Sunday. "Bono was away on his honeymoon," The Edge recalls. "I wrote the music and hit on an idea for the lyrics and presented it to the band when they got back."

The song would articulate the band's own sense of bewilderment at the forces which had been unleashed by the Northern conflict, but it was an incident at a gig in the USA which provided the immediate context for Bono. "I walked out of the backstage door in San Francisco," Bono explained, "and there were 30 or 40 people waiting for a chat and for autographs, and I was scrawling my name on bits of paper as they were handed to me. I got this one piece of paper and was about to write on it when something in me said 'hold on a second'. The paper was folded and when I opened it, there was this big dogma thing looking for signatures – I was about to sign my name on a petition to support some guy I'd never heard of, an Irish guy with Republican connections. And I got worried at that stage.

"As much as I'm a Republican, I'm not a very territorial person. The whole idea of U2 using a white flag on stage was to get away from the green, white and orange. To get away from the Stars and Stripes. To get away from the

> ## "Fuck the revolution," Bono declared on stage.

Union Jack... I'm frightened of borders and I get scared when people start saying that they're prepared to kill, to back up their belief in where a border should be. I mean, I'd love to see a united Ireland but I don't believe you can put a gun to someone's head to make him see your way."

In that sense 'Sunday Bloody Sunday' was a protest song – not against any one act of violence but against a cycle of violence into which all of the protagonists in the Northern conflict seemed to be locked. Adam remembers that it was originally much more vitriolic, with an opening line that would have hung like an albatross around U2's collective neck for years to come: *"Don't talk to me about the rights of the IRA."* But better judgement prevailed. "The viewpoint became very humane and non-sectarian," Adam reflects, "which is the only responsible position."

The urgency of the emotion did not, however, make it an easy song to produce. During the writing of *War*, Bono suffered from writer's block and one of his abiding memories of making the album relates to how his wife, Ali, helped him through this traumatic period, especially in relation to 'Sunday Bloody Sunday'. "She was literally kicking me out of bed in the morning," Bono recalled. "She literally put the pen in my hand."

What emerged was a cry from the heart which effectively articulated for an emerging generation the terrible pointlessness of sectarian hatred and violence. During recording, considerable time was spent on the drum part. Larry Mullen Jnr. was exiled from the studio and located under the front staircase in Windmill Lane, the open spaces above lending his sound the natural reverb that producer Steve Lillywhite was looking for. There, he was given a rare opportunity to use his experience with the Artane Boys Band in a rock context, hammering out a martial rhythm reminiscent of the nationalist marching band material he'd played in that more regimental setting. By chance, The Edge had bumped into Steve Wickham on the way home from a writing session and the violinist was brought into play, his fiddle colourations effectively stirring

> ## "One of his abiding memories of making the album relates to how his wife, Ali, helped him through this traumatic period."

up some old ethnic ghosts and lending the song deeper Irish resonances. "Actually it starts as a folk song and ends up as one of those Salvation Army songs," Bono reflects now. "That was a good idea, but I don't think it came off really. People didn't pick up on that."

A powerful song, it became a live staple, its anthemic quality lending itself to the stadium treatment towards which the band were inevitably being drawn as the *War* tour catapulted them into the big league. The song resurfaced on the mini-album *Under a Blood Red Sky*, also released in 1983, but its apotheosis came during the 1987 and 1988 *Joshua Tree* tour, which was being recorded for the *Rattle and Hum* album and film extravaganza.

The version in the film was recorded on the day of the Enniskillen massacre, 8 November, 1987. This, too, was a horrific military operation, in this instance carried out by the IRA. A bomb was placed at the war memorial in the centre of Enniskillen town in Fermanagh, not far from the disputed border which partitions the six counties of Northern Ireland from the rest of the country. As a crowd gathered there to mark Remembrance Day and to pay tribute to those soldiers from the North who had died in the Second World War, the bomb was detonated, killing 13 people and injuring or maiming numerous others. It was an action which was impossible to defend, and the ensuing wave of condemnation and revulsion shook the Republican movement to its core. Many would remember the Enniskillen bombing as the most appalling atrocity committed in the cause of Irish unity, and the pictures of grieving friends and relatives of those who had been murdered were seen throughout the world. In particular Gordon Wilson, a Methodist whose daughter died beneath the rubble holding her father's hand, emerged as a man of extraordinary dignity and courage, whose appeal for forgiveness cast the barbarism of the IRA's action in a particularly harsh light.

"Fuck the revolution," Bono declared on stage in the McNichols Arena in Denver after the news had come through from Ireland, and the band proceeded to unleash a cathartic, emotional version of the song which reflected their anger – and that of so many Irish men and women – at another senseless, brutal act of violence, in which innocent people had been butchered. "It was the ultimate performance of the song," Bono confided in 1988. "It was almost like the song was made real for the day, in a way that it was never going to be again. Anything else would be less than that."

The acoustic guitar that opens 'Seconds' and drives it was The Edge's idea. "A smart move," Bono observes. "There's a sense in which everyone in this band wants to be something else. Adam is the exception, but I would love to be the guitar player, Larry would love to be the singer and The Edge would love to be the drummer. All this lead guitar stuff never meant much to him.

seconds

A kiss is just a kiss: Bono welcomes Liam Gallagher of Oasis, to Dublin, 1996.

"**i** remember B.B. King talking to Steve Cropper, who is a real rhythm player himself, and he turned round and said, 'That's the greatest rhythm guitar player in the world', pointing to The Edge – who nearly fell over, because that's really where he's at. He was very groove sussed, and we were trying to get that going on *War*."

Adam got a good thing happening on the bass too, and the song began to fall into shape. "It's funny," Bono says. "Very few people mention 'Seconds'. It wouldn't normally be considered one of the big U2 songs, but I met the singer

"I've always felt physically ill at the concept of nuclear fall-out," Bono says. "We are the first generation of people to have to live with that possibility."

from Oasis, Liam Gallagher, recently. He came up to me and he was humming the bass line from 'Seconds'. He said, 'That's a *bad groove*, that's a *bad groove*.' And it is."

'Seconds' is a tour-de-force from The Edge. For the first time (of only three in U2's history to date) he sings lead vocals. In fact it was The Edge's voice that U2 tended to double-track for harmonies. Bono figures his partner-in-crime's singing was under-rated: now that he was out in front, a whole lot of people failed to notice the difference and assumed it was Bono on vocals.

The track offered ample evidence that U2's canvas was broadening. There was musical irony in the juxtaposition of The Edge's jaunty acoustic pop confection with lyrics about the imminence of nuclear catastrophe. There's humour too in the reference to a track by their Island labelmates, Troublefunk: *"They're doing the atomic bomb/Do they know where the dance comes from?"* And in a move that in many ways was ahead of its time, they lifted a sample from a 1982 TV documentary entitled *Soldier Girls*.

"The whole spectacle of these girls going through this incredible routine of training seemed perfect to slip in here in the middle," The Edge told Carter Alan on WBCN in 1983. "It's not obvious but if you listen close you can hear the refrain *'I want to be an airborne ranger/I want to live the life of danger'.* It's very disturbing."

"I remember watching it in the Green Room in Windmill," Bono recalls. "It happened to be on and we made a recording of it. Sometimes things like that just fall into place." Whatever way all the elements slotted together, overall the track was curiously reminiscent of the Beatles – a positive recommendation at the worst of times. Not to be outdone, one close associate insists that the group were subconsciously influenced by the Human League, who had themselves released a track with the title 'Seconds' (about the assassination of John F. Kennedy) on their *Dare* album.

Meanwhile, in global political terms, during the early '80s, there was reason to believe that the lunatics had taken over the asylum. Under Margaret Thatcher's bellicose regime, American Pershing Cruise missiles had been freshly installed in Britain. And in the USA, there was the scary picture of Ronald Reagan, a right-wing fundamentalist president who was quite clearly doddering and incompetent into the bargain. With his finger on the button, you got the impression that Armageddon might be unleashed at any time. Maybe even by accident.

"I've always felt physically ill at the concept of nuclear fall-out," Bono says. "We are the first generation of people to have to live with that possibility. It's all around us, it's in our heads. And it affects the way people feel about the world. I always saw it in apocalyptic terms. For the first time, it became possible – it is possible – to destroy everything."

Ban the Bomb – an anti-nuclear protest in London.

Adam had come up with the bass figure at a soundcheck. The Edge had developed the piece on the piano. Now, the band were five, maybe six tracks into recording *War* and Bono still hadn't got down the lyrics for 'New Year's Day'. "It was an unsettled time," Adam recalled later. "You looked around and there were conflicts everywhere. We saw a lot of unrest on TV and in the media. We focused on these."

Solidarity leader and later President of Poland, Lech Walesa

new year's day

turning those themes into a song was another story. In the end, Bono had to make up the lyrics on the spot. "He'd sing and whatever came out would be the starting point," Steve Lillywhite revealed. The singer had a set of images in his head that he felt would fit the mood of the piece. He began to describe them to the backdrop of the music, doing different versions, refining them as he went along. He was flying on a wing and a prayer, doing verbal incantations and testing everyone's tolerance for the Nth time in the process. But the opening line is beautifully arresting and what emerges is a haunting love song of considerable depth. Everyone was under strain, there were arguments about the vocals and at one stage the track was in danger of being left off the album. In the pressure to get the record finished, some of the lyrical seams were left showing. But it was the only real single on *War* and went straight into the UK Top 10 on release.

"I personally am bloody sick, every time I switch on the radio, of being blasted with this contrived crap," Bono said shortly afterwards. "It would be stupid to start drawing up battle lines but the fact that 'New Year's Day' made the Top 20 indicated a disillusionment among record buyers with the pop culture in the charts. I don't think 'New Year's Day' was a pop single, certainly not in the way that Mickie Most might define a pop single, as something that might last three minutes and three weeks in the charts. I don't think we could have written that kind of song."

What they did write does conform to the basic chart model in one respect at least, however. It is a love song, doubtless written by Bono with his new wife, Ali, in mind. But the impressionistic political backdrop infused the track with a sense of separation and longing that gives it its distinctive resonance. It would end up connecting with the mood of the time in an unexpected way. With the emergence of the Solidarity movement, from 1980 onwards the communist regime in Poland was being challenged effectively

"Everyone was under strain, there were arguments about the vocals and at one stage the track was in danger of being left off the album."

for the first time since the Iron Curtain had been erected. Following a series of strikes, martial law had been imposed, in December 1981, by the head of the Polish Communist Party, General Jaruzelski. Solidarity became a proscribed organization and its leaders were arrested, among them Lech Walesa. "Subconsciously I must have been thinking about Lech Walesa being interned and his wife not being allowed to see him," Bono commented. "Then, when we'd recorded the song, they announced that martial law would be lifted in Poland on New Year's Day. Incredible."

Nothing changes on New Year's Day? You knew what he meant all the same.

war

Initially, U2 conceived of *War* as a knuckleduster in the face of the new pretty-boy pop that was flourishing in Britain in the early '80s.

But it was also intended as a verbal two-fingers to the self-styled cognoscenti who had been stepping up their attacks on U2 as being too worthy and sincere by far, not real rock 'n' rollers.

like a song

"I think 'Like a Song' was addressed to the critics who didn't get what we were about, who thought we weren't really punk enough," Bono recalls. "That's a subject that comes up again and again because people really do fall for this rebel thing. It's such a cliché."

"It made some kind of sense in the '50s and '60s. Against a conservative backdrop, that punk attitude had a real meaning. Now a lot of it is just dressing up." Bono's anger isn't always well articulated in the song itself. "I don't think I got the tone of voice right," he observes. But he hits the bulls-eye once at least, in identifying the selfishness at the heart of most rock 'n' roll posturing. *"When others need your time/You say it's time to go,"* he accuses. The band make a lot of thunderously impressive noise, but in the end 'Like a Song' remains just that. Like a song.

Bono observes the soundcheck.

There aren't many songwriters who would attempt to get away with it. It remains inscrutable: there is no reference to a drowning man in there.

It's to do with the way U2 constructed their songs at the time. "It was the title of a Sam Beckett-style play I'd started about a drowning man," Bono recalls. "I had a few scenes written. There was to be a guy in a chair with a blindfold and there was to be a little ballet thing." In the build-up to recording *War*, The Edge remembers that it was a song that they took for granted. Although most of the work still had to be done on it, they knew that there was the root of a very strong piece in there.

When it came to putting it down, the song took flight, developing into one of the band's most sophisticated and successful artefacts. Rhythmically, Larry and Adam stitch it together beautifully, with more than a little help from The Edge on acoustic. Bono's singing is transcendant and there's a lovely eastern inflection to the counter-melody when Steve Wickham's violin lifts off towards the close.

"Whereas I know some of the songs on the *War* album could be re-recorded and improved on," The Edge told Carter Alan in 1985, "with 'Drowning Man' it's perfection for that song. It's one of the most successful pieces of recording we've ever done."

I have a hunch that the phrase "drowning man" may have featured in the first draft of the lyrics, to be replaced as the song developed by the altogether more musical "take my hand". Whatever the truth in that, 'Drowning Man' has been interpreted as a love song in which the subject and object are

Steve Wickham

drowning man

deliberately merged, with Bono surrendering himself to a higher love, embracing both the sexual and the spiritual.

Looking back now at the reflection of his younger self in the mirror of the lyric sheet, Bono hesitantly describes it as a psalm. Mostly these are written from the point of view of David railing at God – but occasionally the perspective switches and what we read instead are God's words. At the height of his involvement in charismatic Christianity, Bono had been experimenting with the experience of speaking in tongues within the Shalom group. The *feeling* is that some other force takes over, that the rational checks we normally impose are abandoned, that your voice disappears into another voice and that some external power is speaking through you. Bono would search for that higher state, improvising lyrics on the microphone, allowing the words, the feeling – at its best the ecstasy – to take hold. He remembers being up there for the recording of 'Drowning Man'.

It's a song written from the perspective of a loving God. It may, in its way, be entirely presumptuous – but, far more importantly, its cup is overflowing with tenderness.

And it is addressed to Adam Clayton.

> "Bono would search for that higher state, improvising lyrics on the microphone, allowing the words, the feeling – at its best the ecstasy – to take hold."

Adam Clayton

war

the refugee

Steve Lillywhite had a rule that he would not do more than two albums with any one band or artist. It was time for U2, also, to move on to fresh alliances, and to use the opportunity to remodel their sound. They knew what they wanted: a harder, more urban, more rock 'n' roll feel than *October* had exhibited. Among those considered were Jimmy Destri, then of Blondie, Sandy Pearlman – who had worked with Blue Oyster Cult and The Clash, Roxy Music's Rhet Davies, and Jimmy Iovine, who had phoned repeatedly, insisting that he wanted to produce the band.

Producer Bill Whelan

along the way they'd considered the possibility of using an Irish producer. Bill Whelan had already formed a publishing alliance with the band's manager, Paul McGuinness, and they demoed one song at least with him. It turned up on *War*.

"I think when Bono went to America he became more politicized," one friend suggests. "He was hanging out with Cubans in San Francisco. In America, the blacks, the Italians and other immigrants have an *amour* for the Irish. Bono always got that kind of response, so he started to take an interest in what the Irish and the blacks and the Caribbeans had in common. I think that's where 'The Refugee' was coming from."

It was that, and more besides. The Irish film-maker Bob Quinn had been exploring the roots of Celtic culture. In an influential documentary, the *Atlantean* trilogy, he advanced the theory that the Celts had come to Ireland from Egypt and North Africa, taking their music and their art with them. Similarities had been detected between Irish traditional melodies and those of Middle Eastern folk and ethnic music. And in the same vein, art historians were beginning to identify unmistakable connections between Coptic art and the intricate and elaborate artwork hand-drawn by Irish monks in manuscripts like the *Book of Kells*.

That kind of discovery, and the debate it inspired, was hugely important in a country like Ireland, whose culture had been stultifyingly rigid and enclosed in the 50-plus years since independence had been declared in 1921. Among the younger post-'60s generation in particular, there was a growing awareness of the need to look outwards, and to learn from other cultures and other societies. This was now given fresh impetus by the recognition that our own roots and origins were far more complex – and far more interesting – than we'd traditionally been led to believe. Bono saw the *Atlantean* trilogy and later met Bob Quinn. It was almost inevitable that the curiosity which had thus been aroused would find an outlet in a song.

"That was a passion at the time, that Irish music had to be re-invented or re-incarnated. At around the same time, I was trying to get in touch with John Lydon, to see if I could get him to record with The Chieftains. I had this idea that his voice sounded like bagpipes and I thought that they'd be amazing together. Then we met Steve Wickham, who came in and played on 'Sunday Bloody Sunday'. I had spoken with Steve, over many nights, about

Mick Jones and Paul
Simonon of The Clash

how Irish music could be re-appropriated, because it was terribly unhip at the time. That became his project. He went off with that in mind and joined In Tua Nua. [He also later hooked up with The Waterboys.] So a lot of good came of all that."

The Troublefunk reference on 'Seconds' wasn't the only reason to suspect that someone had been doing some serious listening to black music. When *War* was being pieced together, Steve Lillywhite – who'd agreed to become involved one more time when all else had failed – took the Bill Whelan track and put the finishing touches to it. Larry Mullen's thumping tribal drums were mixed right up front and the band engaged in some suitably primitive chanting. The noise was impressive enough: it just didn't sound entirely as if U2 were wearing their own clothes, playing

their own riffs, using their own voices.

"I haven't listened to that song in 10 years," Bono confesses, "but I think it's probably in the wrong key and is trying to be exciting and not quite pulling it off."

Curiously, Bill Whelan, who was credited with producing the track, found his own angle on the theme later in *Riverdance*. If re-invigorating Irish music, and in particular Irish dancing, was the objective, then Whelan achieved it spectacularly, with a successful musical that explored again the connections between Irish, American and – to a lesser extent – African music.

In doing so, along with the show's producer Moya Doherty, Whelan succeeded in re-introducing an erotic, sexual dimension to an ethnic dance culture that had become sterile and antiseptic.

> "I was trying to get in touch with John Lydon, to see if I could get him to record with The Chieftains."
>
> – BONO

45

Bono tied the knot with Ali Stewart on 21 August, 1982. The band were hugely in debt to Island Records at the time and the singer didn't have a whole lot of money to lavish on the occasion. Still, the Island connection had one distinct advantage: the owner of the label, Chris Blackwell, held extensive properties in Jamaica and the Bahamas. He loaned one of them, a house called Goldeneye which had once belonged to Ian Fleming, to Bono and Ali for their honeymoon. 'Two Hearts Beat as One' was one of two songs that Bono wrote there.

two hearts
beat as one

Two hearts: Bono and wife Ali

the second single to be released from *War* – and the band's second hit in Britain – it was another stab at fusing rock and funk and it was at least a partial success. Lyrically, Bono is still struggling to find a voice. *"I don't know how to say what's got to be said,"* he confesses. But even more revealing, perhaps, is the undercurrent of desperation which the song announces.

You can imagine Bono unable to bask in the comfort of his honeymoon house, his restless spirit inevitably contemplating with mounting horror the prospect of entering the studio again with a bunch of under-worked lyrical ideas and half-completed choruses scrawled on the back of cigarette papers and Air India sickbags. *"I can't stop to dance/This is my last chance,"* he says, as if to excuse himself to Ali. And of course he may have been right: if U2 had not taken off with *War*, then it might well have been their last album, on Island at least. And if Island had dropped them, who knows what might have happened then?

"I didn't really write that many love songs in the straight sense because I think – does the world really need any more silly love songs?" Bono asserts. "But this is one. And in many ways I do think that it's beautiful. We're trying to make it groovy and we ain't quite pulled it off. I think if we'd tried it in a different key, we might have discovered a sexier groove and it might have worked better. But we never did that. Whatever the jam was in, I'd sing the song in that key. That's why there was a tightness in the vocals, which I find it hard to listen to now. I was screeching a lot of the time. But I think if a song like that had been delivered differently it would have more appeal to me now 'cos it's a good song."

An outsider visiting Ireland in the late '70s and early '80s might have been forgiven for concluding that the locals knew nothing about carnal delights, and had little interest in the pleasures of the flesh. The dominant ethos was still extremely conservative on sexual issues. The underlying reality was that the people had begun to move on, and the seeds of a more tolerant and liberal society were beginning to take root. But officially, it was a culture where condoms were still available from chemists only on prescription, homosexuality was illegal, and highly restrictive censorship laws ensured that erotic or pornographic books and magazines were almost completely unavailable.

i t couldn't have been more different to New York, Hamburg or Amsterdam. Inevitably these somewhat exotic destinations held a particular allure for four young Irishmen in a rock 'n' roll band, enjoying the freedom of the cities they were visiting for the first time.

"I certainly remember a fascination with prostitution," Bono recalls. "We played Amsterdam and I remember seeing the girls for sale in the windows, lit in red. Thinking about it. Trying to figure out the reality of it, whether there *was* any or not. I was never judgmental about it."

'Red Light' is decidedly ambiguous. It's a love song, which could be addressed to one of the girls Bono had observed in the windows of the flophouses in the Red Light district. Equally, it might be another somewhat parental, albeit affectionate homily directed at saving Adam's immortal soul. Or it could be written from the point of view of a prostitute, watching her clients come and go. Probably, in a way that was typical of U2's songs then, it is any or all of these things at once.

Musically, the band make a stab at evoking an appropriately steamy cityscape. Kid Creole and The Coconuts, who were knocking on the door of stardom at the time, passed through town while U2 were recording the album, and the ensemble's trumpeter Kenny Fradley was hauled in to add a brassy bit. And then there were The Coconuts themselves.

"They came in," Bono recalls. "They wanted the lights turned down to do the recording and I think we had the studio lit in red, for effect. I can't remember which, but one of them started to take her top off. She wasn't undressing. She just took her top off, but we weren't used to that kind

red light

of thing. I remember the temperature in the studio was at an all-time high. Everyone was running around looking for cold water. We were that naive!" [*laughs*].

Lyrically, the song is reasonably strong, but 'Red Light' is widely regarded as one of U2's most unsatisfactory cuts. At least we now know who to blame.

The voice squad: Bono with Kid Creole's Coconuts.

"Homosexuality was illegal, and highly restrictive censorship laws ensured that erotic or pornographic books and magazines were almost completely unavailable."

Bono was beginning to write songs. You can tell by the way he was getting into using characters. And then there were the small poetic flourishes, lines that have a more finished feel to them. He was beginning to know his own strengths, to understand how to channel his creative energies more effectively. He was becoming a songwriter.

surrender

Bono live: never about to throw in the towel.

he'd met Sadie – not her real name – in New York. She was living on the street, hustling and doing whatever was necessary to keep body and soul together. Over 10 years on, she's still at the same game, only by now she's got a smack habit to feed. Back then, he was attracted to her and to the way in which she'd been able to let go of all the trappings of domesticity and respectability. He probably still is.

There's an ambivalence here that involves a huge leap forward from the biblical certainties of *October* and hints at the more complex world of *Achtung Baby* and *Zooropa*. The concept of surrender is a spiritual one, but it's rooted not in any conventional concept of virtue. It wasn't enough for Sadie to be a good wife, to raise a good family, to lead a good life. And so she took to the streets. "You've got to learn to let go in order to really live. That's what 'Surrender' is all about," Bono explains.

There's a reminder of the fascination with suicide on *Boy* when Sadie takes herself up to the 48th floor to find out, in the words of the song, what she's living for. "In one sense everyone's got to jump off. That's what it's all about – the idea that if I want to live, I've got to die to myself."

The rest of the band provide the atmospherics, with The Edge enjoying himself playing a free role on slide guitar. But this is primarily Bono's track as he himself lets go, blissfully surrendering, fading, fading into the background.

"Over 10 years on, she's still at the same game, only by now she's got a smack habit to feed."

The recording of *War* had been exhilarating, tense and finally draining. There were times during the course of their incarceration in Windmill when Steve Lillywhite had had to push Bono to the limits, forcing him to sing until his throat bled. Now, here they were, a track short and with their allotted studio time almost up. The band had enjoyed themselves in the past improvising B-sides and starting and finishing songs in an hour. The results were usually throwaway, but what the hell? They wanted to get '40' done. Steve Lillywhite said to go for it.

40

adam was out of the studio and The Edge stood in, supplying a sweet, resonant melodic bass line that worked beautifully over the simple guitar strum. No point in changing it. At 6 o'clock in the morning, a belligerent bunch of musos in a local Dublin band arrived to begin the session they'd booked. They wanted U2 out. The band had to lock the door and mix the track while Bono was doing his final vocal take. His voice sounds ragged, 6 o'clock in the morning ragged. But whatever chemistry was at work as dawn crept in from the east over Dublin Bay, the band achieve a remarkable serenity. If this was what they'd been looking for throughout *War*, they'd found it in that final hour.

Partly it may be that they knew that their ordeal was over, that there was no point in trying too hard. Keep it simple. Get it down. It'll work out. '40' emerges as a lullaby, a hymn that's suffused with a deep feeling of peace and resignation. For the most part, the lyrics are lifted from Psalm 40, in the Psalms of David. But the desperate plea in the opening track, 'Sunday Bloody Sunday' – *"How long must we sing this song?"* – is revisited here as an incantation, a prayer.

'40' would become one of U2's best known tracks, chosen by the band to close their live shows throughout most of the '80s. The Edge called it a monument to U2, created in an instant.

"I really love that song," Bono says simply now. "I've seen some incredible scenes, I've seen some extraordinary sights, through it. I really love it."

Amen.

The Biblical David beseeches the Lord for copyright protection.

the unforgettable fire

t he tension of the *War* tour had scared U2. There was a danger that they were becoming shrill. There was a danger that they already had. They needed to chill out. Live a little. Absorb influences. Get back in touch with the impulse that had inspired them in the first place. The success of their live mini-album *Under a Blood Red Sky* gave them room to manoeuvre.

(Island U25)

Produced by **Brian Eno.**

Recorded at **Slane Castle, Meath; and Windmill Lane Studios, Dublin.**

Released **1 October 1984.**

For their next studio album, it would help to find a new producer. They thought of Conny Plank. It didn't happen. And then in a flash of inspiration The Edge thought of Brian Eno. It is impossible to speculate what might have happened if Eno had said no. Instead he brought Daniel Lanois with him.

They began the album in Slane Castle with the mobile. The sessions were open-ended, spacious, free. The band did a day's recording naked. "We got into gaffer art," Bono commented. Lanois, for one, lost some pubic hairs as a result.

But Danny was good on rhythms. Larry's playing became looser, funkier, more subtle. Adam's gained in confidence and poise. Gradually Bono learned to sing again. The relaxed, experimental feel of those initial sessions gave the record its fresh, exploratory tone. Not everything worked and, as the deadline approached, they opted to go back into Windmill. Bono was still agonizing over lyrics. Less than two weeks before the band were due to go on tour, he announced that he couldn't do it.

He was given an ultimatum. Do it. The final ten days' recording were a nightmare. One or two tracks sound seriously undercooked. But on balance the exercise was thoroughly successful, producing U2's first album with a cohesive sound.

With *The Unforgettable Fire*, U2 were reborn.

Bono had become a voracious reader. He was still interested in the Bible and in opening up its myriad secrets, but he was casting his net more widely now than ever before. On tour, in buses and hotel rooms, he'd bury his head in whatever he could get his hands on. "It's a pity I didn't keep a diary," he says. "If I could remember what I was reading I'd probably know much more quickly where a lot of the songs came from."

which were rendered all the more stark by the fact that he had drowned himself in the River Seine in 1970.

So often U2 songs begin with the title. A phrase fixes itself in Bono's head, and he carries it around knowing that it has the potential to act as a springboard, that it may inspire the leap of the imagination necessary to begin writing a song. It can take months. It can take even longer. The title goes down in a notebook or on a piece of paper. Sometimes, in the immediate flush of inspiration, a verse

a sort of homecoming

Bono and a sort of horse coming.

he was immersing himself in fiction, philosophy, poetry. And the more poetry he read, the more he began to understand his songwriting mission as a poetic one.

He could occasionally be self-conscious about it. "I am a writer of words," he reflected in 'Dreams in a Box', a poem written during 1987 which he contributed to the Chicago Peace Museum. But there is no doubt that by 1984 and the making of *The Unforgettable Fire*, he had begun to find his poetic voice.

Bono had been reading the work of Paul Celan, a Jewish poet of mixed German and Romanian origin, from a collection given to him by Bill Graham of *Hot Press*. Celan was an intensely spiritual writer, a mystic whose life and death were shrouded in ambiguities. In many ways he may have been a crucial discovery for Bono. On *War*, U2 had stepped back from the charismatic triumphalism of *October*'s most nakedly religious songs, but only so far. Now, Celan's work posed a set of questions that were complex and highly problematic for anyone of narrow, fixed religious convictions. Gradually, Bono, Larry and The Edge were leaving those certainties behind. But Celan, in particular, opened up new avenues of spiritual doubt,

or two will be produced, which may end up in another song entirely.

"Poetry is a sort of homecoming," Celan had written, and it rang true for Bono. For a musician, constantly away from home and on the move, the phrase had a special kind of significance. In a sense, it conjures up the peculiar condition of the transient, the state of statelessness that afflicts those whose experience makes them, occasionally at

51

the unforgettable fire

Poetic champion composed: William Butler Yeats.

least, uncertain of their own roots and their own identity.

In the end, Celan's phrase inspired a meditation that seemed to encompass in one impressionistic reverie many of Bono's familiar obsessions. It is written in a dreamy, cinematic style, the camera briefly capturing vivid images which then dissolve one into the next, a constant sense of movement propelling the song along. *"She will die and live again, tonight,"* Bono sings, and sex and spirituality intermingle, in an unmistakable allusion to the little death and the (little) resurrection.

But while there is a sense in the lyrics that things are falling apart and the centre cannot hold, the extent to which the narrator seems in control of the words, of the ideas, of the poetry, is in itself reassuring.

It's as if Bono is re-affirming his commitment to a life devoted to the search for poetic truth. While it might seem like a veiled reference to 'I Will Follow', the chant *"O come away/O come away/O come away/O come away say I"* is more likely an unconscious allusion to William Butler Yeats' 'The Human Child', and it was towards influences of that kind that he was increasingly drawn.

"A lot of rock 'n' roll is banal ideas well executed," Bono reflects. "Whereas I think a lot of what we do is really very interesting ideas, badly executed."

'A Sort of Homecoming' involved a lot of very interesting ideas well executed. It was a powerful opening to the album.

Gonna use her voice: Chrissie Hynde of The Pretenders.

On the road, U2 are constantly working informally on new ideas. As a matter of course, rehearsals and sound-checks are recorded. Frequently the germ of something new will emerge as the band improvise their way through a series of rhythm patterns and chord changes.

pride (in the name of love)

from a musical point of view, over the years this is how a substantial number of U2 songs began. 'Pride' was among them. The band played Hawaii during the *War* tour, in November 1983. Their live engineer, Joe O'Herlihy, was recording the sound-check. He remembers The Edge leading the way into a series of chord changes. As they rode the rhythm there was a mistake, and the band picked up on it: someone's slip had given a new twist to the piece and they ran it a few more times. Joe recorded the incident in his own personal memory bank: by now he'd learned to recognize these special moments. When the time came to record *The Unforgettable Fire*, he remembered precisely where the roots of 'Pride' were to be found.

U2 songs often proceed along parallel tracks. On the one side, a set of musical ideas is taking shape. On the other, Bono and The Edge are developing bits of titles, lyrics, choruses and whatever other scraps of ideas have suggested themselves. The real heartache starts when they begin the process of bringing these different elements together. Bono was working on something about Ronald Reagan. He had the title 'Pride' in mind for it, thinking about the kind that comes before a fall, thinking of the hubris which was the dominant characteristic of America's foreign policy during the Reagan era. But it wasn't working, and he began to get the feeling he was going to have to switch tack.

An idea can take on a life of its own. It won't do what you want it to do. And so you have to let it find its own way. The band had been to the Chicago Peace Museum and were impressed by the exhibit there dedicated to the black civil rights leader Martin Luther King, who had been brutally gunned down as he stood on a motel balcony in Memphis on 4 April, 1968. Shifting emphasis to the kind of pride that King had inspired in black people, Bono sensed that there was an entirely different song to be written.

At the centre of the song is a series of images that have the grainy feel of wire photos sent back from the front-line of resistance: *"One man caught on a barbed wire fence/One man he resist/One man washed up on an empty beach/One man betrayed by a kiss."* There is no sense that Bono had abandoned his religious beliefs, but the references are more subtle here and there's an underlying awareness of the contradictions that will increasingly qualify the fervour that *October* had revealed.

Recording 'Pride (In the Name of Love)' proved to be extraordinarily difficult. U2 had done a backing track in relaxed circumstances in Slane, but when they moved across to Windmill Lane to finish the record it didn't feel right. They speeded it up, slowed it down and heaped overdub on top of overdub. It was lousy and they knew it. With time ticking away and everyone becoming increasingly agitated, they decided to go for broke. They agreed to ditch what they'd done in Slane and came in the next day to re-record the track from scratch. Sometimes that's the only way to resolve an impasse in recording. Luckily, in this instance, it worked. Almost immediately they knew that 'Pride' was a killer. Chrissie Hynde of The Pretenders was in town and she dropped into the studio to assist with the backing vocals, though the sleeve credits refer to Mrs Christine Kerr. Not surprisingly, it became the first single from *The Unforgettable Fire*, released in advance of the album.

"When I started writing I didn't even know what a couplet was," Bono recalls. But by *The Unforgettable Fire* he had developed a much stronger sense of what the conventions were. When he got it right, then a song lifted and soared: 'A Sort of Homecoming' was a case in point, a tremendously visual, poetic, emotional word-festival. Things didn't always work out so well, however.

Whereas Steve Lillywhite had been highly rigorous and exacting in his attitude to songs, Eno was far more indulgent. Bono tended to come at his themes obliquely. Eno let him get away with it even when he ended up saying very little.

Bono was aware of the junk that had begun to flood Dublin. He knew a couple of friends who'd become involved. Now he wanted to write a song that captured his own ambivalence to the drug. "I'm probably an addictive kind of person myself," Bono admits. And so that was what he wanted to convey lyrically.

There's an openness and sparkle to the music on 'Wire', which skips along on a light funk groove courtesy of an in-form Larry Mullen. The hand of Eno and Lanois is in evidence here, as the band veer in a direction already sign-posted by Talking Heads, whom Eno had also produced. But while the noise is impressive, the lyrics never get beyond mere sketchwork. "There is the fascination of death and of flirting with death that's part of heroin use," Bono reflected later. But none of that is conveyed here. There are moments of sardonic rhetoric that almost work – *"Such a nice day/To throw your life away"* – and the song ends in a kind of a nagging rap. But 'Wire' is an example of how flat a song improvised on the mike can be. *"Is this time, the time to win or lose?"* he asks, *"Is this the time, the time to choose?"*

Bono knew what a couplet was now, alright. But that didn't mean he was William Shakespeare.

"Now he wanted to write a song that captured his own ambivalence to the drug."

the unforgettable fire

When the Americans dropped the atomic bomb on Hiroshima and Nagasaki, it was one of the final and most barbarous acts of World War Two. These two Japanese cities were utterly destroyed, and in human terms the toll was even more horrific.

toll is almost impossible to calculate, though 200,000 is probably a conservative estimate. It was as close as we had ever come to Armageddon, a terrible spectacle of such frightening immensity that anyone who was close to it could never, ever forget – the whole world, it seemed, transformed into a gigantic charnel house.

Iwakichi Kobayashi was a survivor of the holocaust that had engulfed Hiroshima and Nagasaki. He drew a picture to illustrate his memory of what had happened. Japanese television picked up on the theme and invited other survivors to submit their own paintings. It became a kind of exorcism, a therapeutic outpouring of grief and horror at the atrocity which had been visited on innocent people by the military machines of both the USA and Japan.

The Japanese created an exhibition of the paintings

the unforgettable fire

Hiroshima: a city destroyed.

and drawings from survivors of the holocaust, entitled *The Unforgettable Fire*, and it was housed within the Hiroshima Peace Memorial. During the early '80s, some 60 of the pictures had been taken on tour; they went on display at the Chicago Peace Museum, and U2 saw them there. "Painting was part of the therapy to help these people purge themselves of their internalized emotions," The Edge told Tristan Logan of *Boston* magazine at the time. "The image of that purging quality, coupled with the insight it gave into the horror of nuclear holocaust, stuck in Bono's mind. Later we found the title fit the new record in many ways, especially in reflecting its multicoloured textures."

It was Bono's magpie instinct at work again. In a reversal of the norm that would be typical of the band, Bono thought of *The Unforgettable Fire* as the name of the album first. It was too good a title not to use it for a song as well – though what Bono produced by way of a lyric had little or no connection with the original source of the title.

"It was a soundtrack piece I'd been messing around with on the piano at home," The Edge reflected later. "It was a beautiful piece of music but I couldn't see how one could approach it lyrically or vocally. It was knocking around for quite a while, and myself and Bono were out in his house doing work on material for the record and I found this cassette of the piano piece and we decided to mess around

a total of 67,000 people died immediately as a direct result, and thousands more were scarred, injured and maimed. But it was a catastrophe truly like no other in terms of its psychic impact: the effects of radiation from the bombs would last for generations, producing genetic mutations of the most chilling kind, and causing widespread leukaemia and cancer. The final death

with it. I had the DX7 keyboard and worked on a treatment. Within an hour, we'd written a verse section with Bono playing bass, and we virtually wrote the song there. Obviously it changed with drums and bass in the studio, but it was the first 20 minutes in Bono's house that counted."

Bono was still in a state of semi-permanent writer's block. "Writing songs scares the living daylights out of me," he said at the time. "It's been a huge problem and I just ran away, I guess." Even in a situation where they had the melody and the music, he was finding it hard to get a fix on the lyrics.

"I see the rhythm of words as being important," he reasoned afterwards. "They build up slowly and often I don't think it's ready yet – though everyone else may think it is, I can't let it go. That's why a lot of the songs tend to be sketches. 'The Unforgettable Fire', it's a sketch: *'Carnival/wheels fly and colours spin/face to face/in a dry and waterless place.'* It builds up a picture, but it's only a sketch." Some sketches, however, work better than others. "It doesn't tell you anything," Bono adds, but he's right only up to a point. Again this is an emotional travelogue, images shuffled through the memory to underscore the song's heartfelt sense of yearning. It is a love song that links thematically back to 'A Sort of Homecoming', but it's imbued with a deeper sense of foreboding that seems to anticipate the end of a relationship.

"It's classical almost," The Edge told Carter Alan in 1985. "I see it as a music piece rather than as a song. Bono, in a very unconventional way, explores numerous melodies over sections. Instead of repeating melodies – you know, verses and choruses, which is what everyone does – we've got three chorus melodies and two verse melodies. It has a certain symphonic feel for me because there are so many intertwining themes. I know we could have recorded it better but, I think, for all its flaws, I just see it as a great piece of music."

The symphonic feel is heightened by the addition of a string section, arranged by Noel Kelehan – an unlikely ally for U2, since he was most familiar to both Irish and international audiences as the conductor of the RTE Light Orchestra, in successive Eurovision Song Contests. The important thing, however, is that the strings work, lifting the track beyond conventional rock aesthetics. Its horrific starting point notwithstanding, it was one of U2's most beautiful creations.

Van Morrison's legend looms large in Irish music. He emerged as one of the king-pins of the Belfast beat scene in the early '60s with Them. Signed to Decca, the band moved to London and had a cluster of hits, including classics like 'Baby Please Don't Go' and 'Here Comes the Night'.

promenade

the garage-band nugget 'Gloria' was deemed worthy only of a B-side. Unhappy with what he considered an exploitative recording deal, and disillusioned with the business, Morrison disbanded Them and left for the States. There he recording the magical *Astral Weeks*, which still ranks among the greatest rock albums of all time. On it, Morrison forged a new kind of song-poetry. The themes on *Astral Weeks* were firmly rooted in the Belfast that the singer had grown up in and left behind, but there was a powerful stream-of-consciousness running through the

The tower of song: Bono's historic residence in Bray, Co. Dublin.

the unforgettable fire

Eno's hand was in evidence.

> "A spiral staircase led from the living room up to the bedroom. Above the bed was a glass roof, opening up a spectacular view of the night sky."

songs, with Morrison digging deeper and deeper into the inner-self to uncover a quality of poetic truth that was new for rock 'n' roll.

From U2's perspective, Morrison was crucial. Following a period in seclusion, he had re-emerged in the late '70s and, the man's reputation as an abrasive genius notwithstanding, his music reflected a renewed sense of inner contentment. His interest in language, and in squeezing out new meanings from it, was undiminished. Van Morrison stretched words, broke them down, created new ones, and – occasionally in despair at the limits which this discipline imposed – plunged into a kind of primal articulation, letting the inner self rise to the surface and express itself. But guiding this search for descriptive, expressive resources beyond language was a profound interest in spirituality. Morrison was an Irish artist, with an Irish sensibility, influenced by Irish music and Irish melodies – but he was also a soul singer who was not afraid to reveal his spiritual concerns.

U2 could never merely follow the Morrison model, but it was reassuring to them, nonetheless, that he had managed to infuse his work with such a powerful sense of

Gerard Manley Hopkins.

spiritual mission. It was inevitable that Bono would listen to and be inspired by his music, and on 'Promenade' that influence is unmistakable. Morrison's straining at the leash of linguistic limitations had something of Gerard Manley Hopkins in it, and the same thought strikes you about 'Promenade'. Words are used for their sound as much as their sense, which was not new for Bono – but here there is a poetic surefootedness in the writing that marks a significant step forward. After the explosiveness and controversy of the *War* tour, Bono had spoken about the need for U2 to re-invent themselves. "Today was the last U2 gig," Bono said on the evening the tour finished. "But I'm not talking about the end of U2. This is the end of a cycle. We must develop new areas now. U2 is just beginning." He had spoken too about the need to be sensitive and atmospheric: 'Promenade' was the third track on *The Unforgettable Fire* which that description would have fitted.

"I find it very difficult to listen to *War* now," Bono admits. "There is so much anger there and the effect of that is to tighten up the voice, so that it becomes higher and more shrill. I don't like the way I sound at all. But on *The Unforgettable Fire* I learned to relax again. I learned to sing again." He had understood from listening to Van Morrison that sometimes it's better to whisper.

And so there's an intimacy to 'Promenade' that's appropriate to a song that's about intimate, personal experience. Bono and his wife Ali had moved from one side of Dublin Bay, in Howth, across to Bray – another slightly faded seaside resort just beyond the southern border of county Dublin. He was living in the Martello Tower there, which he'd had re-designed. A spiral staircase led from the living room up to the bedroom. Above the bed was a glass roof, opening up a spectacular view of the night sky. The tower overlooked the Carlisle Grounds, where Bray Wanderers played their League of Ireland football games. All along the promenade are amusement parlours, snooker halls, fast-food outlets, restaurants and guest houses. That background is evoked in impressionistic strokes, but 'Promenade' is unmistakably a love song that celebrates the spiritual dimensions of sexual desire. *"Turn me around tonight/up through the spiral staircase/to the higher ground."*

It's where we all want to go, if we know how to get there.

One of Brian Eno's rules is that there are no rules. Sometimes, if you work too hard at something you kill it.

Occasionally when you're doodling, something emerges which is transcendent. Inspiration can strike in the most unexpected situations. You can frame the maxims in different ways. You can hone them till they're razor sharp. You can even develop them, as Eno did, into a set of Oblique Strategies. "The first I wrote was 'Honour thy error as a hidden intention', a reminder not to have too fixed a view about what was appropriate in a given piece," Eno explained to David Gan, "to accept the possibility that sometimes the things one doesn't intend are the seeds for a more interesting future than the one one had envisaged."

It is impossible to speculate about what Adam might have intended when he began to amuse himself with a sliding bass figure, in a break during recording, after U2 had put down a version of 'Bad' in Windmill Lane. Musicians do this kind of thing all the time and more often than not the germ of an idea is lost once somebody walks in with a cup of coffee.

"I started playing along with Adam, totally unaware that Brian was listening in the other room," The Edge recalled. "He happened to have some treatments set up for the vocal Bono had been doing and he applied those to the guitar. He thought it was really nice, so without bothering to put it on multi-track, which is the 24-track tape machine, he just recorded it straight down to stereo tape. It was very much a live performance. There was no way we could mix it or re-do any of the instruments." There was probably a temptation to get Bono to stick a vocal on top, but the singer must have been relieved when that option was dismissed. One less lyric to write. Whew!

The track is pensive and exploratory. In no way an attempt to celebrate Independence Day, it should be taken rather as a kind of musical diary-entry. This is how we were feeling on 4 July. Eno captured the moment for posterity. That was a vital part of his genius.

4th of july

"I started playing along, totally unaware that Brian was listening in the other room."

– THE EDGE

Naturally high: The Edge recording in Slane Castle.

bad

Some of U2's biggest songs happened almost by accident. 'Bad' stands in a line from 'Party Girl' through '40'. You could conclude that it was destined to become a live favourite.

The needle and the damage done.

> "It's only after six months of touring it and talking to different people that you get to the inner truths of the song."
>
> – ADAM

It began with an improvisation by The Edge, the other guys in the room joining in. "I think we did three takes," The Edge recalls, "and that was enough to give us our basic track. There are overdubs but it's almost live, and it's got that feel. There's one moment where Larry puts down the brushes and takes up the sticks and it creates this pause, which has an incredibly dramatic effect. That's the sort of thing that you don't plan." But when it happens, it feels absolutely right.

For the second time on *The Unforgettable Fire*, we are given to understand that Bono is addressing a heroin addict. There is a sense throughout 'Bad' that he doesn't know what he wants to say, and that he doesn't know what he's saying either. But, in a way, he says it eloquently anyway.

To begin with there's an empathy in 'Bad' which gives the song resonance. The accusatory tone of War has been abandoned. *"If I could,"* Bono sings, *"Yes I would/If I could/I would let it go/Surrender, dislocate."* It's an honest admission of his own vulnerability to the temptation that drugs like heroin represent. "It relates to what I was trying to do, much more overtly on Zoo TV," he states. "With those characters, I wanted to admit to those things, those sides of yourself, that want to run away from responsibility, and that

find people who have run away attractive. That was there on 'Bad' too. I've always had a real respect for responsible people but I also have a real respect for irresponsible people. There is that side of me that wants to run."

'Bad' begins on a kind of drone, but it's the light, shuffling rhythm track, with Adam throwing in a dub-influenced bass part, that gives the track its addictive propulsion. "I think the experience of working with Brian and Daniel Lanois was a revelation to Larry," The Edge says. "Instead of his goal being technique or drumming ability, he became aware of new approaches to rhythm. He became aware of percussion." Eno's philosophy afforded him a new kind of freedom to explore and improvise. "We grew on this album, a lot," Larry told Carter Alan, and it was true of no one more than himself. In many ways 'Bad' is a personal triumph for him.

Bono, meanwhile, was engaging in his own inarticulate speech of the heart. Like 'Wire', there's nothing in the night-lit world of 'Bad' that makes it clear this song has to do with junk. But there is a restlessness throughout that in itself speaks volumes. You begin to imagine the narrator prowling his room in the darkest hour before dawn, wrestling with the temptation to take the plunge. There is a desire in here that's almost suicidal, a desire to go over the edge to experience whatever the other side might throw at him. The feeling is so intense that he can't express it clearly. His thoughts emerge in disconnected fragments. He repeats himself. There are things he isn't saying. If you wanted to get tough about it, you'd argue that 'Bad' says nothing. But it's a trip – a tense, nervy, intoxicating, exhilarating trip. And musically, it is marvellous.

"Comprehension had never been particularly important to me," says Adam, who worked as Bono's sounding-board, sitting in on the singing during the recording of *The Unforgettable Fire*. "It's much more important how the lyrics feel. If it doesn't sound right, then I'll consult him and try and figure out what's going on. But it's an instinctive thing. I find that it's only after six months of touring it and talking to different people that you get to the inner truths of the song, which is not always something Bono intended. Gradually the sand and debris is swept away and the core is revealed."

Desperation, dislocation, separation, condemnation, revelation, in temptation, isolation, desolation. All of those qualities are there in Bono's performance, except one. The time for condemnation was over. For now.

Sometime in New York City – probably when the *War* tour hit Manhattan – Bono wrote the bones of 'Indian Summer Sky'. "Most of the writing was cinematic and very fast," Bono says. "It had a sense of wanting to break through a city to an open place."

indian

summer sky

a friend of Bono's had spent some time in Toronto. He felt troubled, torn in two by a city that was "cool" and "shiny". "There had been a lot of massacres of Red Indian people in that area," Bono reports, "and he felt in some way as if there were troubled spirits still there. What I was trying to get across in 'Indian Summer Sky' was a sense of spirit trapped in a concrete jungle."

The song is imbued with an epic quality: on the one hand wind, ocean, sky and earth, on the other heart and soul, more heart and more soul. At one point, it anticipates 'With or Without You' on *The Joshua Tree* as Bono sings, *"You give yourself to this the longest day/You give yourself you give it all away."* It's possible that the chorus – *"So wind go through to my heart/So wind blow through my soul"* – sounds as much like Talking Heads as it does, simply because of Brian Eno's involvement. He had, after all, produced *Remain In Light*. The influence seems unmistakable, but there's nothing forced or unnatural in U2's music here.

"In many ways," Bono reflected later, *"The Unforgettable Fire* was a contrast between bricks and mortar and music with the sky over its head." In that it was a product not just of Bono's Martello Tower but of the initial phase of recording in Slane Castle. But it also reflected the increasing liberation of Bono's spirituality. He was beginning to move to the rhythms of nature. Now you could move your hips to U2. Now you could dance.

And it felt good.

> "What I was trying to get across in 'Indian Summer Sky' was a sense of spirit trapped in a concrete jungle."
>
> – BONO

Under Adam's watchful gaze, Bono, The Edge and Eno string it up during sessions for *The Unforgettable Fire*.

59

the unforgettable fire

The difference between the production styles of Steve Lillywhite and Brian Eno could not be more starkly expressed than by this track. Lillywhite was prepared to experiment alright, but Eno went much further.

elvis presley
and america

Elvis Presley: rock 'n' roll genius.

h e saw a piece that had been recorded as utterly malleable. You could open it up, slow it down, stand it on its head, reverse it – anything that might work was worth a shot. And so on an experimental day, when Daniel Lanois and he were fishing around for ideas, they slowed down the backing track from 'A Sort of Homecoming' and played it for Bono without telling him what it was. Eno encouraged the singer to improvise over it.

"It was partly a reaction to the Albert Goldman book, which tried to portray Elvis as the archetypal rock 'n' roll idiot," Bono explains. "But the way he held the mike, the way he sang into the mike – this was his genius. But his decline just tore at me, and when I picked up the mike it was a completely off the wall thing and I just began to sing." Bono approached the track like a jazzman, letting his voice take the song and following it, improvising the lyrics as he went along. Bono saw it as a dry run. The lyrical ideas could be sifted through and refined later. But Eno had other plans.

"He forced Bono to change his approach to recording," The Edge remembers. "Whereas previously with Steve, seven or eight different tracks would be collaged into a single vocal, Brian started insisting, whenever it was practical, on doing one take. He was much more interested in continuity, in the performance."

It still came as a shock to Bono when Eno told him that the cut was finished. It was one of Eno's oblique strategies in action: overtly resist change. And another: emphasize the flaws. "It was such an inspired performance," The Edge said flatteringly, "that we decided to leave it as it was." Not everyone would be so complimentary. Among the band's most supportive critics, Dave Marsh in the USA and Neil McCormick of *Hot Press* in Ireland hated the song. It wasn't what Bono was apparently trying to say about Elvis that rankled, it was the fact that 'Elvis Presley and America' so obviously sounded like a work-in-progress.

"I think that it does evoke that decline, the stupor, the period when – if you've seen the clips of him – he forgets his words and fumbles," Bono argued at the time.

It wasn't a bad shot at post-rationalization, but one thing's for sure: it may have been a useful harbinger for the journey to the heartland of rock 'n' roll that *Rattle and Hum* would involve, but 'Elvis Presley and America' would never be regarded as a U2 classic.

The Unforgettable Fire had been coined as a phrase to describe the terror of the holocaust. However, U2 had seen another meaning in it. Just as 'Pride' could be conceived as a song about Ronald Reagan and written about Martin Luther King, it was possible to ascribe another sense to a phrase that played on Bono's imagination.

f ire, passion, belief – these were things that U2 had written about, things that they had dedicated their music to. Elvis Presley had lit a fire that was burning still. So too had Martin Luther King. With 'MLK', he became the hero of *The Unforgettable Fire*, the man whose memory was evoked in the end to soothe the anxieties which had riddled the album and which had crept up on U2 increasingly as the recording had progressed.

It was becoming a trademark. '40' had ended *War* – as 'Scarlet' should have ended *October* – on a healing note. Now that *The Unforgettable Fire* was done, it was time for a spiritual, and 'MLK' provided it. It was a lullaby, a song of reassurance and reconciliation. A song of hope. *"Sleep, sleep tonight/And may your dreams/be realised,"* Bono sang, and it was made to be sung by thousands joined together in a gesture of communion. "Those people who were fighting for civil rights," Bono remarks, "they understood that music better than they understood 'Pride', which was rock 'n' roll music. They understood the tribute."
Let it rain, rain on he.

mlk

▌ "Those people who were fighting for civil rights," Bono remarks, "they understood the tribute."

MLK: Martin Luther King.

the joshua tree

july 13, 1985. Live Aid. In front of the biggest television audience for a live music event ever, U2 stole the show. Sales of *The Unforgettable Fire* soared. Suddenly U2 were not just a big band. They were one of the biggest in the world.

(Island U 26)

Produced by **Brian Eno and Daniel Lanois.**

Recorded at **Windmill Lane Studios, Dublin; and STS, Dublin.**

Released **March 1987.**

It gave them some breathing space. The Edge wrote the soundtrack for Paul Mayerberg's film *Captive*. Bono went travelling, listened to the blues. Did 'Silver and Gold' for the *Sun City* album project with Keith Richards and Ronnie Wood, recorded with Clannad. The whole band did two tracks with Robbie Robertson.

In '86, they emerged in fits. For *TV Gaga*. *The Conspiracy of Hope* tour in the US. *Self Aid* in Ireland. A different band! They did dirty, loud, noisy cover versions of Eddie Cochran and Bob Dylan. They'd travelled a long, long way from the cultivated European atmospherics of *The Unforgettable Fire*.

Bono was listening to roots music, folk, the blues. He was thinking about songs, reading about the Deep South. The Edge had looked east on *Captive*. The band moved west with *The Joshua Tree,* into the arms of America. Bono's songwriting had more focus now. Greater depth. He was dragging himself up there alongside Dylan, Morrison, Lou Reed. "It's our most literate record yet," he said. That was an understatement. It went straight to No.1 in the U.S. and the U.K. In America it became the fastest-selling album of all time. It also delivered the first platinum-selling CD.

In the arid wasteland of the Nevada desert, the Joshua Tree survives despite the dirt, bone-dry sand and stone in which it is embedded. Somewhere down there is water. Somewhere down there is the source of life. Somewhere down there is hope. The challenge is to find it.

Sometimes you can hear it in your head first. A slow, dramatic, swelling keyboard drone. A jangling rhythm part on guitar coming in over it. It sounds good – in your head. It feels like the start of something – an intro. But now you have to get it down on tape. Already there's some slippage. The first few steps you take never seem to capture the full glory of what you could hear, but if you come any way close, the momentum will carry you forward.

Bono and Ali in Ethiopia, 1985

where the streets have no name

t he Edge in his house in Monkstown fooling around on a four-track Tascam home recording studio. Sticking down the keyboard on his own. Listening back to it. It'll do. Rewind. Then the guitar. The rhythm holds good. Try some variations on the chord. Little flicks off the major. Now you can see the bigger picture again. Imagine a bass. The drums coming in. It does feel good. The beginning of a song...

'Where the Streets Have No Name' is one of those ones that seemed as if it didn't want to be born. "The way we write, we sometimes feel that the song is written," The Edge told John Waters, "the song is already there, if you could just put it into words, put it into notes. We have it, but it's not realized yet.

"If you saw us working in the studio sometimes, you'd be scratching your head trying to figure out what we were doing. Mostly, if we get the feeling that we're onto something good, we eventually do get there. And 'Where the Streets Have No Name' is a great example, because that took weeks of work to arrive at."

It nearly drove Brian Eno mad in the process. The more the band worked on the song, the more he resented it. At one stage he became so frustrated at the amount of time being devoted to 'Where the Streets Have No Name' that he wanted

to erase the multi-track. "That's right," The Edge recalls. "We weren't in the studio at the time and he asked the assistant engineer to leave the room. He'd actually decided to do it. But the assistant engineer wouldn't go. He stood in front of the tape machine, saying, 'Brian, you can't do this'. And so he didn't. But it was close."

In the end it was Steve Lillywhite rather than Eno who mixed the finished product. "It took forever to get that track," Daniel Lanois told *Rolling Stone*. "We had this giant blackboard with the arrangement written on it. I felt like a science professor, conducting them. To get the rise and fall, the song's dynamic, took a long time."

Rise and fall? That makes it sound almost sexual – a thought that mightn't be too far from the truth. Bono certainly sounds restless and agitated as he launches into a confession: *"I want to run/I want to hide/I want to tear down the walls/that hold me inside/I want to reach out/And touch the flame/where the streets have no name."*

"It's been a theme all the way through the group's music," he says, "this sense of wanting to run, wanting to give in to the urge of the hunter. I always think there's two modes – hunter and protector. Or for me there is anyway. If I gave in to one I'd be an animal. And if I gave in to the other, I'd be completely domesticated. Somewhere between the two is where I live."

We all feel the crushing burden of domesticity to one degree or another at different times. 'Where the Streets Have No Name' expresses the corresponding desire to cut and run. But it also captures the desperate need for anonymity that someone in Bono's position frequently feels: where the streets have no name, neither do the stars.

The title undoubtedly draws on the time Bono and his wife Ali spent in Ethiopia during 1985. They'd gone there as volunteers, working with aid agencies on the ground, distributing food and assisting with health and educational initiatives. Bono came home to Ireland, to the Western world, with a profound sense of the vacuum at the heart of contemporary living. "The spirit of the people I met in Ethiopia was very strong," Bono says. "There's no doubt that, even in poverty, they had something that we didn't have. When I got back, I realized the extent to which people in the West were like spoiled children."

One of the strengths of the song is that it is never quite clear where the streets with no name are, or precisely what the phrase is intended to mean. He could be talking about Heaven. Maybe even offering us a glimpse into some kind of private hell. "I can look at it now," Bono says, "and recognize that 'Where the Streets Have No Name' has one of the most banal couplets in the history of pop music. But it also contains some of the biggest ideas. In a curious way, that seems to work. If you get any way heavy about these things, you don't communicate. But if you're flip or throwaway about it, then you do. That's one of the paradoxes I've had to come to terms with."

> "He could be talking about Heaven. Maybe even offering us a glimpse into some kind of private hell."

i still haven't found what I'm looking for

Some things stick in the memory. The Edge held a party in his newly reconstructed house in Monkstown on the south coast of Dublin, on New Year's Eve, 1986. By this stage the bulk of the work on *The Joshua Tree* was done and the band were relaxing. But Bono couldn't quite let go.

Haven't Found What I'm Looking For' had to have its roots in gospel. But he also sensed that the theme was big enough to allow him to go for broke, to write an anthem.

'I Still Haven't Found What I'm Looking For' is beautifully written and elegantly constructed. The band trip lightly along on a groove that's a model of restraint, with an acoustic rhythm guitar break from The Edge where others might have preferred an instrumental solo. Bono's singing is soulful and heartfelt. No one puts a foot wrong.

"I used to think that writing words was old-fashioned," Bono confessed. "So I sketched. I wrote words on the microphone. For *The Joshua Tree*, I felt that the time had come to write words that meant something, out of my own experience."

Left: The Staple Singers: spreading the gospel.

O ne of his most attractive qualities is the naked enthusiasm he shows for the band's own music. And so he explained to me that this was an album of songs, that U2 had finally learned what the word meant, and that he was convinced that they had just made by far their best album to date as a result. "There's one in particular," he explained, "that's amazing." And then he started to sing it to me. "It goes like this: *I have climbed/the highest mountain/I have run/through the fields/only to be with you/only to be with you.*' And it's got this refrain," he expanded and sang on till he came to it. "*But I still haven't found what I'm looking for.*"

The bass drum of some thumping dance track was whacking away next door, and the hubbub of party voices reigned all around – and yet I'll swear that I could hum the song the next day. It was that catchy. A perfect piece of pop music, it went to No. 1 in the US when it was released there as a single, and no one could have been in the least bit surprised. From the start, Bono clearly knew that he was onto a winner.

The song had entered the world under another title, 'Under the Weather'. It also had a different melody. But once The Edge had come up with the title and the theme of spiritual doubt had crystallized in Bono's imagination, then the momentum became inescapable. Dermot Stokes, who was writing more extensively for *Hot Press* at the time, had given him a tape of blues and gospel music, including tracks by The Swan Silvertones, The Staple Singers and Blind Willie Johnson. Eno, who had listened to a lot of gospel, further stimulated his enthusiasm. Now Bono knew that 'I Still

You could sense it straightaway. 'I Still Haven't Found What I'm Looking For' was the real thing – though not everyone seemed to agree with that. In 1991, Negativland, an underground band based in San Francisco, released a record entitled 'U2'. It was a piece of attention-seeking pop larceny: they had re-mixed and re-modelled 'I Still Haven't Found What I'm Looking For', interspersing it with excerpts of an interview conversation between Bono and the American DJ, Casey Kasem. That it was a scam, both creatively and commercially, was underlined by the fact that U2's logo dominated the cover. One automatic reaction was that their fans might be conned into buying something under false pretences.

Island Records stepped in and took out an injunction to prevent further sale or distribution of the record. From the start it was a no-win situation for the U2 organization. Negativland pleaded that there was no breach of copyright because 'U2' was a parody. And they argued that U2 were defining themselves as corporate rock animals by crushing what was essentially a subversive artistic statement. Which is all very well. But could U2 – or their record company – risk giving any and every scam merchant in the USA carte blanche to use and abuse their logo and their recordings on any pretence whatsoever?

"What was scary to me was that people who were criticizing us weren't really listening to the records," Bono told David Fricke of *Rolling Stone*. "The records were not propagating any kind of 'men of stone' thing. *The Joshua Tree* is a very uncertain record. 'I Still Haven't Found What I'm Looking For' is an anthem of doubt more than faith."

"They argued that U2 were defining themselves as corporate rock animals by crushing what was essentially a subversive artistic statement."

65

Before recording *The Joshua Tree*, the band decided to rehearse in Danesmote, a period house in Rathfarnham on the outskirts of Dublin.

The Joshua Tree than 'With or Without You'. On one level it is that rare thing in the U2 canon – a love song – and it works as such, capturing an emotion that most people in serious relationships must have felt at one time or another when Bono sings, *"I can't live/with or without you."* But this is no silly love song of the kind that Bono despises. In fact, the more you delve, the more you become aware that beneath its surface restraint lies a tangled web of complex anxieties. Concise it may be, but 'With or Without You' is anything but straightforward. There is, of course, a spiritual dimension to the song as erotic love and agape love

with or without you

Shadows and tall trees.

> "The thing is to challenge radio," Adam told *Rolling Stone.*

the room they occupied was beautiful, with high windows and natural light flooding in. The rehearsals went so well that they decided to do the album there.

"We had experimented a lot in the making of *The Unforgettable Fire*," The Edge recalls. "We had done quite revolutionary things like 'Elvis Presley and America' and '4th of July'. So we felt, going into *The Joshua Tree*, that maybe options were not a good thing, that limitations might be positive. And so we decided to work within the limitations of the song as a starting point. We thought: let's actually write songs. We wanted the record to be less vague, open-ended, atmospheric and impressionistic. To make it more straightforward, focused and concise."

You could say that there are few better examples on

converge again in Bono's personal mythology, and he returns to the theme of self-surrender and ego-loss. But what does he mean when he confesses, *"My hands are torn/my body bruised/She's got me with/nothing left to win/and nothing left to lose"*? And who is "she"?

Bono doesn't like being specific about personal songs of this kind. Never did. "In 'With or Without You', when it says, *'And you give yourself away/And you give yourself away'*, everybody in the group knows what it means," he explained in 1987. "It's about how I feel in U2 at times – exposed. I know that the group think I'm exposed, and that the group feel that I give myself away. I think if I do any damage to U2 it's that I'm too open. For instance, in an interview, I don't hold the cards there, and play the right one because I either have to do it or not do it. That's why I'm not going to do many interviews this year. Because there's a cost to my personal life, and a cost to the group as well."

"And you give yourself away": a phrase to turn over and over, and to look at every which way. A lot of anxiety, doubt and even guilt wrapped up in it.

"The thing is to challenge radio," Adam told *Rolling Stone*. "To get 'With or Without You' on the radio is pretty good. You don't expect to hear it there. Maybe in a church."

What's more, U2 got it to No. 1 in the singles charts. "Paul McGuinness didn't want to release it as a single," Gavin Friday reveals. "But I told Bono that it was a certain No. 1. It was one of the biggest arguments I ever had with Paul, and in the end Bono sided with me. In fairness to Paul he did come up to me afterwards and apologize. He said 'You were right'. And of course I was."

In the sabbatical he took during 1985, Bono travelled extensively. Almost uniquely among rock stars, it would have rankled with him to do Live Aid and not to know first-hand what was happening in Ethiopia. So he went there as an aid worker with Ali.

Sandinista leader and, later, President of Nicaragua, Daniel Ortega.

his partner shared a genuine concern for the underprivileged, and especially people in emerging countries, marginalized by the machinations of those holding the reins of political, economic and military power in the West. And so they also travelled to Central America, under the auspices of Amnesty International, to observe and spent time in both El Salvador and Nicaragua. It was natural for an Irish man and woman to identify with the Nicaraguan experience – that of a small country struggling to establish its own freedom and identity, being bullied by a much bigger and more powerful neighbour. On the streets, Bono saw terrible poverty, a direct result of the American economic blockade and US support for the civil war being waged by the Contras. But he also saw the dignity which the people maintained in the face of the calamities visited upon them. It was an insight into the dark side of US foreign policy that would be hard to forget. They also got close enough to the brutal campaign of murder and oppression being waged with US backing in El Salvador, to come to only one conclusion.

"The spirit of the people in Nicaragua is being beaten down," Bono said at the time. "They've no food and no supplies. I was at a rally of Daniel Ortega's and you can tell from the look in people's eyes that they wanted so much to believe in their revolution. But people think with their pockets a lot of the time and you can't blame them for it, women trying to bring up children, and fellas with no work. It's just very sad to see the stranglehold America has on Central America in practice. When you go into a restaurant and they give you a menu, there's 15 items on the menu and they don't tell you at first that they've only got one. You have to ask 14 times before they tell you, no, we just have rice."

It would not have been in Bono's nature to remain silent. As Martin Luther King had emerged as the hero of *The Unforgettable Fire*, now *The Joshua Tree* became a prayer for the dispossessed and for victims of military oppression. The

bullet the
blue sky

USA had been good to U2. It had embraced them, given them success, transformed them into one of the most successful and important groups of their era. But the things that were being done by Americans in Central America, ostensibly in the name of freedom and justice, were appalling. When it came to it, U2 would be prepared to bite the hand that had fed them.

'Bullet the Blue Sky' howls with anger and with fear. In El Salvador Bono had seen government fighter jets flying

the joshua tree

> "I don't believe that there is one, single, perfect spiritual way and, in realizing that, obviously, you become a lot more open."
>
> **– THE EDGE**

overhead in a mission. He had heard the bark of guns in the distance that followed. That's the reality someone else wakens up to every day. 'Bullet the Blue Sky' was an attempt to confront U2's own audience with a sense of what that might mean. But that is only a starting point, as the song travels backwards, searching for the heart of the darkness into which innocent people were being plunged. Irangate, the details of which had emerged during 1986, had exposed the greed, duplicity and corruption which had taken over Washington during the Reagan era. "People were so behind everything Ronald Reagan stood for," The Edge reflected around the time of *The Joshua Tree*, "but now I think when we go back to America we'll see a broken country. Either that or people refusing to look – which is a more frightening prospect."

"I still believe in Americans," Bono added. "I think they're a very open people. It's their openness which leads them to trust a man as dangerous as Ronald Reagan. They want to believe he's a good guy. They want to believe he's in the cavalry, coming to rescue America's reputation after the '70s. But he was only an actor. It was only a movie. I think the picture's ended now and Americans are leaving the cinema a little down in the mouth." 'Bullet the Blue Sky' made one other connection, linking the disastrous US foreign policy under Reagan to his own religious fundamentalism and that of the Christian tele-evangelists who had flourished in his version of America. U2 recognized that imperialism is fuelled by a righteousness that denies others their *own* right to believe, and to express those beliefs.

"I would say that none of my fundamental beliefs have changed," The Edge said during 1986, "but they've broadened and matured and been tempered with a wider experience of (a) what's good about the rest of the world and (b) what's bad about religion everywhere. I basically assume that every single religious group, or community, has a problem, is in some way screwed up. I don't believe that there is one, single, perfect spiritual way and, in realizing that, obviously, you become a lot more open."

The mention of the preacher Jerry Falwell inspired anger, bordering on contempt. "He preaches that God dresses in a three-piece polyester suit, is white, speaks in a Southern accent, is from an Anglo-Saxon background and has a wife and children. And then you say, how does that relate to a Chinese peasant? And you realize that it doesn't at all."

Or to a Southern black? The song contrasts the burning crosses of the Ku Klux Klan with the liberating sound of John Coltrane's saxophone breathing into the New York night. America: land of paradoxes. Everything that's great about the world, and everything that's repulsive about it, rolled into one. That's what 'Bullet the Blue Sky' was about.

A sax supreme: the great John Coltrane.

You couldn't escape the shadow of heroin in Dublin in the 1980s, nor the spectre of addiction and death that trailed in its wake. 'Wire' had dealt with this theme. So had 'Bad', with greater effect. Addressed to a junkie acquaintance from the band's old Lypton Village days, its resonance was so powerful and its emotion so true that it had become a centrepiece in the band's live shows during *The Unforgettable Fire* tour, one of the original and enduring U2 anthems of mass popular appeal.

running to stand still

now U2 returned to the theme, in a song which was clearly inspired by Lou Reed's towering 'Walk on the Wild Side', an influence which reflected the fresh non-judgemental stance of Bono and the band to the drug problem that was endemic on the streets, and in the estates where they had grown up in Dublin.

'Running to Stand Still' is inescapably located in that terrain, with the early lyrical reference to the seven imposing blocks of flats that scar the urban landscape of North Dublin and distinguish Ballymun, where Bono had grown up, from the rest of the city, evoking a potent image of desperation and decay. *"I see seven towers/but I see only one way out,"* Bono sings, and you know what he means. "I don't come from the viewpoint of someone who is completely unsympathetic to drug users," he reflected in a *Hot Press* interview, following the release of *The Joshua Tree*. "I really understand the attraction. I understood it then, when I was in my teens, and I understand it even more now because of, for instance, being on stage for two hours and then not being able to sleep for six or seven or eight hours."

Besides, numerous friends, acquaintances and fellow musicians in Ireland had found themselves in thrall to the China girl. Christy Dignam, lead singer with Aslan – one of the brightest hopes among the first wave of post-U2 bands in Dublin – had endured a very public flirtation with the drug. And then in January 1986, Philip Lynott of Thin Lizzy – a legendary and inspiring figure among Irish rock bands – had died of liver failure brought about by drug abuse and specifically, heroin addiction. When it comes that close to home, you realize that there is no point in being judgemental.

"A thing that really bothers me personally is that for two years myself and Ali lived in Howth, on the same road as Phil, in a little cottage that we rented at the time," Bono confided, "and I would see him everywhere else but on that street. Every time I saw him he'd say, 'Why don't you come down for dinner? You know, you have to come down for a bite.' And I would say, 'You know, you have to come up for a bite. You have to drop up.' Every single time. And I never did call down and he never did call up. That's what came back to me. I never did call down."

The song is imbued with a real sense of tenderness and compassion. But it isn't directed solely at those who are

Ballymun, Dublin: two of the seven towers.

the joshua tree

victims of heroin addiction. In 'Running to Stand Still' Bono goes further, empathizing with the central character who is willing to put everything at risk in order to transcend the crushing drabness and narrow horizons which blighted the lives of so many in a city of high unemployment and squalid living conditions.

"I heard about a couple," Bono explained about the genesis of the song, "and both were addicted, and such was their addiction that they had no money, nothing to pay the rent – so the guy risked everything on a run. He went and smuggled into Dublin a serious quantity of heroin, strapped to his body, so that on the one hand there was life imprisonment, on the other hand, riches. Apart from the morality of that, what interested me was what put him in that position. *You know I took the poison from the poison stream/and I floated out of here.*" Because for a lot of people there are no physical doors open any more. And so if you can't change the world you're living in, seeing it through different eyes is the only alternative. And heroin gives you heroin eyes to see the world with. The thing about heroin is that you think that's the way it really is, that the old you who worries about paying the rent is not the real you."

Three amigos: Adam, Bono and the late Philip Lynott of Thin Lizzy.

Musically, 'Running to Stand Still' was improvised almost to tape using 'Walk on the Wild Side' and Elton John's 'Candle in the Wind' - which they'd segued into during 'Bad' on the previous tour - as a launching pad, but lyrically it was finely honed. It became one of the most important songs on *The Joshua Tree*. Not only because it would emerge as a great Dublin anthem, but for other perhaps more crucial reasons too. In its lack of moral certainty and its refusal to judge its subjects harshly, it looked ahead to the chaotic landscape the band would describe – and embrace – through *Achtung Baby* and *Zooropa*, in which the only certainty is uncertainty itself. That made it one of the band's most mature and compelling creations to date, a haunting, challenging piece of pop poetry that still resonates with lyrical truth almost ten years on.

If the USA was groaning under the scandalous excesses of the Reagan era in the '80s, things in Britain were little better. The logic of the Conservative Prime Minister Margaret Thatcher's free market economic policies had led to a huge increase in the numbers of unemployed, taking the figure to record heights of well over three million. Among those most disastrously hit were the mining communities of the north of England.

red hill mining town

under Thatcher's direction, and the chairmanship of Ian McGregor, the National Coal Board began to implement a policy of closing down what were deemed to be uneconomic mines. A miners' strike followed, with the National Union of Miners, led by Arthur Scargill, fighting the pit closures tooth and nail. It was destined to be one of the most bitter and protracted industrial disputes in recent history in Britain, and the devastation wrought was immense.

During the summer of 1984, Bob Dylan had played During the summer of 1984, Bob Dylan had played Slane Castle, just outside Dublin, and early in the day Bono had interviewed him for *Hot Press*. It gave Dylan the opportunity to invite the U2 singer on stage, to join in an encore of 'Blowin' in the Wind'. Thrown a verse to sing by Dylan, Bono realized that while he recognised the song, he didn't know the words: he was forced to wing it. In some ways that unplanned live collaboration saw Bono cross the great divide in musical terms. More than anything, it confirmed for him just how much he still had to learn about the great tradition of singing, songwriting and musicianship.

A friendship developed which saw him delving into Dylan's back catalogue and retracing the connections between the Irish and American folk traditions. He was listening to Bruce Springsteen, too, opening another window into the blue-collar world of labour songs. This growing awareness of the power of the folk tradition was reflected in the band's participation in a 25th-anniversary tribute on the *Late Late Show*, on national television in Ireland, to the folk scene veterans The Dubliners. For the

what people are getting at," he said at the time. "'Red Hill Mining Town' is a song about the miners' strike and the only reference to Ian McGregor is *"Through hand of steel and heart of stone/Our labour day is come and gone"*. People beat me with a stick for that but what I'm interested in is seeing in the newspapers or on television that another thousand people had lost their jobs.

"Now what you don't read about is that those people go home and they have families and they're trying to bring up children. And, in many instances, those relationships broke up under the pressure of the miners' strike. *'The glass is cut, the bottle runs dry/Our love runs cold in the caverns in the night/We're wounded by fear, injured in doubt/I can lose myself but I can't live without/'Cos you keep me holding on.'* I'm more interested in the relationship at this point in time because I feel other people are more qualified to comment on the miners' strike. That enraged me – but I feel more qualified to write about relationships because I understand them more than what it's like to work in a pit."

> "What the song did capture eloquently was the sense of doom that surrounded the death of the small close-knit mining communities."

Miners' leader and arch-foe of Thatcherism, Arthur Scargill.

occasion U2 chose a Peggy Seeger song that had originally been sung by Luke Kelly, and performed it with impressive restraint and authority. 'Springhill Mining Disaster' tells the story of how greed and exploitation in a coal mine in Nova Scotia ended in catastrophe. Bono delivered the song with passion and conviction, winning respect in the process.

All of these strands came together in 'Red Hill Mining Town'. It was criticized in some quarters for not being politically specific enough, but there is no doubt whatsoever about where Bono's sympathies lie. "I know

What the song did capture eloquently was the sense of doom that surrounded the death of the small close-knit mining communities. It was considered by the band for release as a single, and a video for it was shot by the film director Neil Jordan, who was to make *The Crying Game* and *Interview With the Vampire*. The band were unhappy with what Jordan produced and the video was quietly buried.

Which may explain why 'Red Hill Mining Town' never became a major part of the U2 live set. It deserved better than to become a lost gem.

the joshua tree

Bono was trying to find ways of communicating his increasing sense of unease about the USA. 'Bullet the Blue Sky' had come spitting out in a spirit of anger. 'In God's Country' was more measured; it had an air of resignation. The image of the desert was at the heart of *The Joshua Tree*. "It has a spiritual aspect," The Edge reasoned, "which the record has, and also a great deal of mystery, which I like."

in god's country

Symbol of America: the Statue of Liberty.

adam went further: "The desert was immensely inspirational to us as a mental image for this record. Most people would take the desert on face value and think it's some kind of barren place, which of course is true. But in the right frame of mind, it's also a very positive image, because you can actually do something with blank canvas, which is effectively what the desert is."

That's the kind of thinking that informs 'In God's Country'. It sounds a bit like U2 playing U2 until The Edge drops in an Ennio Morricone-style guitar figure in the break. Bono, meanwhile, is restrained. Coming to him in a dream, the USA is characterized as a desert rose, a siren whose dress is torn in ribbons and in bows. *"We need new dreams tonight,"* Bono sings. He's thinking about the dearth of new political ideas. "Except in Nicaragua," he says looking back. "That's why the revolution there was so important."

"It's not your first reason for being on stage, to effect change in the political climate of a country," Bono said at the time. "I don't know what the first reason is, but that's not the first reason. But I like to think that U2 have already contributed to a turnaround in thinking."

Maybe 'In God's Country' would turn a few more heads around. Then again maybe not. You could argue that the chorus was too radio-friendly for that.

"Coming to him in a dream, the USA is characterized as a desert rose, a siren whose dress is torn in ribbons and in bows."

After Live Aid, there was less pressure on U2 to produce a follow-up to *The Unforgettable Fire*. The natural life-span of that record had been given an enormous boost by the band's cathartic performance in front of a global television audience. They didn't need to rush a new album. And so they took some time out. They stopped being U2. Individually and sometimes collectively, they went in search of fresh stimuli. Bono's appearance changed enormously. He was searching for new musical roots, listening to folk, blues and country. And that search was reflected not just in the way he was thinking but in the way he looked, too.

trip through your wires

I t also connected with the musical changes that Ireland was going through in the mid-'80s. Mike Scott had relocated to Dublin with The Waterboys and had become obsessed not just with Bob Dylan and Van Morrison but also with the Irish folk tradition. The Hot House Flowers were also in the ascendant, and making similar links. Both tended to turn up for spontaneous sessions in the strangest of places, so that Dublin became a city of buskers. Keeping that kind of company, the lead singer with one of the most successful groups in the world might have been inclined to think that he should be able to strap on an acoustic guitar and sing a song without the back-up of a 30-person road crew and $1 million worth of PA. It was against that backdrop that 'Trip Through Your Wires' was conceived.

An old friend, Billy Magra, had become involved in a new RTE late-night youth television programme, *TV Gaga*, as producer-director. As a supportive gesture, to add to the programme's credibility – and hopefully its ratings – the band agreed to appear on the show and to unveil two new numbers. The word went out: they would sound like nothing U2 had ever done before.

Mike Scott of The Waterboys.

the joshua tree

On the night, the band trooped on looking like extras from some B-movie remake of *Easy Rider*. They performed 'Womanfish' – a song which subsequently disappeared apparently without a trace – and 'Trip Through Your Wires'. And it was as had been promised. There wasn't an echo effect in sight, nor any of the bright, clean, melodic guitar colourings that had been U2's trademark. Instead, we witnessed The Edge getting down 'n' dirty in a bar room bluesy romp, a drinking song that featured Bono wailing away crudely on a Dylan-esque harp solo. On the night it looked and sounded like a work-in-progress. Clearly it was. The version on *The Joshua Tree* is far tighter and more disciplined but the spirit of the shambolic *TV Gaga* performance is retained.

"It was a hootenanny, a big yahoo," Bono told Carter Alan. "We kind of made it up at the moment and I just blew into the harp. The thing about Dan Lanois and Brian Eno in the studio is that they're very supportive of the idea of a session. Dan will be in there with his tambourine, standing beside Larry, looking him in the eye and whacking a cymbal here and there. They get really carried away with it and we get carried away with them getting carried away with it. It's just a vicious cycle in the right sense of the word. Yeah, 'Trip Through Your Wires' was fun."

"It could be about an unconventional sexual encounter and the attendant feelings of confusion and guilt."

Lyrically it's relatively throwaway. It can be seen as another paean to the contradictory charms of America, personified as a woman. It could be about an unconventional sexual encounter and the attendant feelings of confusion and guilt. Or it can be read simply as an exercise in personal myth-making of the kind Dylan initiates would have been more than familiar with: the singer broken down by the ravages of living the hard life being put back together by the love of a good woman (or even a bad one!).

Sex 'n' drink 'n' rock 'n' roll? It might have been Bono's own personal basement tape. It had Dylan's influence written all over it, but it also made sense in the wider context of the musical and spiritual journey being undertaken by the band on *The Joshua Tree*.

When U2 were on tour in New Zealand in 1985 they met Greg Carroll. A Maori, he worked doing front-of-house for the promoter on the band's Kiwi dates, beginning in Auckland. "There are five volcanic islands which make up Auckland," Bono explained, "and the tallest is One Tree Hill. Greg took me there on my first night in New Zealand."

one tree hill

One Tree Hill, Auckland, New Zealand.

Carroll had been around the music and media scene for a while and when they saw him in action, the U2 crew were suitably impressed. He was a bundle of energy, a live wire. "Paul McGuinness thought this guy's so smart we can't leave him here. Let's take him with us to Australia," Bono explained. Within a short time, Greg Carroll had become a valued member of the organization.

Their world tour over, the band returned to Dublin. Greg Carroll came too. He worked as Bono's assistant and, in the few months he spent in Dublin, became like a brother to the singer. He was well loved and widely respected by those who knew him both within and outside the U2 camp.

What happened was horrific. A nightmare. On the run-up to recording *The Joshua Tree*, he took Bono's Harley Davidson on a courier run. It was a bleak, rainy night. The roads were abominably wet and visibility was bad. On one of the main routes out from the city centre, a car pulled out in front of him and Greg, going full tilt, ploughed into it. He was killed instantly. The experience shattered everyone in the U2 camp but Bono was particularly badly wounded.

"It was a devastating blow," he told David Breskin. "He was doing me a favour. He was taking my bike home. Greg used to look after Ali. They used to go out dancing together. He was a best friend. I've already had it once with my mother. Now I've had it twice. The worst part is the fear. After that, when the phone rang my heart stopped every time. Now when I go away I wonder 'Will these people be here when I get back?' You start to think in those terms."

"For me, it inspired the awareness that there are more important things than rock 'n' roll," Adam Clayton reflected. "That your family, your friends and indeed the other members of the band – you don't know how much time you've got with them."

Even six months later, Bono found it hard to talk about, choking back tears in an interview. "The emphasis," he reflected, "among family and friends when we had a No. 1 record and were a big band was on how much you'd got – and not how much you've lost. The sense of loss came home through losing Greg Carroll. But the sense of loss has continued – I feel it even now."

It was sufficient to inspire one of Bono's finest lyrics, its imagery superbly evoking the seafaring heritage of Carroll's Maori ancestors. Not only that, "One Tree Hill" also produced a magnificent vocal performance which showcased Bono's extraordinary development as a singer. A spiritual tour de force, it is a hymn of praise and celebration which describes the traditional Maori burial of their friend on One Tree Hill and links it poetically with themes of renewal and redemption, with the river running, running down to the sea.

Those who heard 'One Tree Hill' would be similarly affected. Replete with chord-shifts inspired by Eno, sweet African-tinged guitar from The Edge and a sensuous rhythm groove courtesy of Adam and Larry, it was – and remains – among the great U2 tracks, a fitting tribute to one of the band's faithful departed.

"Greg Carroll's funeral was beyond belief," Bono said. "He was buried in his tribal homeland, as a Maori, by the chiefs and elders. And there was a three-day and three-night wake and your head would be completely turned around. And ours were, again and again."

> "On one of the main routes out from the city centre, a car pulled out in front of him and Greg, going full tilt, ploughed into it."

Bono premieres 'Trip Through Your Wires' on RTE's *TV Gaga*.

Bono had gone west in his reading. He was interested in Flannery O'Connor, Raymond Carver, Norman Mailer. Looking for insights into the people of the vast place that had embraced them. Ways of understanding the ordinary stock first and then the outsiders, the driftwood – those on the fringes of the promised land, cut off from the American dream. He read *The Executioner's Song*, Norman Mailer's superb account of the life of Gary Gilmore. 'Exit'

wasn't about Gilmore. It wasn't about Charles Manson either. But it trawls the area occupied by either or both, getting inside the head of a protagonist who's careening into psychosis.

Musically 'Exit' is like nothing U2 had ever done before. The antithesis of their bright, ringing, optimistic inspirational selves, it was dirty, angry, loud, discordant, repetitive, noisy, black. If the intention was to invoke a sense of evil abroad, then it was effective, with Larry's blistering drum attack and Adam's low-down insistent muddy bass creating a powerful sense of being inside someone's skin, of feeling their palpitations en route to some unspeakable denouement.

"You could say that this is forbidden ground for U2 because we're the 'optimistic' group," Bono confided at the time. "But to be an optimist you mustn't be blind or deaf to the world around you. 'Exit' – I don't even know what the act is in that song. Some see it as a murder, others suicide – and I don't mind. But the rhythm of the words is nearly as important in conveying the state of mind."

That was the point of 'Exit': to convey the state of mind of someone driven, by whatever powerful urges, to the very brink of desperation. The undercurrent of religious imagery reflected a new awareness of the dangers of fanaticism implicit in faith. But there was no other message in 'Exit'. Except this is how it is out there: deal with it. And in a way, it was a method of purging the band's own demons, their own anger and fury at the vicissitudes fate had thrust upon them. It was a way of coming to terms with death and with grief. It was an exorcism.

As such, it was not without its own psychic cost. In the USA, a man accused of murdering Rebecca Shaeffer, a TV actress, claimed that he was inspired by listening to 'Exit'. It may have been no more than a smart defence lawyer coming up with a half-plausible plea of mitigation, but it wasn't the kind of accusation you wanted hanging over you, however spurious. But then, there was a whole list of positive lessons to be learned from *The Joshua Tree* too.

Firing on all cylinders during
The Joshua Tree **tour.**

> "It was a method of purging the band's own demons, their own anger and fury at the vicissitudes fate had thrust upon them."

During 1986, U2 had agreed to participate in the *Conspiracy of Hope* tour in the USA with Sting, Lou Reed, Bryan Adams, Peter Gabriel and Joan Baez, among others. The tour was both a money-raising and a consciousness-raising expedition, undertaken on behalf of Amnesty International.

mothers of the disappeared

the band had developed a close relationship with that organization through Jack Healey, an Irish–American former priest, who put together the Conspiracy tour. He had helped in making connections for Bono in Nicaragua and El Salvador. Now, in a variety of shapes and guises, Amnesty concerns were resurfacing on *The Joshua Tree*.

In particular, Bono had been struck by the accounts he'd heard of murder squads operating under the Argentinian military junta through the '70s and '80s. Those bleak decades before the Falklands War – or the war in the Malvinas – precipitated a return to democracy during which hundreds of student opponents of the military regime had been arrested and were never seen again, dead or alive. In Argentina they became known as "the disappeared", and an organization called Mothers of the Disappeared had been formed to campaign for full disclosure of what had happened to those who had been lifted – and to work towards the arrest and trial of the police and military personnel who had been responsible for fashioning and carrying out the State policy of torture and murder.

'Mothers of the Disappeared' continues the tradition of '40' and 'MLK' – but it is less a celebration, less a lullaby, than a lament. It enters with disturbing sound effects courtesy of Eno, and it never loses its ominous, mournful quality – The Edge's guitar is barbed wire, and Bono sounds like Dylan's man of constant sorrow, his yodel a high, lonesome sound, a *caoineadh* if ever there was one. The song is an act of witness but there is no optimistic note of reassurance struck to close the album. Too much evil in the world. Some things just can't be explained.

Even Bono was prepared to acknowledge that now.

Bono and Lou Reed perform for Amnesty International's *Conspiracy of Hope* tour.

rattle and hum

having shot to No.1 on both sides of the Atlantic, *The Joshua Tree* went on to sell 12 million copies worldwide. It was the record of a radically different band to that which had set out on the *War* tour in 1983. And yet when TV stations wanted to show live footage of U2, all they had was the *Under a Blood Red Sky* video. It was time to consign that version of reality to history.

(Island U27)

Produced by **Jimmy Iovine.**

Recorded live in **Tempe, Arizona; Denver, Colorado; and New York. Also at A&M Studios, Los Angeles; Sun Studios, Memphis; STS Studios, Dublin; The Point Depot, Dublin; and Danesmoat, Dublin.**

Released **October 1988.**

The movie was Paul McGuinness' idea. Whatever he had in mind, the band would inevitably screw it around. Conceptualize it. Complicate it. Make it as difficult as possible. And then make it more difficult again. So they did. Business as usual.

They wanted to explore American music. Travel back to the source. Hook up with some seminal figures. Take risks. Deflate the myth. Acknowledge that in the grand scheme of things they were only beginners. Right. And make the biggest, the best, the most dramatic, the most explosive rock movie ever.

Can I get back to you on that one, darling?

They could have done a straight concert film and a live double-album. "And made a lot of money for very little work," Bono argued. "That's what big rock bands do. They take the money and run."

Instead, U2's restless desire to keep moving got the better of them. Part documentary, part travelogue, part concert film, *Rattle and Hum*, the movie, is big, loud, sketchy, humorous, gauche, powerful, revealing. *Rattle and Hum*, the album, is sprawling, eclectic, eccentric, throwaway, inspiring, magnificent. Hammered in the press, it sold 14 million copies.

The myth wasn't going to be easily deflated.

There were people who ridiculed the choice of the Beatles' 'Helter Skelter' as the opening track on *Rattle and Hum*. In fact, it would be hard to pick anything more appropriate. *The Joshua Tree* had catapulted the band into the front line, right up there as contenders for the title that no one really wants: the biggest rock 'n' roll band on planet Earth. On a tour that was scheduled to run over 264 days and through 15 countries, they would do 110 shows at 72 venues in front of a paying audience of 3,160,998 fans. In addition, there was the San Francisco Save The Yuppie free concert, with an audience of at least another 20,000 people. And, meanwhile, chunks of all this mayhem were being filmed for a major rock 'n' roll film. It was a roller coaster ride all right, in which everything was capable of being turned upside down.

helter skelter

The Helter Skelter Man: Charles Manson.

in one obvious sense, U2 were on top of the world. In another, they had been plunged into the vortex, where every aspect of their operation was under scrutiny, and every element of their increasingly hydra-headed organization under severe strain. None more so than the band themselves.

"'Helter Skelter' was exactly what we were going through on *The Joshua Tree* tour," Bono said. "It was one of the worst times of our musical life. First a falling light cut me up, and I had to have stitches in my chin. My voice failed for the first week because of dry heat – the press came to the opening show and I couldn't sing. We were on the run the whole time and I busted up my shoulder and was in a lot of pain. And I found that I was drinking a lot just to stop the pain."

Recorded at the McNichols Arena in Denver on 8 November, 1987, it featured in the black and white footage of the film *Rattle and Hum*. "The line about Charles Manson was just an off-the-cuff remark on the night," Bono recalls. "If I got up people's noses, that's fine. But I still think it was relevant. We were travelling around the United States and I had a few incidents coming up against the hard-core spontaneous combustion of violence that seems to happen there. I've always been fascinated with that and still am."

Look no further than the sign marked 'Exit'.

"The line about Charles Manson was just an off-the-cuff remark on the night," Bono recalls. "If I got up people's noses, that's fine. But I still think it was relevant."

rattle and hum

In 1845, Ireland lost its potato crop. It was the signal for an economic and social catastrophe of ghastly proportions. That the worst ravages of what became known as the Great Famine might have been averted is incontrovertible.

van diemen's land

being exported. Meanwhile, as successive potato crops failed as a result of blight, the death toll mounted. In the long run, two million were to die and as many emigrated to the USA in what became known as the coffin ships. Hundreds of thousands died en route, of starvation, typhoid and other diseases associated with malnutrition. Many did find their way to the promised land, bringing their music with them – thus to provide one of the key tributaries leading to the hybrid that would become known as rock 'n' roll.

In Ireland, meanwhile, experience of the famine dovetailed with the nationalist sentiment burgeoning throughout Europe. In 1848, an uprising was planned but it petered out miserably and the leaders were arrested. Among them was a Fenian poet, John Boyle O'Reilly, who was deported to Australia for his role in orchestrating the rebellion. In Irish folk culture, the name given to Tasmania – where citizens who had fallen foul of the Crown and the courts were frequently transported – was Van Diemen's Land; it was already the title of a familiar rebel ballad. But U2's 'Van Diemen's Land' – like 'Sunday Bloody Sunday', the ultimate cathartic version of which would be captured in the *Rattle and Hum* film – is not a rebel song. Written and sung by The Edge against the sparse backdrop of his own plucked electric guitar, it is a sad and moving reflection on the continuity of suffering, injustice and violence, with the scarlet coats of the Fenians now being replaced by the black berets of the IRA.

"It's an emigrant's song – or an immigrant's song," Bono comments. "That's what justifies its place on the album. But I have to be very focused in a record, and for me that record was set in only one place."

As it happens, The Edge's plaintive appeal for justice without violence, recorded in The Point Theatre where U2 were rehearsing, provides one of the most beautiful and striking moments in the film, with Phil Joanou's cameras sweeping kinetically down the River Liffey that runs through the heart of the city and out into Dublin Bay, a place from which at least some of the emigrants of the 19th century embarked.

John Boyle O'Reilly had been bound for Australia. U2 were travelling deep into the heart of the USA. All of us, to one degree or another, are on the run. Driven – but by what?

An evicted family during Ireland's Great Famine

enough food was being produced within the 32 counties of Ireland to feed the population. But the dictates of the market and the laissez-faire economic policies of the time prevailed. Throughout 1845, '46 and what became known as Black '47, the food that was being produced in Irish fields on the back of Irish labour was

The first single off *Rattle and Hum*, 'Desire' confounded expectations. If anything on *The Joshua Tree* half-pointed in this direction it was 'Trip Through Your Wires' – but that was sprawling and indulgent, a drunken slice of bar-room raunch.

Iggy Pop: he helped teach U2 how to rattle and hum.

by comparison, 'Desire' was loaded, cocked and ready to go off in the listener's hand. "We talked about getting some songs with interesting drum lines," Larry explained to Steve Turner, for *Rattle and Hum*, the book, "so instead of spending time jamming as we used to, we each went away and did research and came back. This is what we came up with."

The Edge claimed that they'd been listening to Iggy Pop's coruscating '1969', which may indeed have been the case, but this rhythm was sired by one Mr Bo Diddley and made its first global impact on the charts via The Rolling Stones, out of Buddy Holly's 'Not Fade Away'. On its release, 'Desire' went straight to No. 1 in the UK, and U2 were understandably pleased. They'd originally recorded it in STS Studios in Dublin as a demo. They re-recorded it in A&M Studios in Los Angeles, and it was much tighter and more accurate. "But it lacked feel," The Edge says. So they went back to the original, 2 minutes and 58 seconds of it, in all its dirty magnificence.

"We were going back to rhythm and blues as part of our wanting to understand America," Bono explains. "We'd been reading the Beats and various travel writers. Then we started to get into the music. Travelling through America, you're listening to different radio stations, rhythm and blues, country, soul, jazz, and you realize that rhythm is the sex of the music. So I think we got into dealing with those subjects, including desire, when we were making that jump musically."

The Edge had never been an R'n'B fan. Now he'd begun to see the great emotional strength of the music. "At the time, I think I had begun to realize that music had become too scientific. Too often, listening to modern records, you'd hear a producer rather than musicians interacting. That's something we were trying to get back to in our own music. I liked about 'Desire' the fact that it was totally *not* what people were listening to. It was a rock 'n' roll record, not a pop song."

For Bono, however, it was also a reflection on the *condition* of being a rock star. "I wanted to admit to the religiosity of rock 'n' roll concerts and the fact that you get paid for them. On one level, I'm starting to criticize these lunatic fringe preachers, *"stealing hearts at a travelling show"* – but I'm also starting to realize that there's a real parallel there between what I'm doing and what they are."

'Desire' was the beginning of a process. Increasingly, Bono would consciously begin to own up to the contradictions in his own and the band's position. It was a reflection of the fact that U2 had come of age that they could produce with such enormous relish something that, on the surface at least, was so utterly basic.

And you can be sure that the irony of *that* wouldn't have been lost on a band that had travelled a long way to get back to where they once belonged.

> "I liked about 'Desire' the fact that it was totally not what people were listening to. It was a rock 'n' roll record, not a pop song."
>
> **– THE EDGE**

rattle and hum

The road can be a good place to write. The stimuli are all around – the new sights, sounds, smells, experiences that provide the base metal from which songs can be wrought.

Bob Dylan: the dark side of Hawkmoon.

hawkmoon 269

also, there are lacunae, hours spent in transit or holed up in some hotel room that need to be filled. An experienced hand works out the best way of using that down-time. A Pro Walkman does for capturing chord progressions, melodies, rhythms. The lyrical ideas can be jotted down in a notebook: a potential title here, a memorable phrase there, a couplet, a chorus, a verse. Nuggets that may sometime open the door into a song.

The Edge had the Walkman doing overtime during *The Joshua Tree* tour. 'Hawkmoon 269' was one of the structures he sketched, just himself and an acoustic guitar, onto a cassette. It was there in raw form, a piece in search of a lyric.

"Hawkmoon is a place in Rapid City, Dakota," The Edge told me around the time of the release of *Rattle and Hum*. "We passed by it on the Amnesty *Conspiracy of Hope* tour and Bono, ever a man with a notebook handy, thought 'That sounds good'. So he used that as a point of departure for the song." It wasn't the only one. Bono remembers a crushing hangover that heightened the sense of dislocation that frequently infects musicians on the road, and the refrain comes straight out of that particular black pit: *"When the night has no end/and the day yet to begin/As the room spins around you/I need your love."*

Maybe it was symptomatic that it became such a demon to record. Bob Dylan came along to play on the track and contributed a kind of inebriated hurdy gurdy effect that probably accurately captures the state of mind he was in on the day. The band piled in, moving convincingly from

Take 268: Adam checks the monitors.

restraint to abandon, but the battle to put a final shape on it continued. "It was actually mixed 269 times," Joe O'Herlihy laughs. "That's where the title came from."

Bono looks unhappy even discussing it now. "That was my favourite song on the record," he says, "but we actually physically wore down the tape doing that number of mixes, and as a result, some of the tautness of the rhythms aren't there, the way they should be. So I have a bad reaction to listening to it now, based on what it should have sounded like."

Not that anyone outside the camp would notice. Beginning as a love song, it transforms into a howl of lust, a huge molten volcano of a piece that climaxes in the most intense gospel chant of U2's career: *"Meet all your love in the heartland"*, the backing trio of Edna Wright, Carolyn Willis and Billie Barnum repeat, building the chant higher and higher until it comes to a dead stop.

"I'm sure there was enormous sexual frustration in the performance of that song," Bono admits. "I don't know how long we'd been away but at this point we were fully grown card-carrying men of 26, 27, 28. We were recording in Sunset Sound, with all the shit that happens around there going on. Search-and-destroy choppers looking for drug busts. Sunset Strip. Hookers. Every neon sign advertising sex in some shape or form. You could feel all that coming through in 'Hawkmoon'."

It's there in the rhythms, in Larry Bunker's thunderous timpani explosions and Larry Mullen's crashing cymbals. It's there in Bono's tortured metaphors and his yowling vocals. It's there in The Edge's blistering, dirty guitar. It's there in Adam's palpitating bass.

'Hawkmoon 269' may feel less than perfect to the band but perfection is hardly what it's about. Robert Palmer may have sung about being addicted to love but this was the real thing. Even better than the *real* thing.

It is 11 November, 1987. In between dates, the band decide to do a free gig on the back of a truck in an open space in San Francisco city centre, by the Embarcadero. Their own equipment is already on its way to Vancouver for the band's next show, so they borrow a sound system from – who else? – The Grateful Dead. Given the proximity of the location to the city's financial district – and in honour of the stock market crash of the week before – Bono dubs it the "Save the Yuppie" benefit.

the opening number they perform is a rough, improvised version of Bob Dylan's 'All Along the Watchtower'. In contrast to his first attempt at a Dylan cover, when Bono joined the maestro on stage at Slane for 'Blowin' in the Wind', on this occasion he clearly knows the words. Not that he's unduly constrained by that small detail.

The red guitar, on fire in 'Desire', reappears here, as Bono improvises: *"All I've got is a red guitar/three chords and the truth/All I've got is a red guitar/the rest is up to you."*

all along the watchtower

The band don't seem to know the chords quite as well as Bono does the lyrics, however, and there are some startlingly odd moments of musical disjointedness. The first 30 seconds of the guitar intro are missed by the recording engineer and The Edge has to dub it in later. "Otherwise, everything else is as it was performed live," The Edge confirms.

As it happens, the occasion becomes more memorable for its off-stage antics. Aware of the fact that the mayor of San Francisco, Diane Feinstein, has offered $500 as a bounty for bringing any of the city's numerous graffiti artists into custody, Bono climbs to the top of the adjacent fountain sculpture and sprays "Stop the traffic – rock 'n' roll" on it. A warrant is issued for his arrest but, the graffiti having been cleaned off by the following day, the attempt to bring the singer to justice eventually peters out.

In the long run, Bono puts it all down to mid-tour madness, but there's no mistaking the satisfaction U2 feel when Diane Feinstein is replaced as mayor soon after the gig and her successor, Art Agnos, abolishes the bounty and, instead, sets up a fund to sponsor the work of graffiti artists in the city.

> "In the long run, Bono puts it all down to mid-tour madness."

Left: The former mayor of San Francisco, Diane Feinstein, with the President of America, Bill Clinton.

83

rattle and hum

One of the criticisms which had been levelled at U2 during the squalls that surrounded their Self-Aid performance in Dublin was that, in the USA, they were still playing to predominantly white audiences. The implication was that they had failed to cross the class and racial divide in the States, despite their overt celebration of Martin Luther King in 'Pride (In the Name of Love)' and 'MLK'.

i still haven't found what i'm looking for

"All I've got is a red guitar, three chords – and a hat."

my own impression at the time was that Bono has been stung by these accusations, angered at the suggestion that any artist or band could somehow be held accountable for the audience that chose – or chose not – to acknowledge them.

It may, however, have been a critical catalyst, inspiring the band to begin their odyssey in search of the roots of rock 'n' roll in black music, and in particular through rhythm and blues, gospel and soul. It must have felt like a remarkable vindication, then, when they first got wind of the fact that 'I Still Haven't Found What I'm Looking For' was being covered by a gospel group, trading under the name of The New Voices of Freedom, in Harlem. The choir had sent a tape of their version of the song to Island Records, who passed it on to U2. Bono, Adam, Larry, The Edge and Gavin Friday went to check out the choir in their Harlem church and were impressed. As *The Joshua Tree* tour wound up to hit New York, a collaboration seemed like an attractive option.

The band suggested some rehearsals, to see if the different versions of the song could be integrated. The result provides one of the outstanding moments in the movie *Rattle and Hum*, a gloriously exuberant, thrilling musical encounter in which the common spirituality of the different participants is celebrated, tentatively at first and then with a rare and infectious abandon. Later, the choir joined the band for their date at Madison Square Garden and, although more formal, the performance is hardly less compelling. Bono's vocals are superb, as he trades licks with the two soloists George Pendergrass and Dorothy Tennell, creating the atmosphere of a Pentecostalist gospel service at its most transcendent.

The New Voices of Freedom's own version of 'I Still Haven't Found What I'm Looking For' was released as a single on the New Jersey label Doc Records. The song was later recorded by The Chimes, who had a hit with it in the USA and the UK. You could say that it's on its way to becoming a standard.

Bono in pensive mood.

freedom for my people

In the film, it was the kind of moment that inspired scepticism. U2 go for a stroll in downtown Harlem, to meet The New Voices of Harlem, followed by the cameras. There, they happen on a busker, one Mr Sterling Magee, with his harmonica sidekick, Adam Gussow, performing 'Freedom For My People'. The band hang about and observe, under the watchful artificial eye of the camera.

it's easy to see the point that's being made: a bunch of rock 'n' roll superstars still have something to learn from a rough 'n' ready street performer. In *Rattle and Hum*, U2 undertook their musical odyssey as both fans and pupils. But the presence of the camera made the value of that gesture a little harder to take at face intent: inevitably, it introduced an element of self-consciousness that a cinema audience would find it difficult to overcome. On record, however, 'Freedom For My People' – written by Sterling Magee, Bobby Robinson and Macie Mabins – drifts in and out, a found piece of street noise that acts as an appropriate prelude to what follows.

rattle and hum

It was backstage at Slane, interviewing Bob Dylan for *Hot Press*, that Bono was given his first lesson in the importance of tradition.

Brendan Behan: unknowingly contributed a few words to the U2 canon.

silver and gold

dylan, who was almost as familiar with Irish ballads as he was with the work of Woody Guthrie and the country blues of Leadbelly and Robert Johnson, mentioned the McPeakes from the north of Ireland. Bono looked at him blankly. "There's no particular musical roots or heritage for us," he explained about U2. "In Ireland there is a tradition, but we've never plugged into it."

"Well," Dylan insisted, "you have to reach back into the music. You have to reach back." There is no doubt that Bono was struck at that moment by an inadequacy at the core of U2's schtick, and he resolved to go about rectifying it. Part of the answer was to

begin to move in different musical circles, and Bono did. Taking a break in New York late in 1989, he hooked up with Peter Wolf of the J. Geils Band. They visited a Rolling Stones session being presided over, coincidentally, by Steve Lillywhite and became involved in a jam. With Keith Richards playing the piano, Wolf and Jagger traded vocals and harmonica licks. Bono was forced merely to watch – he didn't know any of the R'n'B standards that they were familiar with. They listened to some John Lee Hooker – and Bono was hooked on the raw power of the voice, the rhythm and the stinging guitar.

To some extent the experience was humiliating, but Bono was spurred into action. Back in his hotel room, in a fever he wrote his own take on the blues. He had just been in Ethiopia with his wife Ali, working in a camp there to assist in the process of post-famine renewal. He had seen first-hand the impact of Western economic policies on the African continent and his sense of outrage is palpable in 'Silver and Gold', a song about imperialism, greed, exploitation and repression.

Bono's magpie instincts as a lyricist came to the fore again. He borrowed the line *"I am someone"* from the black civil rights leader Jesse Jackson. And he plundered the Irish literary landscape for a couplet deriving from Brendan Behan: *"I have seen the coming and going/The captains and the kings."* But in writing the song from the perspective of a black political prisoner, he had also made a crucial leap of the imagination, a significant artistic advance that would assist enormously in the writing of *The Joshua Tree*.

The original acoustic version was recorded with Keith Richards and Ronnie Wood for the *Sun City* album. On *Rattle and Hum*, the whole band are on board and the result is inevitably heavier, Bono entering into the spirit of the performance with an improvised anti-apartheid rap, ending in a pre-emptive strike against the inevitable accusations of political posturing. "Am I buggin' you?" he asked sardonically. "Don't mean to bug you."

Curiously it was the throwaway line "OK Edge, play the blues", introducing the guitar break, that generated the most flak. But then The Edge's solo is quintessential Edge, and underlines just how far from the blues *he'd* been reared.

"Well," Dylan insisted, "you have to reach back into the music."

The improvisations that had kick-started so many U2 songs weren't coming quite so easily. The Edge realized that they needed new ways of writing, and his response was characteristically sensible. He decided that he would learn. He had come up with the basis for 'Desire' and 'Hawkmoon 269' on the acoustic guitar. Now add to that list 'Angel of Harlem'. From a musical perspective, something curious happened.

The angel herself:
Billie Holiday.

because he was at the centre of things on acoustic, The Edge found it more difficult to identify a space for himself on electric lead guitar. He was going to have to master some Steve Cropper-style licks to slot in and around the Stax-like horns on a sweet soul ballad of this kind.

Bono had been thinking about Billie Holiday. A friend of his, a girl called Alexis whom he'd met in San Francisco when she was 15 or 16, had moved to London and kept in touch. She'd given him a biography of the singer they called Lady Day. His fascination had been primed, and as U2 travelled around the States, picking up on gospel, jazz and R'n'B stations, it was intensified. 'Angel of Harlem' was written on the road but it's got the pulse of New York in its veins, with John Coltrane, Charlie Parker and Miles Davis making cameo appearances alongside the star of the scenario.

The lyrics have a strong visual, cinematic feel, but it was the Memphis Horns that completed the picture. Anyone familiar with Southside Johnny and the Asbury Jukes will know where this one is coming from. "Funny, I can hear Dylan in it more than Stax," Bono smiles now, and the reference makes sense. What's important, however, is the sheer mastery of it all.

On their musical odyssey through the American heartland, the band had decided to swing by Sun Studios in Memphis and to line up a session there. With the Memphis Horns in attendance and Cowboy Jack Clement at the desk, they recorded what became a tribute not just to Billie Holiday but to the vast legacy of great music that America had bequeathed to the world. Upful and celebratory, it remains one of U2's finest moments.

"It's a jukebox song," Bono says. "We don't have many jukebox songs, maybe six or seven, but that's one that people play in bars."

And anywhere else they need to get that *rush*.

angel of
harlem

87

rattle and hum

The Joshua Tree tour was half-done. The idea for *Rattle and Hum* had been worked out, and it was clear that the band were going to have to do some serious recording. Rather than de-camping, returning to Dublin – where it was winter – and attempting to re-focus there, someone suggested heading for the West Coast and working in LA. If the album was going to be *about* America, then it made sense to hang out there, in the place where the multifarious by-products of the American Dream could be seen at their most extreme.

love rescue me

t he Edge took a house out in Beverly Hills with his wife Aislinn and their kids. It was the house where the Menendez brothers later murdered their parents. "We were the last guys there before them," Bono laughs. "I was staying in the mews and that was where I wrote 'Love Rescue Me'."

If "wrote" is the right word. After a night of debauchery, Bono was sleeping fitfully and had a bizarre dream about Bob Dylan. He woke up and, under the cloud of a massive hangover, began to write the lyrics of the song he thought he remembered Dylan singing in his dream, about a man people keep turning to as a saviour, but whose own life is increasingly shattered, and who could do with a shot of salvation himself.

Shortly afterwards, Bono got a call, asking him if he wanted to pay a visit to Dylan – and thus, with a weird synchronicity, he ended up finishing the song later that day with the man in his dream. "I thought it was a Dylan song," Bono recalls. "So when I met him I said, 'Is this one of yours?' and he said, 'No, but maybe it could be'. So we worked on it together, which was great."

How much of the finished product is Bono and how much Dylan remains unclear. "Listen, I'd polish his shoes, I really would," Bono says. "A lot of people want their heroes to not let them down. I think it's a duty of heroes to let you down in some ways." Bono told Neil McCormick of *Hot Press* that Dylan had recorded a lead vocal for the track that was astonishing, and which taught him more about phrasing than

he ever imagined he still had to learn. It was withdrawn, apparently at Dylan's request, because of a potential clash with his Traveling Wilbury commitments. "But one wonders," McCormick commented, "was the despair and regret of 'Love Rescue Me' a little too close to the bone?"

It's certainly all there in a lyric that is powerful, poetic and unremitting in its harsh, tormented glare. *"In the cold mirror of a glass/I see my reflection pass/I see the dark shades of what I used to be/I see the purple of her eyes/The scarlet of my lies/Love rescue me."* Beginning as a country

ballad, the song is transformed by the entry of the Memphis Horns, lifting it into the realms of country-soul à la Otis Redding. "I don't think I fully pull it off in the singing stakes," Bono admits. "At that point, I was still allowing black influences into my voice, whereas now I am fully content to be white. Pink even [laughs]. I like it as a musical influence but in the voice it's dangerous for me."

Right: The Menendez brothers: 'Love Rescue Me' was written in the house they would make notorious.

Early in 1986, B.B. King landed in Ireland for shows in Dublin and Belfast. After his Dublin date, he hooked up with U2, who were at the gig. "We discovered a common bond," Adam Clayton recalled. "When we met him, there was a whole world of understanding there." B.B. asked for a song and Bono came up with the basis of it pretty quickly. "Writing songs for other people can be so easy," Bono reflects. "You're out of your own head and into someone else's. It comes quickly and you write it down."

when love comes to town

the challenge is to finish the job – typically, Bono engaged in a spot of brinkmanship, completing the lyric in the bath in his hotel room just before he was due to present it to B.B.

A hand-written note, scrawled to B.B. alongside the lyrics that the singer shoved under B.B's hotel room door, indicates that Bono had always envisaged sharing the vocals in the context of *Rattle and Hum*. Legend has it that when King met Bono after reading the lyrics he asked, "How old are you? They're heavy lyrics. Heavy lyrics." On the Texas leg of *The Joshua Tree* tour, B.B. opened for U2, and the sequence featuring 'When Love Comes to Town' was shot in Tarrant County Arena, in Fort Worth. The album version was recorded in Sun Studios, where so much seminal rock 'n' roll had been produced by its original owner, Sam Phillips.

"You go into the Sun room, and it's a modest room," Adam recalled later. "It's got the old acoustic titles on the wall and the pictures of Elvis and Roy Orbison and Jerry Lee and Carl Perkins – it's just history. You don't take a lot of technology into a studio like that – just the smallest amount of equipment you can do with. And you try to get back to that feeling of making rock 'n' roll *without* having huge banks of Marshalls and whatever. Just strip it back and play the simplest thing you can."

Simple, maybe. But 'When Love Comes to Town' brilliantly fuses gospel and blues influences, taking B.B. back to where it had all started for him, singing in a gospel quartet in Mississippi. With the redemptive power of love as its theme, it goes back even further for its clinching biblical metaphor as the two singers trade verses: *"I was there when they crucified my Lord,"* B.B. sings, *"I held the scabbard when the soldier drew his sword/I threw the dice when they pierced his side/But I've seen love conquer the great divide."*

Bono is free-wheeling. "It's like that line from Brendan Kennelly's *Book of Judas*: 'The best way to serve the age is to betray it'," he says. By *Rattle and Hum*, U2's faith had become truly inclusive. You could feel it in the grooves.

> "How old are you? They're heavy lyrics. Heavy lyrics."
>
> – B.B. KING

That's entertainment!
Bono with B.B. King.

"We don't write many straight love songs," Bono says. And it's true, in the conventional meaning of that term. But U2 do write about love all the time. In fact love in its many facets and guises is the terrain their music most frequently occupies. 'Heartland' is a love song.

heartland

"Let's see, have I forgotten anything? Oh yes, a bottle of milk!"

> "America both fascinates and frightens me."
>
> – BONO

i t was written during 1986 for *The Joshua Tree*. Recorded at Adam Clayton's home in Rathfarnham, it was one of the five or six tracks that remained unfinished from those marathon sessions. When it came to the cut, the band went for 'Trip Through Your Wires' in preference; it was a question of flow and balance. "It was too laid-back," Bono reflects. "We wanted stuff we could play live. On *The Unforgettable Fire* we'd gone that sort of ambient route, so on *The Joshua Tree* we wanted to toughen it up a bit." 'Heartland' was something they could profitably return to later.

It gelled with the theme of *Rattle and Hum* perfectly.

If *The Joshua Tree* had attacked the duplicity and deceit at the heart of US political machinations, its follow-up was a much more affectionate document, in its new songs celebrating popular culture and the country that had provided the breeding ground for the blues and rock 'n' roll. 'Heartland' emerges as a love song to the nation. Ireland had frequently been characterized as a woman by poets like James Clarence Mangan in 'My Dark Rosaleen' and William Butler Yeats, who cast the country as Caitlín Ní Houlihín in a variety of works. Now Bono was applying for the same kind of poetic licence. He passed the test with honours.

'Heartland' was Daniel Lanois' favourite track on *Rattle and Hum*, and not just because he shared the production credits with Brian Eno. He felt, overall, that the album was too clear, too focused, too contained. From one perspective, it lacks the sense of mystery which Eno and himself had always striven for.

"We'd always had this thing in the band where we talk about the sex of the chord," Bono explains. "So if you don't play the third, the chord becomes bi-sexual somehow. It could be either major or minor. And the track becomes unresolved musically if you use ninths or sixths and you don't play the third. In American music, and particularly the blues, those things become very clear musically. Danny loves 'Heartland' because it's back to those suspensions."

It is back to the dreamy, poetic language of the finest moments on *The Unforgettable Fire*, too. Like all great affairs of the heart, there is an element of obsession here, an acknowledgement of the pain alongside the pleasure to be discovered in love.

"America both fascinates and frightens me," Bono said at the time. "I can't get it out of my system. The German film-maker, Wim Wenders, who directed *Paris, Texas*, has said that America has colonised our unconscious. He's right. America is everywhere. You don't even have to go there – it comes to you. No matter where we live it's pumped into our homes in *Dallas*, *Dynasty* and *Hill Street Blues*. It's Hollywood, it's Coca-Cola, it's Levis, it's Harley Davidsons. There's good and bad in all of these, but either way you've got to deal with it."

You don't even have to go there – but it's better if you do. There is a sigh at the heart of 'Heartland', a sense of a love that, for all its trials and tribulations, is being fulfilled. And then Bono takes off, soaring into a gorgeously controlled falsetto to convey a sense of infinite rapture.

And two hearts beat as one.

You're trying to make sense of the madness around you. Album sales are going through the roof. The tour is like a military operation, only that it sometimes feels as if Sergeant Bilko is in charge. There are hundreds of people on board now and they all want a piece of you. The record company wants a piece of you. The media wants a piece of you. The fans want a piece of you. And your family – they're entitled to a piece of you that you can't give them.

And on top of all that – the usual mayhem, only worse – someone had the bright idea of making a fucking film of the tour. Something inside keeps telling you that it could be a catastrophe.

god part II

t here's so much money at stake and so little control you can exert. They get in the way, shove cameras up your nose, follow you around – as if you didn't feel that you were in a goldfish bowl already. You remember Washington DC. Falling on the stage. Dislocating your shoulder. Being wheeled into an ambulance. Looking up and seeing Phil Joanou – you'd nicknamed him ET – and his cameras. You said: "ET", you said, "what the fuck are you doing in my ambulance?" And he said: "Hey, you wanted me to make a documentary!" Madness. Complete fucking madness.

And if you whinge about this kind of thing, if you complain – it's like, "You ungrateful bastard, you. You've got money, success, hit records, hot and cold running groupies, stretch limos, champagne on ice everywhere you go – and you're complaining?" As if that was what it was all about. It makes you think about what it must have been like for Elvis. Why he hid himself away in Graceland and ate a mountain of cheeseburgers. It makes you think about what it must have been like for The Beatles, for John Lennon.

That was why you decided to open the set with 'Helter Skelter'. Now the word was out that Albert Goldman was about to do a hatchet job on Lennon. Goldman. His Elvis book stank. Made Presley out to be a rock 'n' roll idiot. Now the same asshole was going to do John Lennon over, and portray him as a rock 'n' roll fool. As a bully. As a reptile. Albert Goldman. What the fuck would he know?

There's a song in all this. Make it a tribute to Lennon. Jimmy Iovine knew him. Worked with the Plastic Ono Band.

Bruce Cockburn: kicked the darkness
until it bled daylight.

rattle and hum

The God couple: John Lennon and Yoko Ono.

'God Part II', you could call it. Send up all that Hollywood sequel stuff. That's a new twist. Give Goldman a going over himself. Get some of that pent-up bile out of your system. Say some things about Lennon. Own up to some things about yourself. Have some fun doing the whole thing in the Plastic Ono mould. Only re-vamped. Upgraded. Look for a new dynamic. A good excuse to check out how this grunge thing feels. Nice and quiet and then WHAM! IN YOUR FACE! Keep it tight, restrained and then USE THE SLEDGEHAMMER. BAM! Jimmy should be able to handle that.

'God Part II', you call it. It's hard alright, a sort of a half-way house between *The Joshua Tree* and the future. It's got Lennon written all over it. It's got drum loops for Larry to kick against, which is interesting. It's got you being all nice and reasonable and then WAH! Throwing a bit of a tantrum. You get a chance to quote Bruce Cockburn: a good line of his, that one about kicking the darkness till it bleeds

daylight. You use the opportunity to show your own darker side. To be a bit irresponsible. To reveal your anger. And to do a Lennon yourself, trying to wrap up the truth in a single phrase. "I believe in love." Because it's true. You do. Not that it cut much ice with Yoko. "That was a nice cover version you did of John's song," she'd said when you met her. Cover version! At least she didn't look for royalties.

Looking back on it later, with a bit of distance and detachment, it's not a track you'll make a passionate case for. The thing that stops it coming off is the singing: it does sound like a bit of a tantrum. You can laugh at that now yourself, but there's not a lot of humour in the song or on the record. Vitriol is at its best with wit.

What the hell. 'God Part II' may not be the best thing you've done by a long shot but it was necessary. It helped. Sometimes that's the point. Whatever gets you through the night, it's alright. It's alright.

Sometimes you have to get away from it all to write. One of U2's strategies was for Bono and The Edge to head off into the country somewhere, to isolate themselves, the better to let the muse speak through them. When *The Joshua Tree* tour finished, they took a short break, and then began the process of writing new material for *Rattle and Hum*. They retreated to a house in Connemara owned by John Heather, that they rented on occasion.

The Beatles: an influence on *Rattle and Hum*.

The Edge was working on the basics of 'Desire' – the Bo Diddley rhythm, the main riff. He also had this beautiful chord sequence and melody that Bono immediately saw potential in.

He worried it around for a while, looking for a way in lyrically. Eventually it came. "It became a meditation on commitment and what that means," Bono says. It became 'All I Want Is You'.

Musically, there were more shapes to be thrown yet. If *Rattle and Hum* had begun with The Beatles via 'Helter Skelter', it would end with them too, in a string coda that was reminiscent of 'A Day in the Life'. Ironically, it was the wayward genius behind many of The Beach Boys' finest moments, Van Dyke Parks, who contributed an arrangement that leaned back in the direction of Europe, bringing the whole album to a haunting, ethereal finale that would not have been out of place on *The Unforgettable Fire*. But it is just one of many fine elements on a track that promises much and delivers more in its epic scale, with Larry's deceptively languid drumming and Adam's melodic bass meshing beautifully.

'All I Want Is You' is a love song and Bono doesn't usually talk about these things – but on this occasion he does. "That's clearly about a younger version of myself and my relationship with Ali," he reflects. "It takes a huge generosity of spirit to be around somebody who's in the position I'm in, and who can expose you. If you're a very private person, as she is, that's something you have to be very careful about. That's why I often write about other people's experiences as well as my own, and in all of my love songs you'll find that there's a few stories.

"That's a song about commitment, really. I don't think being married to someone is so easy, really. But I'm interested in the idea of marriage. I think it's madness but it's a grand madness. If people think it's normal, they're out of their minds. I think that's why a lot of people fall apart, because they're not prepared for what it is. Once they've made that commitment, they think that's the end of it, now they can rest easy.

"I'm very restless. I am not the kind of guy who would normally settle down with a family and one person. I'm just not. I'm a tinker. I like to travel. I like to move around. The only reason I'm here is because I met someone so extraordinary that I just couldn't let that go. So a lot of the sense you get from the work is that some of the characters want to run, to get to the airport and just fly away. And other characters could never be away from this."

He looks around at his living room. "I think that's a great dynamic for songs."

Onwards to *Achtung Baby*!

> "That's a song about commitment, really."
>
> – BONO

all i want is you

elina Scott in Central Park, New York. A mike stuck in Bono's face. Selina Scott! Every teenager has watched her on TV and gone, "Wow!", and here she is flattering Bono, talking about his interest in social justice, his trip to Ethiopia, his involvement in the *Sun City* anti-apartheid project. Bono's so pleased with himself he feels like saying "You're right. What a guy." Just about contains the impulse.

(Island U28)

Produced by **Daniel Lanois.**

Recorded at **Hansa Ton Studios, Berlin; Dog Town, Dublin; STS Studios, Dublin; and Windmill Lane Studios, Dublin.**

Released **November 1991.**

The Giants' stadium, later that evening. No problem Selina, come on in. Bring your mike. Bring your camera. Keith Richards is there. Lou Reed is there. Would you have a few words? For a 60-minute special on U2?

Lou can be curt. When he doesn't like Selina's questions he tells her where to get off. "Man, you got a lot of shit to deal with," he says to Bono.

Maybe he misunderstood. Maybe Selina was just playing devil's advocate. But to Lou, she seemed to be casting aspersions on the idea of U2 being interested in social justice. Bono's face flushed and he felt – numb. Then the anger hit. It was stupid to let shit like this get to you but she had seemed so – sweet.

It was gnawing at Bono. Then he saw a line somewhere about U2 marketing idealism. And he thought, that's it. We've got to get rid of this baggage. It doesn't matter how sincere you think you are. It doesn't matter how long you spend trying to explain things. Perceptions are more important than truth.

You're a rock 'n' roll star. Your job is riddled with contradictions. Time to put them on the agenda. Time to blow everything that's gone before into smithereens. Enter *Achtung Baby*. Enter Zoo TV.

And then U2's whole world started to fall apart.

Wartime Germany. The Allies are wreaking havoc. Cities being bombed. Buildings are being pummelled to the ground. Thousands dying. In the midst of all that chaos, a moment of surreal humour. The walls of Berlin zoo have been knocked down. Look, there they go. The animals are escaping! The citizens of Berlin emerge from their bunkers in the morning. There are rhinos, pelicans, flamingos in the streets. For them, it is a brief respite, a moment of illusory freedom in the ruins of a city, before being recaptured.

achtung Baby was a nightmare to record. It nearly killed everyone in the band. Bono remembers East Berlin as being brown: a dark, depressing shade of brown. Some days were better than others, of course, but there was a lot of tension, a lot of rancour, a lot of frustration in the air. On one of the darker days, Bono remembered the animals wandering around the city in their brief moment of ascendancy. He decided that a trip to the zoo would be in order. U2 bought ice-creams and walked round the zoo like school kids. Phew! Rock 'n' roll, as somebody said.

Bono was interested in the zoo. He'd read a novel about setting free the animals, a kind of introduction to Dadaism. Going right back to Lypton Village and the Virgin Prunes, that was his world. He began to feel that things were coming full circle, that maybe it was time to re-introduce characters like the Fool. On-stage at The Point in Dublin, at the end of the *Lovetown* tour that followed *Rattle and Hum*, he had talked about going away and dreaming it all up again. Dreaming, that was the thing. They'd been moving in the direction of the literal. Now, they needed to become Dadaist again. It was time to stop making sense. Or to stop making obvious sense, at any rate.

He was ready. Ready for the laughing gas. He was ready. Ready for what came next.

He was interested in the zoo as a metaphor. So there was a certain surge of recognition when they landed in Berlin to record the album. This place was like a fucking zoo alright. After the Wall had come down, the city was disappearing by the second. Every businessman in Europe seemed to be there, buying it up by the yard. And every hooker had flown in, too. It was a goldrush in full swing, without the gold.

zoo station

Trabant city: we got us a convoy.

When they called the train station Zoo Bahnhof, they knew what they were on about. It had been the gateway to the East, when the world was divided by the Cold War. Zoo Bahnhof was right on the crossroads. The idea of going and dancing there appealed to the band. Now, in the brave new world of re-unified Germany, the place was peopled with dealers and pimps, pick-pockets and transients. Now, *there* was a metaphor for all human life.

Zoo Station. Right at the heart of the contradiction. Sam Shepard had said that was where to be, and he was right. The point was that the song would open the album with a statement of intent. Forget the previous reference points. You are about to embark on a journey into the unknown. So are we.

The first verse reads as if it could have been written from the point of view of a child about to be born: "(I'm) ready to say I'm glad to be alive/I'm ready, ready for the

> "Every businessman in Europe seemed to be there, buying it up by the yard. And every hooker had flown in, too."

achtung baby

push." And that suspicion lingers throughout, as if Bono is drawing inspiration from having watched his own first child struggling to find her bearings in an unfamiliar and sometimes hostile world. *"In the cool of the night/in the warmth of the breeze,"* he sings, *"I'll be crawling around/on my hands and knees."*

Lovetown: at this stage U2 decided to dream it up all over again.

But then a new child *is* being born here. Bono was unhappy with his vocal performances when the band began to record *Achtung Baby*. "Let's just try something that's

It had been bugging Bono for a long, long time. You switch on the radio and hear a soulful voice bellowing out something that sounds almost spiritual. It turns out to be a promo for a bank. You flick on the television. There's this incredible piece of footage that could be straight out of *Vanishing Point*, only it looks richer, denser, more expensive. It's a car ad.

it was around the time of the release of *Rattle and Hum*. "You can't tell the difference between the ads and the records any more," Bono said to me, clearly rattled by the way in which music was being co-opted and manipulated to serve the needs of commerce. And yet wasn't rock 'n' roll itself about commerce, about selling records? That thought was there as an undercurrent in 'Desire', a song about turning people on, that had Bono stuttering about *"Money, money, money, money, money, money"*.

'Desire' had been recorded with Paul Barrett and Robbie Adams handling engineering duties in STS studios in Dublin. Another song, started in the same session and then put to one side, had been called 'The Real Thing'. They took the multi-track of that to Germany and tried to work on it in Hansa Studios. But the atmosphere was so overloaded with melancholy that nothing happened. They couldn't crack it.

Back in Dublin, they set up in Elsinore, a mansion on the Dalkey coastline, near where Bono and The Edge live, to which the band give the name Dog Town. It was there that *Achtung Baby* began to come together. The Berlin session had been racked by a mixture of creative divisions, personal tensions and an abiding sense of dislocation. Gradually these were overcome in the more relaxed, informal atmosphere of the new surroundings. The spirit of Berlin hung over the record, but now the darkness and claustrophobia could be turned to creative effect. By the time it came to finishing 'Even Better than the Real Thing', the band had rediscovered their sense of fun, tarting it up à

> "It gave Bono a different sound, and also a new persona to play with."

gonna put me in a completely different place," he told Flood, who was engineering the sessions. They agreed to distort the voice, making it sound as if Bono were singing through a megaphone. It created a completely different emotional feel, changing not just the voice but everything around it. It gave Bono a different sound, and also a new persona to play with. It was a return to the child-like world of Lypton Village alright – a case of travelling back to go forward: *"Time is a train/makes the future the past/Leaves you standing in the station/with your face pressed up against the glass."*

The band sounded different too. The drums were hard, insistent, industrial. There were moments of sunlight, as the train emerged from the underground, flashes of openness captured on The Edge's guitar. But this was the beginning of a journey into the dark underbelly of human experience and the suggestion of a child's-eye view only made it more poignant.

la Marc Bolan in a tribute to the kind of glam rock that was on *Top of the Pops* when they were hitting their own teens.

"It had been called 'The Real Thing', which is a really dumb title for a song," Bono reflects. "So with these new eyes that we had, we thought 'Even Better than the Real Thing' is actually where people live right now. People are no longer after experiences of truth. They are looking for true experiences, for the moment. People are no longer obsessed with the question 'What is the truth?' They want to know 'What is the point?' And the point is the moment. That's where we live right now, in this rave culture. Interesting things come out of that because living in the present, in the now – and not looking to what's around the corner – is very dangerous politically, ecologically, in relationships, to the family. But that's where people are at right now."

U2's interest in dance had been stimulated by their own plans to open The Kitchen in the Clarence Hotel. Besides, there was an imperative always to be at the cutting edge of youth culture, to know what was going on, to absorb whatever lessons might need to be learned and to apply them smartly to the evolving band gestalt. 'Even Better than the Real Thing' was evidence enough that Larry and Adam could mix it with the best of the new Manchester dance groups in the rhythm department but there was more than a hint of irony in U2's appropriation of the old Sly Stone gospel routine, the backing vocals pleading *"Take me higher"*, before Bono delivers the chorus with what amounts to serene detachment.

The intention was to indulge the voyeuristic emphasis on appearance, to slide knowingly down the surface of things. The infatuation with the moment is superbly captured in the clubbers' heroic self-projection: *"We're free to fly the crimson sky/The sun won't melt our wings tonight."* But underlying these erotic chimerae is something tragic. What else but the sound of a relationship

cracking up could explain the lines *"Well, my heart is where it's always been/My head is somewhere in between/Give me one more chance/Let me be your lover tonight"*?

Meanwhile, the joke was on Coca-Cola, who had been using "The real thing" as their advertising slogan for years. It almost came full circle when Richard Branson approached the band, seeking permission to use 'Even Better than the Real Thing' for his campaign to launch Virgin Cola.

But that would have been one irony too far. The band refused.

even better than the real thing

> "Underlying these erotic chimerae is something tragic."

Marc Bolan: the real thing.

> "The Berlin session had been racked by a mixture of creative divisions, personal tensions and an abiding sense of dislocation."

achtung baby

Sometimes it can seem as if you're digging a hole. Another day, another recording session. Nothing seems to be coming right. You flounder around for six hours, and at the end of it you know that inspiration has gone on an extended holiday. But now that you're into the process there's no option but to keep going. And so you flounder around some more. And then suddenly: BANG!

one

U2 were in Berlin for three months and they delivered two songs. It was as bad as that. And one of them happened entirely by accident. They were in the throes of working on 'Mysterious Ways' and looking for a middle eight. The Edge came up with two alternatives. Bono heard one of them and he thought "massive new song"! He improvised a melody over the chords and it sounded good.

"The Edge put the other middle eight on at the end of it and that just became the song. The melody, the structure – the whole thing was done in 15 minutes," Bono recalls.

Naturally, the band were excited. It was one of those happy accidents, those moments when the log-jam of ideas

breaks and a song comes flooding through. Tapes of the work-in-progress were being delivered to Eno, who was coming back with comments and responses; in due course, he got this first, inspired draft of 'One'. The next time he showed up in Hansa Studios he was in buoyant mood.

"Brian arrived and he said that he liked all the material we had," Bono recalls. "We were surprised because everyone was freaked out about it. Then he said 'There's just one song I really despise, and that's 'One'.'"

Bono laughs. "He felt it needed some serious deconstruction. So we went about that, and that's why it works. Because you can play it on acoustic guitar now and it works, but if you had heard it on acoustic guitar first, it wouldn't have had the same feeling."

Flood remembers the session well. It was one of those special occasions alright. "It was very, very quick," he says. "Bono sang 90 per cent of the melody and a lot of the lyrical ideas off the top of his head. It just came together. There was a moment and we caught it."

It is extraordinary to think just how close 'One' came to not happening. Given the shambolic and often haphazard way in which U2 operate in the studio, there's always a sense that songs are written by accident, but this was a particularly extreme case. And yet it emerges as one of their finest creations, a ballad of great depth and beauty that's open to a multiplicity of interpretations.

"I think it was based loosely on the position I was in regarding my last girlfriend and my wife," Bono's old Lypton Village associate, Guggi, reflects, offering one interpretation. "It's about everything that goes with the breakdown of one relationship and starting up another. I was with my last girlfriend, Linda, for 14 years. And then I got a little studio down in the City Arts Centre. I was working there and then I heard that this German painter was coming over to live here for six months, to work, and it turned out to be Sybil. That's how I met her. We started painting together and it sort of went from there. And I was very close, physically close, to Bono at the time because he was around and we were spending a lot of time together. And I think a lot of that is captured in the song."

'One' is a song about relationships. The implication of guilt, felt by someone who has just walked out on a long-term love, is there alright when Bono asks, "*Have you come here for forgiveness/Have you come to raise the dead/Have you come here to play Jesus/To the lepers in your head?*" But the song is also a meditation on the extent to which

Zoo TV: the medium is the message.

their Berlin sojourn was testing the band's own sense of unity. "That's an extraordinary thing about songwriting," Bono relates. "What something is in essence, you don't have to play to it. In fact if you play against it, you often get much more.

"'One', of course, is about the band," he adds. "Have you seen the *Live at Sydney* film? It was after Adam flipped out in Sydney, and we'd had to do a show without him. We had just two nights to film, and the first was gone because he wasn't there. So we had one night to get it and we knew he was in a bad way. But he looks amazing in the film and there's a real boldness to his playing, against the odds. I don't know how he kept it together.

"We thought that was going to be the end, to be honest with you. We didn't know if we wanted to go on if somebody was that unhappy and not enjoying himself. And that performance of 'One' suddenly becomes what it is about that night. It does have that quality as a song. Going around Europe, when the stuff was going on in Bosnia, sometimes 200 miles from where we were playing, you'd get a similar kind of feeling – that that was what it was about."

Three videos were made for 'One', each drawing on a different interpretation of the song. One, directed by Mark Pellington and built around an image of buffalo being herded over the side of a cliff, was based on the work of the artist David Wojnarowicz, who had died of an AIDS-related illness in 1992. It led to speculation that 'One' was a song about AIDS and that the lyric represents a conversation between a father and his HIV-positive gay son. It always seemed like a somewhat liberal interpretation to me.

"It was part of one of the layers of the story," Bono argues. "If a song deals with any kind of sexual or erotic subject matter, then the spectre of AIDS has to be present. But it's not the only threat to relationships. Everything out there is against the idea of couples. The concept of fidelity is constantly undermined in every ad, every TV programme, every film, every novel you read. Sex is used to sell commodities. It has become a commodity itself. In fact, it's always *been* a commodity.

"If sex is even close to the centre of our lives, how come we've relegated the subject to where it's the property of the dullest of minds, to pornographers and the like? I still think it's virgin territory because you're prone to juvenalia in it, the 23 positions in a one-night stand type of boast, but there's much more out there than that."

With the Berlin session in the bag, the tape of 'One'

The Edge adds foreground.

was taken back to Dublin. What they had was a good foundation but it still needed what The Edge calls "foreground". They put lots of overdubs down but still couldn't get a mix they were happy with. That was when Eno came in and, with razor-sharp instinct, did a mix based on his personal prejudices, ruthlessly throwing out what he didn't like. It was the breakthrough they needed. They got a picture of an arrangement that would work.

Flood remained unconvinced. "I was the nagging doubter," he recalls. "I always felt it was a bit straight, until we did the final mix. It was all hands on deck. Bono didn't like a line in the vocal and we basically spent the whole day re-doing it. From that, we went into mix mode and it was me, Eno, Lanois and Bono sitting at the back, all doing different moves, getting the mix to be quite emotional.

"There's a point in the process when the technology gets lost and you can actually use the desk as an instrument. It started to happen on that mix. We got to just after the '*Love is a temple*' section at the end and The Edge said, 'I've got this great idea for a guitar riff'. So on the mix, there were three of us on the desk, the rest of the band vibing around and The Edge at the back of the studio, playing the guitar part live to the half-inch.

"Personally, I feel that the song has such a strong emotional content – and we managed to completely honour and improve on that, the way we mixed it."

> "Eno came in and, with razor-sharp instinct, did a mix based on his personal prejudices, ruthlessly throwing out what he didn't like. It was the breakthrough they needed."

99

achtung baby

What are the themes of *Achtung Baby*? You could put the same question to ten people and get ten different answers. When Bill Flanagan asked The Edge, he reeled them off: betrayal, love, morality, spirituality and faith. Betrayal came first.

It's in his kiss: Judas and Jesus in the Garden of Gethsemane.

until the end of the world

it was in the air. The Edge's marriage was falling apart. So was Guggi's. There was a lot of tension in the band. Now that they were working with rhythm loops, Larry wasn't even sure what his place was anymore. If he'd been paranoid, he could have felt that he was being pushed to one side. Maybe he was paranoid. On the other hand, maybe he was being pushed. There was that morning where the others had succeeded in leaving him stranded. Larry had spent hours languishing in his East German hotel, wondering what was going on till eventually he was crawling up the walls. He'd had to phone Dublin to get the number of the studio to make contact. When he got

in to Hansa, in the end, he was furious and he let everyone know it. Betrayal. It was in the air alright. There'd have to be a song about it.

Bono had been reading Brendan Kennelly's *Book of Judas* and thinking about Sinead O'Connor. Judas Iscariot was a remarkable character. The more you thought about him the more enigmatic he became. The redemption couldn't have happened without him. So was he the ultimate insider? Did he understand the role that had been allotted to him? It was interesting when you thought about how he betrayed Jesus: with a kiss! What had been going on between them anyway?

Written for Wim Wenders, 'Until the End of the World' is about an encounter – possibly an illicit one – in which sex is high on the agenda. There's a hint that only men were involved, in the line: *"I was down in the hold/just passing time."* There's also a strong suggestion of prostitution: *"I took the money, I spiked your drink/You miss too much these days if you stop to think."* And there is an unmistakable reference to oral sex: *"Surrounding me, going down on me/Spilling over the brim."* But it doesn't stop there. *"In waves of regret, waves of joy,"* Bono sings, *"I reached out for the one I tried to destroy."* And you know that he must be thinking of an orgasm that's drenched in feelings of guilt.

All of these elements are in there, of course, but the song is about betrayal and it's written from the point of view of Judas Iscariot. ("There you have it," Bono quips. "Jesus singing about Judas. What more could you want?") The line *"In the garden I was playing the tart/I kissed your lips and broke your heart"* is the key, referring to the scene in the Garden of Gethsemane, and there's no mistaking the implication of a homoerotic bond between Jesus and the man who betrayed him.

On the other hand, there's a sense that Bono is writing about himself and his own capacity for betrayal. "That's about a man playing the tart," Bono says definitively. "I don't think I know any women who are tarts, but I know a lot of men. So that's not an anti-woman thing."

Or could it be about someone Bono felt had betrayed him? In truth it is about all the betrayals and indiscretions that were so central to the experience of U2 at the time. In many ways *Achtung Baby* marked the end of the world as the band had known it. "That's something that comes up in Wim Wenders' film-making," Bono remarks. "How hard it is to love. The impossibility of it all."

Especially when you realize that there's no one you can really trust. No one you can trust absolutely.

You could listen to *Achtung Baby* every which way. You could turn it upside-down. You could look at it from a dozen different angles. It doesn't matter. No matter what way you come at it, there is blood on the tracks. And nowhere is this more evident than in the ballad 'So Cruel'.

the saddest things. I was their best man, and we all went through that. But that was only one part of it. There were lots of other things going on internally within the band and outside it, and I was working through all of that. People are desperately trying to hold onto each other in a time when that's very difficult. Looking around, you see how unprepared for it all people are, and the deals they make. I think there's very few people writing about this, really."

Looked at from another angle, 'So Cruel' deals with possessiveness,

so cruel

jealousy and obsession – that part of the brain where sex and power are connected in a heady and addictive cocktail. Scott Walker was an acknowledged influence on the song. "His is a very delicate mode of expression on the outside," Bono told Joe Jackson of *Hot Press*, "though too often it is laced underneath with a lot of pain and rage." So, too, was Roy Orbison, for whom Bono and The Edge had written 'Mystery Girl'. The arrangement is something Flood takes credit for, highlighting a subtle piece of studio chicanery that transforms the song.

"If you haven't got a song there in the first place, none of this would make a blind bit of difference," he says, "but I think the way we shifted around the rhythm was very important. It was put down as a very straight-feeling backing track. The bass is played, but in the studio we doctored it to change the emphasis of where the bass line lay. That turned it into something that had a more unique feel about it, meshed against the song. That was one track where the technology available to us was crucial to the end product."

But in the end it is the poetry that makes it memorable. *"Her skin is pale like God's only dove/Screams like an angel for your love/Then she makes you watch her from above/And you need her like a drug."*

Left: So cruel: shades of Scott Walker.

to describe it as bittersweet would be an understatement. 'So Cruel' is the desolate complaint of a lover who has been spurned but who remains in love with his tormentor. It is dark, bitter, intense and masochistic. As a statement about marital infidelity, the sense of betrayal that accompanies it and the rage that almost inevitably follows, it would be hard to surpass. Bono is clearly drawing on the experiences of those close to him, and particularly on the emotional turmoil that The Edge and Aislinn had been going through.

"That's in there, but it's unfair to lump it all on The Edge and Aislinn splitting up," he explains. "That was one of

achtung baby

Blame it on the wardrobe man. Fintan Fitzgerald, who handles that end of the U2 operation, bought Bono the mad goggles. In the dark days in Berlin, when nothing was happening, it became a kind of routine. Bono would stick on the fly shades and look at the world through the eyes of a character who was only barely forming in his imagination. It was childish, playful. But gradually he began to feel that there was something in it. Slowly but surely 'The Fly' was born.

the fly

Bono: come Fly with me.

the band had been hammering away at a piece with the working title of 'Ultraviolet'. It kept going on and on, round and round, through the recording of the album. "There were some good ideas there, some good sounds," says Flood, "but it had this depressive sort of air about it. It was as if it was never going to burst out."

Back in Dublin, after more heartache, the piece schismed into two parts. One became 'Light My Way'. The other was 'The Fly'. In the first place, the song had been too Leonard Cohen, Bono says, but the sunglasses cured that. Fintan Fitzgerald also gave him a book of Jenny Holger's truisms. "I became very interested in these single-line aphorisms," Bono states. "I'd been writing them. So I got this character who could say them all, from 'A liar won't believe anybody else' to 'A friend is somebody who lets you down'. And that's where 'The Fly' was coming from."

Flood contributed the distortion in the voice, creating the distance that Bono needed to get fully into the part. Daniel Lanois helped with the lyric.

"I thought it was a fascinating character," Bono recalls. "I thought I'd really get a chance to do something with him, especially live, because there had been rumours of megalomania circulating and I thought – well, let's give them a megalomaniac! Here goes!

"The faces of the people in Miami, or wherever we started the tour, when that character walked on stage, was a sight to be seen. I couldn't see it as clearly as everyone else because I had the goggles and the boil-in-the-bag Elvis suit on. But I remember feeling it. It was just a sense of 'Oh no, it's true'. And that was a great feeling."

A complex of undercurrents had come together. "I didn't recognize the person I was supposed to be, as far as what you saw in the media went," Bono told Alan Light in *Rolling Stone*. "There's some kind of rape happens when you are in the spotlight and you go along with it."

'The Fly' was a way of breaking free from that stereotype. It was about subversion. It was also about rebellion. With its hip-hop beats, distorted vocals and hard industrial edge, Bono described the song – the first single release from *Achtung Baby* – as the sound of four men chopping down *The Joshua Tree*.

One of the aphorisms that didn't make it into the final recorded version was "Taste is the enemy of art". "Once you find yourself tip-toeing as an artist, then you know that you're in the wrong place," Bono told *Rolling Stone*. "It's like you have a rule book but you don't remember where you got

it." 'The Fly' allowed Bono to tear up the rule book and start all over again.

There was a touch of Flann O'Brien's surreal humour in the mix. "There are characters in Dublin," The Edge commented, "and I'm sure everywhere else, who sit on their stools by the bar all day. And they know everything. They seem to have moles in the White House and they seem to know exactly what's going on in Moscow. They're bar-stool philosophers with all these great theories and notions. Some of the things they say can be incredibly smart. And yet they are probably mad. I think that's what Bono was playing with."

It allowed Bono to say things about himself and his role as an artist that might otherwise have proven difficult. Without doubt, it's intended as an ironic commentary on the rest of the album. *"Every artist is a cannibal, every poet is a thief/All kill their inspiration and sing about the grief,"* Bono proclaims.

But then 'The Fly' is packed with little explosions of truth, some of them universal, others personal. *"It's no*

secret ambition bites the nail of success," 'The Fly' announces, and it's a powerful image that's rooted in Bono's awareness of the reasons for his own gnawed fingernails. There's a revealing little coda – like the blandishments of a husband, who hasn't shown up for the dinner that's turning into a cowpat in the oven, phoning home.

"It was written like a phone call from hell, but the guy liked it there," Bono told David Fricke of *Rolling Stone*. "It was this guy running away – 'Hi honey, it's hot but I like it here'. The character is just on the edge of lunacy."

Aren't we all? With the Gulf War erupting in the middle of recording, there was a sense in which 'The Fly' represents everyman, disorientated, dislocated, spooked and on the run from the sheer craziness of the world around him. And then there was Bono playing the Fat Lady for the first time, crooning in a gospel falsetto: *"Love we shine like a burning star/We're falling from the sky."*

We should have known it was all over when she began to sing.

Apocalypse Then: the Gulf War.

> "It was written like a phone call from hell, but the guy liked it there."
> – BONO

There is a feeling throughout *Achtung Baby* that man is but an awe-struck observer at the banquet of love. That woman is the superior being. That all she has to do is click her fingers – or crack her whip – and he will obey.

mysterious ways

Larry lays down a funky groove.

"Lanois and Bono argued solidly for over two hours – a bitter, intense argument during which no holds were barred."

images of dominance and submission abound. They're there in 'Zoo Station', 'One', 'Who's Gonna Ride Your Wild Horses?', 'So Cruel' and 'The Fly', with the narrator abasing himself in front of the woman with whom he's obsessed, crawling around on his hands and knees, obeying even her most capricious injunctions and falling at her feet in an abject display of adoration. 'Mysterious Ways' continues in the same vein, with the celebrated couplet "*If you want to kiss the sky/better learn how to kneel... (on your knees boy!)*".

"It's a song about a man living on little or no romance," Bono says. "It's a song about women – or about woman – but it's addressed to him." Bono talks a bit about theology and about El Shadi – the third and least used name

for God in the Bible, which translates as "the breasted one". "I've always believed that the spirit is a feminine thing," he says.

'Mysterious Ways' is not about a particular woman. It is about women in general, and the way they entrance – and often dominate – men. "Ali often says, 'For God's sake will you let me down off this pedestal?'" Bono laughs. "At times I do tend to idealize women. It's easy to fall into the trap of separating them into angels and devils for the sake of the drama. But there's no way that there's ever anything anti-women involved. Our songs are not politically correct. They are written from a man's point of view. He's wrestling with different things, there's a flash of anger and hurt here and there. But I don't think women come out badly."

'Mysterious Ways' is one of the album's most upful, optimistic tracks. It had begun with a bass riff, Adam kick-starting the musical framework and Larry laying down a suitably funky dance, rhythm groove. Then they hit a wall. "A load of different ideas were tried," says Flood. They accidentally side-tracked into 'One', and then came back to 'Mysterious Ways'.

Daniel Lanois went into the studio in Berlin early one morning to try out a few ideas before the band got in. He didn't like what he was hearing and was becoming increasingly frustrated; then when Bono came in and started to sing, he seemed to be pushing the song in the opposite direction entirely. In a dark, tense period for the band, this was the nadir. Lanois and Bono argued solidly for over two hours – a bitter, intense argument during which no holds were barred.

"That's why I love Danny so much," Bono laughs now. "He cares about the record he's making as much and more than any band or artist he's working with."

But it wasn't funny at the time. Joe O'Herlihy remembers it as a brutal and bruising showdown.

"I really thought they were going to have a fight," Flood adds. "But I think it was just a product of the fact that this was such a hard record to make. Going into it everyone knew what we didn't want. It was like, you know what you want to throw out – but you're not quite sure of the place you want to go.

"It takes a series of mistakes, errors, learning, two steps forward, three steps sideways to actually get there," he concludes.

U2 spend a lot of their time in the studio talking. It's one of the great luxuries of their position. Most bands are tightly tied to a schedule and a budget.

U2 have both the creative freedom and the financial clout to define their own terms. But once they do commit themselves, then all hell breaks loose. When someone is committing the guts of $250 million for your tour, they want to know that you're going to show up for the first date. And since the record company can anticipate turning over at least that amount again on sales of the album, they want to be certain that it'll be ready and in the shops by the time the touring machine is being cranked into action. Sometimes it's difficult to know which is the harder part: the early phase of groping, searching, arguing. Or the later one of making commitments, of finishing stuff under the gun, of agreeing to disagree to get the product onto the streets.

That's how it was with 'Who's Gonna Ride Your Wild Horses?' That song had so many different incarnations. It was mixed a dozen different ways, and the pros and cons of each of them were debated in detail. Often, along the way, chinks of light appear that might reveal the best way forward for a song, but five mixes on they've been forgotten. Should Larry lighten up on the drums? Should he push them harder? What about that first rhythm track that The Edge put down? Where has the acoustic gone? Adam. We're losing Adam! Sometimes the discussions go round in circles. There are mixes produced that would be unrecognizable from the finished product. And then it's time to be decisive.

Achtung Baby was particularly fraught. Daniel Lanois was producing but at times he seemed uncomfortable with what was going down. Eno was afforded the luxury of being a dilettante, dropping in to listen to what had been happening, and making comments and suggestions. Flood was there all the way through, at the desk, keeping track of everything and coaxing the process forward with a combination of quiet determination and good humour. And when things were getting really hairy, there was always the option of calling in Steve Lillywhite as a fresh pair of ears. They used him on 'Even Better than the Real Thing'. And

when it came to the crunch, when decisions had to be made about 'Who's Gonna Ride Your Wild Horses?', they brought him in again.

"Steve mixed it and he went for the sonic blast of it," Bono says. "It started out as one of those Scott Walker things but we felt it was too rich. Daniel probably felt that the way we went in the end was too FM. It's a song I feel we didn't quite nail on the record because there was another whole set of lyrics that were dumped and I wrote those quickly and off we went. But we did another version which was released as a single which was better."

who's gonna ride your wild horses?

It had been more of a love song. Now it was about sexual jealousy. The lyrics may have been hurried but it has its share of telling psychological insights into the battlefield of love, all the same. *"Well, you lied to me/'cos I asked you to,"* Bono sings, and you don't need to be told what the context is. And it comes back, in the final chorus, to oral sex: *"Who's gonna taste your salt water kisses?/Who's gonna take the place of me?"*

"It's been said to me alright", Bono concedes, "that there's a lot of references to oral sex on the record. It's a very equal position. But I hadn't thought about the cumulative effect. I guess there's something for everybody. Don't try this at home [laughs]."

A trio of axe-grinders.

achtung baby

Sometimes it could get too intense in Dublin. Everyone watching your every move. The stupidest things being reported on, often inaccurately. It had become hard for anyone in the band to go out and be loose.

trying to throw your arms around the world

L.A. - City of the lost drinkers?

that was one of the reasons for deciding to stay in Los Angeles through the winter of '86. There was a sense of freedom there that Dublin didn't allow. When they began searching for a place to stay, the estate agents showed them a dozen fancy pads. "You don't want to see this place," they told The Edge. "It's more like a military compound. There's no air conditioning. No carpets. No en-suite toilets." The Edge said they'd take it.

It was a massive place. They could do anything they wanted to it, because it was up for demolition in the not-too-distant future. So they put down roots and went through the full LA experience. "We started to live at night a lot more," Bono says. "We started to spend our time downtown, away from the high altitude in every sense, travelling down these astonishing freeways into the belly of downtown LA."

Downtown LA is an extraordinary scene: people stepping over bodies on the way into banks in the morning. Bobby Fischer - the chess giant - was rumoured to be living downtown in a box. At night the place was full of illegal drinking joints and other nefarious clubs of various shades and stripes. There was a small community of lost souls inhabiting this twilight zone, and U2 embraced it.

"It was really important for me," Bono says. "Things that other people were going through at 18 or 19, I was going through then. You know, getting loaded and being a bit of a tinker. Not caring where you woke up. Ali was really good about it. She was coming over, but she recognized that this was a stage I might need to go through.

"I had an amazing time down there. A famous graffiti artist came up, and he did the house in graffiti. I was getting into painting again, and I was painting in my underwear – as you do in LA! Ann-Louise was over to try and make some sense of the project we thought it would turn out to be. So for the laugh I painted myself with war paint and I came out in my underwear, got Ann-Louise on the back of my bike and rode around Beverly Hills. And they have coaches that go around there to see the stars' houses and when they arrived at our place you just saw all these astonished faces. It was great. That looseness we discovered musically and personally was so important for the records that followed."

On the lyrics sheet of *Achtung Baby*, 'Trying to Throw Your Arms Around the World' is followed by a thanks to The Flaming Colossus, the infamous Hollywood celebrity late-nite bar. "That song explains the feeling that you want to be as creative and as completely and utterly into your music as possible," Joe O'Herlihy reasons. "But at the same time you're trying to bring that on board as well. 'Trying to Throw Your Arms...' reflects what you're trying to give all sides."

It revives 'The Fly', presenting him this time from a more sympathetic perspective, as a guy who goes on the town and finds himself staggering home in the early hours like a lost soul. *"Sunrise like a nosebleed/Your head hurts and you can't breathe/You been tryin' to throw your arms around the world/How far are you gonna go/Before you lose your way back home/You've been tryin' to throw your arms around the world."*

"That's a song about drunk ambition," Bono says. "As in 'I'll be home soon'. There's just warmth in that image." And great insight. *"Nothing much to say I guess/Just the same as all the rest/Been tryin' to throw your arms around the world."* Bono knew the character he was writing about very well.

On most occasions it would pass unremarked. A bit of a chuckle, back to the top of the take and away we go again.

but not this time. It was after 'Ultraviolet' – as it had been titled – had split into 'Lady with the Spinning Head' and 'Light My Way'. 'One' was already in the bag and they had a shape for 'Light My Way'. Over an a-rhythmic drone, it would start with a confessional statement from Bono, a preamble about restlessness and irresponsibility that would put into context what was to follow. Then the band would punch their way in on a Motown telegraph-key rhythm, giving the piece the feel of a pop song. It was about half-way through when Larry dropped one of his drumsticks. You could hear it on the track, as clear as daylight. Everyone carried on. Larry got going again and they finished the take. Then someone threw a curve-ball. Maybe we should leave it in. That bit where Larry dropped the drumstick. He wasn't being funny.

"Given the choice," Eno would ask later in a piece about *Achtung Baby* written for *Rolling Stone*, "how much do you allow a record to exhibit warts-and-all spontaneity and how much do you repair?" Put like that, it sounds like a reasonable question. But when you're the drummer and it was you who dropped the stick – at first, you think maybe they're winding you up. Then you realize they aren't, that they're for real about leaving this stupid little cock-up on the record. What are they trying to do? Make a record that, finally, ruins the band? That insults its fans? That exposes us all as incompetent? The debate lasts for three hours. At times it feels like people are trying to sabotage the record with dissent. When Bono first produces the chorus, it inspires a degree of mirth. *"Baby, baby, baby,"* he sings, *"light my way."* What's so funny?

People hadn't heard Bono use the word "baby" like

that before. He'd often scat things one way and then change them later, but it became obvious that this was the lyric of the song. It didn't feel right. And besides something was niggling about the smartness of it: was it not condescending to use the term for a woman anyway? "There was a lot of debate, and a good deal of laughter, about Bono actually coming out and going 'Baby'," Flood recalls. "It was less to do with the political correctness of it than whether he could actually get away with singing *"Baby, baby, baby/Baby, baby, baby"* and so on. That was very funny for a long time. But he got away with it alright."

It was meant to sound like a pop song. Weren't the words "trash" and "throwaway" among the buzzwords they identified to define the musical terrain they'd wanted to occupy? As a chorus, you could hardly get more throwaway. It was like a decoy. The rest of the song could be as heavy as Bono wanted, a statement wreathed in anxiety and

Author Raymond Carver: the sound of silence.

ultraviolet (light my way)

despair about the terrible price that people pay for love.

Compare this with your average silly love song. *"There is a silence that comes to a house/Where no one can sleep/ I guess it's the price of love/I know it's not cheap."* It isn't the only powerful image in the song but, as Bill Flanagan pointed out, the bit about the quiet that comes to a house where nobody can sleep had unconsciously been borrowed from a Raymond Carver poem, 'Suspenders'.

The magpie had been at work again.

> "There was a lot of debate, and a good deal of laughter, about Bono actually coming out and going 'Baby'," Flood recalls.

achtung baby

acrobat

During the run up to *Achtung Baby*, U2 had been listening to KMFDM, Sonic Youth, The Young Gods, My Bloody Valentine. As far a rock 'n' roll was concerned, the emphasis was on a hard-edged industrial kind of sound. The Edge was particularly into some of the speed-metal stuff that was in vogue. At the time, they'd also developed an interest in Roy Orbison, Scott Walker, Jacques Brel – in torch songs.

Super: Sonic Youth.

In terms of lyrics, that was the way The Edge wanted to go, towards a more personal kind of writing. The challenge that U2 had set themselves for the album was to do justice to both impulses.

Everything was in flux. *Rattle and Hum* had been so successful it was embarrassing. It had also been savaged by the press. Having started out as a band in the slipstream of punk, U2 remembered what they had felt about the supergroups of the late '70s. Were they now about to become what they had despised?

Their strategy had been radical. Take everything you know and throw it out. Work with the music you don't know, in a place you don't know, in a way you haven't worked before. Disorientate yourself.

Well, they succeeded in that – but they succeeded in disorientating Daniel Lanois even further. 'Acrobat' was a case in point. "Daniel had such a hard time on that," Bono says. "He did so well, but he was trying to get us to play to our strengths and I didn't want to. I wanted to play to our weaknesses. I wanted to experiment. With hindsight, some of the experiments didn't come off so well, to be honest."

For most writers, 'Acrobat' would have been a slow song but The Edge cranks up the guitar and does a part that's half 'Where the Streets Have No Name', half 'Bullet the Blue Sky'. Larry's drumming adds to the sense of urgency, whipped along by Adam's driving bass. It was a brave attempt by a rock 'n' roll band to find a distinctive, hard edge, for what was essentially another love song.

But it is the lyrics that make 'Acrobat'. At its heart is an awareness of the ravages of time, and what it does to people and to relationships. But beyond that, there is the self-awareness that, itself, comes only with experience. Not for the first time on the record, Bono acknowledges his own weakness and inadequacy. He is more conscious now than ever before of the contradictions in his own position. *"And I must be an acrobat/to talk like this/and act like that,"* he sings. It was as far from the righteousness that U2 had so often been accused of as you could get. Or was it? "I think he was taking a swipe back at the press with that line *'Don't let the bastards grind you down'*," suggests Gavin Friday.

"The record," Brian Eno said of *Achtung Baby*, "came to be seen as a place where the incongruous strands would be allowed to weave together and where a probably disunified (but definitely European) picture would be allowed to emerge."

He might as well have been writing about 'Acrobat'.

It was Gavin Friday who interested Bono in Jacques Brel. Gavin had run the Blue Jaysus club in Dublin's Waterfront cafe and for a few glorious months, it became one of the city's most celebrated nights-out with Agnes Bernelle, Gavin Friday, Maria McKee and Bono, among many musicians and comedians, likely to show up with something new to perform, in the spirit of the cabaret. Despite its distinctly European flavour, 'Love Is Blindness' had been written during the *Rattle and Hum* period. It was Blue Jaysus material, a song that could have been performed with the accompaniment of a lone piano. In Bono's head, it might have been sung by Nina Simone, one of his all-time favourite singers.

love is blindness

it takes us back – again – to the shadowy world of deceit, infidelity and betrayal. It depicts love at the end, the very end, of its tether. It is as bleak and as despairing a view of the world as you're likely to get, reflecting the emotional climate in which the entire album had been made. "All one's relationships, with your family, with your friends, with the members of the band – everything started to disintegrate with that record," Adam Clayton told John Waters. In terms of its mood, 'Love is Blindness' had the dark, sensual and decadent feel of pre-war Berlin. But its sentiments made it the perfect conclusion to *Achtung Baby*. *"Love is blindness/I don't want to see,"* Bono sang – a desolate acknowledgement of the terrible reality that it is sometimes better not to know. The Edge plays a mournful, ejaculatory guitar solo, stabbing out thick emotional blues notes that linger and then fall away like tears. "A more eloquent prayer than anything I could say," Bono reflects.

And then darkness falls.

"It is as bleak and as despairing a view of the world as you're likely to get."

Jacques Brel.

109

zooropa

**Zooropa
(Island U29)**

Produced by **Flood,
Brian Eno and The
Edge.**

Recorded at **The
Factory, Windmill
Lane Studios,
Dublin.**

Released **July 1993.**

it began with the packaging of *Achtung Baby*. Instead of the single dominant image on previous U2 albums, the sleeve was a pack of cards. The Edge's spangled trousers. Bono in heavy make-up, a naked woman behind him. Larry with tomatoes. A psychedelic Trabant car. Bono in Fly mode. Adam in drag. A game of hide and seek.

There was a message. You thought you had us pigeon-holed: now try sticking all this in that little box. The poses were silly, over-the-top, humorous, sexy, ordinary. You want to see the real U2? Well, here we are. Even better than the real thing!

Zoo TV developed out of the same impulse. It began with the proposition "Everything you know (about U2?) is wrong". It concerned media distortion. Sensory overload. Indulgence. The truth behind the lies – and the difficulty in ever being able to dig deep enough to find it.

The Fly and MacPhisto came alive during the *Zoo TV* tour. You want an egomaniac? Meet Mr. Fly. Someone you can laugh at and jeer? Hey, presto – Mr. Phisto. It wasn't just satire. It was camouflage. It was U2 in disguise. But it was also U2.

Bono was enjoying himself. He discovered that he liked putting on masks. It was fun being MacPhisto, arriving in St Peter's Square to get the Pope's blessing, pushing children out of the way. Method acting! The best fun he'd ever had with someone else's clothes on.

The whole band were enjoying themselves in this crazy hall of distorting mirrors. The energy being generated on tour was phenomenal. You couldn't do indoors in winter. A break in the tour was coming up. They discovered they didn't want to come down. Better to turn this energy into noise. Better to make a record. *Zooropa* here we come!

One of the most important things is to find a location. Then you get a sense of who's actually singing the songs. What they're really about. The emotional as well as the physical terrain. The Edge and Bono had been reading William Gibson's cyberpunk futuristic novels. "He has this location," Bono explains, "the sprawl, he calls it, the city in the future where a lot of stuff is set." Bono wanted to paint a similar kind of picture with noise.

zooropa

during the *Zoo TV* tour, the band had been working with Roger Trilling, and part of the deal was to create the sense of a future that would be attractive, as opposed to the typical sci-fi scenario where what's in store is a wasteland. But other undercurrents were at work too. With the collapse of Communism and the expansion of the European Union, borders were coming down all over Europe. Not always to the good. Civil war was breaking out in the former Yugoslavia and the horrors that would befall Bosnia were beginning to take nightmarish shape. Nazism was on the rise in the newly re-unified Germany. "Looking at all that," Bono says "*Zooropa* seemed like a great image of a European location that was surreal."

During the *Zoo TV* tour, The Fly had taken on a life of his own. He had insisted on having his own dressing room. He began to crowd Bono's space, successfully replacing the singer as the band's frontman for a significant part of the set. He brought his friend MacPhisto on board. And between them they got to the designers who were putting the show together. They filled the gigantic screens with every conceivable kind of bizarre imagery. Some atrocity from the Gulf War? No problem. Bang it on. A clip from a blue movie? Go ahead, sweethearts. Do your stuff.

More of those mad aphorisms that had been premiered on 'The Fly'. TV ads. Copylines. Scenes from a Nazi movie. Members of the audience enjoying their 15 seconds of fame in the *Zoo TV* video confessional. Hey, this is the information age. We're on the brink of a tele-visual revolution. Let's put it all up there.

It was frightening. Fascinating. So much potential. So much potential for disaster. Not a time to lie down and leave it to the buccaneers and the pirates. Time to engage. Time to help to make the future according to your own vision.

"We were opening this kind of *Bladerunner*-type

world," Bono says. "It starts with this neon winking and blinking and these two characters come out of it. There's this image of the 'overground'. It was a time when everyone was all indie and grey and dull – the 'underground'. The overground was like coming out into the bright light of the modern city. It's an amazing place to be, walking around these modern cities like Houston or Tokyo. And the idea was coming out into that, embracing it, going after it."

But first there was the small matter of re-appropriating the language on which *Zooropa* was being founded. Steve Turner, who wrote the book accompanying the *Rattle and Hum* album and film, had begun sending Bono a digest of articles from all around the world. "I kind of stopped reading books and novels so much, and I started

Big Head strikes again!

zooropa

reading more magazines," Bono recalls. "There's something to all that. I wanted to get away from the weight of where I was going. I wanted to fly. There was enough melancholy around."

'Zooropa' begins with the Audi slogan *"Vorsprung durch Technik"*, and in the first three verses there are references to advertising copylines from Daz, Fairy Liquid, Colgate and Zanussi, among others. "And I have no religion," the protagonist proclaims, "and I don't know what's what." But far from seeing that as a weakness, the thrust of 'Zooropa' was that uncertainty could be a positive point of departure.

Right: Cyberpunk author William Gibson looks to the future.

"There's a line in, I think, the New Testament," Bono told Joe Jackson of *Hot Press* before *Zooropa* was released, "which says that the spirit moves and no one knows where it comes from or where it's going. It's like a wind. I've always felt that way about my faith. That's why on 'Zooropa' I say I've got no religion. Because I believe that religion is the enemy of God. Because it denies the spontaneity of the spirit and the almost anarchistic nature of the spirit."

There was certainly a touch of anarchy about how 'Zooropa', the song, was put together. Joe O'Herlihy had

captured a couple of good sound check jams at the beginning of the *Zoo TV* tour. The Edge took the best bits as the basis for a backing track, fed them into a digital editor and created a song structure. The band did a separate jam for the sombre, ethereal opening. "I found sections of this jam," Flood recalls, "did a weird atmospheric mix of it and then when we were starting to piece the album together, I tried to cross-fade that into the beginning of 'Zooropa' as it stood then."

Everybody felt that Flood's intro worked. "The whole mad guitar stuff that happens on the second half was Eno treating a lot of guitars," Flood adds. That worked too. Then, at the last minute, everyone had misgivings about the original jam that formed the backing track for the first half. Now that there was a shape to the song, the band could play it through. Bono even tossed in an odd lyrical reference to 'Acrobat' as a coda. "In the end," Flood explains, "for the first half we just used what had been replayed and on the second half we used what was the jam, with some elements of the replay on it."

You can just imagine the producer at the console, as the band depart back into Europe for another date. "Don't worry, baby," he says. "It's gonna be alright." 'Zooropa'. Better by design team.

Zooropa: *Bladerunner* **on tour.**

During the *Zoo TV* tour, U2 had entered another kind of celebrity zone. *Achtung Baby* had been their hippest album to date, claiming a place for them at (what was perceived to be) the contemporary cutting edge of rock.

the successful Paul Oakenfold remixes of 'Even Better than the Real Thing' and 'Mysterious Ways' had won U2 a new cult respectability in clubs. They'd moved on some ways from the sombrero-toting hombres of *The Joshua Tree*, alright. With the opening of The Kitchen on the menu, they'd gone in search of the best clubs in the world for inspiration. They'd begun to understand the appeal of glamour, of fantasy. Glamour had begun to understand the appeal of U2 too. Adam had hooked up with Naomi Campbell in what was, for a time, one of rock 'n' roll's most celebrated and then notorious liaisons. Kate Moss and Christy Turlington had become friends of the band, visiting Dublin frequently. And when Bono was getting his digest of magazines from Steve Turner, what was he finding there but pictures of himself in full Fly PVC rock star chic, on the cover of *Vogue* in the company of Christy Turlington herself?

"Magazine girls, my head's in a whirl/To be a superman," Bono had pleaded in 'Alone In The Light', a song written in 1977 but never recorded, which predicted at least two of the themes of *Zooropa*.

In some ways it was a natural drift. When you're operating at high altitude, you tend to make friends with other people who are operating in the same rarified sphere. But – on Bono's part at least – it was also a conscious decision. You can either embrace this stuff or be ashamed of it. What was there to be ashamed of? Much better to live the contradiction and report back on it.

'Babyface' – *"cover girl with natural grace"* – could have been written with any of the band's new model friends in mind, The Edge explains. But it was done with a twist. Bono had always been intrigued by the way in which the media turn consumers into voyeurs. It had been highlighted

by the CNN coverage of the Gulf War, which had reduced a terrible human catastrophe to the level of a take it or leave it video game. What's on television tonight? Shit, they're showing more bombs on Baghdad. Turn it off. Boooooring. At first it made you complicit, sitting in your living room watching the slaughter. Then it desensitized you. You went to bed with a nagging feeling that you were turning it off, not because what was happening was outrageous, but because there wasn't much action.

By comparison, pornography – beamed into your home by satellite television – could seem like a benign calling. In the narrative of *Zooropa*, the camera moves up away from the couple in the opening song and goes in through a window in one of the high-rise buildings in the imaginary city of the

future. There's a guy inside, watching a television. He has a remote control and he's slowing down the images. He's turning up the contrast and playing with it. "It's a song about watching and not being in the picture," Bono says. "About how people play with images, believing you know somebody through an image – and thinking that by manipulating a machine that in fact controls you, you can have some kind of power. It's about the illusion of being in control."

The irony is that 'Babyface' is delivered with all the tenderness of a love song. And, in its own way, maybe that's what it is.

Adam Clayton and Naomi Campbell.

The band took a mid-tour break at the beginning of 1993. It was different this time. The *Zoo TV* shows had provided a whole new creative stimulus that they wanted to keep surfing on. They didn't feel like coming down.

The Edge, in particular, needed to keep going. His marriage had split up irrevocably, and for the first time he knew what it was like to wake up to an empty house in Dublin. It drove him back into the studio, where he began to demo new material.

Sorry, Edge is a little tied up at the moment.

Searching through the vaults, he came across a song called 'Down All the Days' that had been intended for *Achtung Baby*, but didn't make the cut. He liked the backing track, with its loop taken from the passage in Leni Riefenstahl's Nazi propaganda film, *Triumph of the Will*, where an 11-year-old boy is shown playing the drum at the 1936 Olympic Games. There was a hard, dirty, industrial feel to the instrumentation, making it a prime candidate for some kind of rap. At first they had considered the possibility of Bono reading – or rapping – 'In Cold Blood', his poem on the dehumanising effect of media coverage of violence and war, over it. But when that didn't work out, The Edge took over.

"One day he was just mucking around and did the idea of the deadpan style over it," Flood recalls. "It was great. Then there was just the process of finishing it off, with Bono doing the high stuff afterwards, and Eno adding the arcade sounds on keyboards. That was one of the easiest tracks to do."

The Edge had become more involved in the lyric writing, acting at times as Bono's editor, suggesting cuts and bouncing couplets off him. 'Numb', however, was entirely his own, and it probably wouldn't be unfair to conclude that the chorus reflected his emotional frailty at the time, with Bono adopting his fat lady voice to testify *"I feel numb"* in a soulful falsetto that contrasted oddly with The Edge's flat delivery of the main vocal. But it also suggested that he was on the road to recovery because, if nothing else, 'Numb' was an exercise in surreal humour, capturing the jaded rock star frozen into physical and emotional immobility by the self-imposed strictures of his position. *"Too much is not enough,"* Bono sings to break the litany of don'ts that comprises the main vocal line, *"gimme some more of that stuff... love."*

"It's arcade music," Bono told *Hot Press,* "but at base it's a kind of dark energy that we're tapping into. It's us trying to get inside somebody's head. So you hear a football crowd, a line of don'ts, kitsch soul singing and Larry – who had come up with the melody for the hook – singing for the first time in that context. What we're trying to do is recreate that feeling of sensory overload."

The video for 'Numb', produced by Kevin Godley, was equally over-the-top, an absurd send-up of bondage games with The Edge being subjected to all kinds of arbitrary humiliations. But the song achieved its apotheosis when the band performed it in the Olympic Stadium in Berlin, where the Riefenstahl film loops had originally been recorded.

"That was a trip," Bono reflects. "There was uproar. There were people at the gig who could be – and probably were – the sons and daughters of the people in the film. But we wanted to point out, before anyone else did, the similarities between rock gigs and Nazi rallies."

> "It's a kind of dark energy that we're tapping into" – BONO

lemon

You wouldn't have any inkling that 'Lemon' was about Bono's mother unless you were told. "Here's one for you," Gavin Friday had said conspiratorially. "The lyrical idea for that developed out of an old home movie that Bono saw."

it happened completely by chance. Someone had approached one of Bono's family at the airport and told him about the existence of this ancient footage in which Bob and Iris Hewson featured. Turned out it had been packaged by one of those companies that put kitsch music on top. It was eerie watching it. The image of his mother, on-screen, haunted Bono. "She was wearing lemon," Gavin recalled. "That's where the title came from."

From that starting point, the song became something else entirely: a meditation about film itself and the pleasure of looking. "The cinema is where we get to be nosy," Bono reflects. "Where we go to look into people's lives, without them minding. People like to stare at

The Edge: Simply the vest.

zooropa

other people up close. But because of my position, I don't get to stare at people so much, so film is important for me, in that it allows me to do that."

'Lemon' is a complex song that flickers with different meanings depending on how you view it. But it is about seeing yourself more clearly through seeing someone else. *"Through the light projected/he can see himself up close,"* Bono sings, and it doesn't involve a huge leap of the imagination to picture him seeing his own reflection in the poignant image of his mother in her youth.

John Boorman: turning money into light.

He borrows a line from John Boorman about the film-making process when he talks about *"turning money into light/To look for her"*. And in that phrase, it becomes a song about imagination itself, about the muse, about the female spirit with which U2 have always associated creativity.

There are hints of voyeurism too. "It's about the experience of looking rather than touching," Bono says. "I think my favourite image is the image of glass, where he melts the sand so he can see the world outside." The end product may sound fluent but it came together in fits and starts. "It began as a crude form of thing," Flood recalls. "Eno decided that there was one bass-line he didn't like, so he just took it out. He treated a couple of guitars and those big string things, he just put on the track."

With the band flitting back and forth between various European cities in which they were gigging, and the studio, that was the way they had to work. They'd play for four or five hours in the middle of the night and Eno and Flood would divide up the end product between them. They'd work separately, pushing the songs forward, tinkering with stuff, adding whatever they saw fit and getting down rough mixes. The band would come back in, repeat the process and hope that they were actually going somewhere.

The Edge added a piano part at the bridge. Then himself and Eno contributed the Talking Heads-style block vocals. They were getting down to some serious mixing when Bono finished the lyrics and did a vocal. Then, finally, Flood decided that they'd have to replace the drum machine with a real drum track and Larry obliged.

It was the last track to be finished. There was a deadline alright, but the days when they'd had to stick down '40' inside an hour were long gone. Sometimes they wondered if the greater latitude had actually made things harder for them.

"They were on tour and flying back after each gig," Flood recalls. "They'd come in to the studio about midnight. I'd have been mixing. They'd listen and make suggestions, maybe do some music. They'd go home to bed. I'd carry on till about four or five in the morning. Then they'd come in at midday, make some suggestions on the mixing or do some more music. There was a whole two-week period where it was like that, which was absolute lunacy.

"With 'Lemon', I was mixing all night and I knew, by nine-thirty, ten in the morning, that all the madness had come to a point where this is it. This really worked. Then I left. They heard what I'd done and really liked it. That was my last day on the album because I had other commitments. After I was gone, they spent another three days trying to perfect the balance, but ended up going back to the one that I had.

"It was a very strange sensation because for me it had been the ultimate feeling of everything coming together. You're digging through the dirt. You have all the frustration, all the lunacy that was going on. And finally you reach a moment where you know that that's it."

The Edge had doubts about it all along, the way it drew so many disparate elements together. When it was finished, however, he too knew it was a U2 song.

Whatever that is.

"The cinema is where we get to be nosy," Bono reflects. "People like to stare at other people up close. But because of my position, I don't get to stare at people so much, so film is important for me, in that it allows me to do that."

During the mid-'80s, Bono had read one of Wim Wenders' books, *Emotion Pictures*. Wenders wrote about the way in which the USA had colonized the unconscious of the rest of the world through popular culture.

bono was also reading Sam Shepard's plays at the time. Shepard had worked on the screenplay of *Paris, Texas* with Wenders and when it came to making *The Joshua Tree*, U2 had in mind a landscape similar to that depicted in that extraordinary film. When Bono met Wenders, he mentioned this. A bizarre synchronicity was revealed.

"He told me that when he was driving across America," Bono relates, "and preparing for *Paris, Texas*, he was listening to *Boy*. He had just one cassette in the car and that was it."

Wenders and Bono established a firm friendship, so it was no surprise when the director asked the band to do the title track for his *Stay (Faraway, So Close!)* movie.

The band watched the film and used it as a jumping off

stay (faraway so close)

point for their own take on the theme. "The film was about angels who want to be human and who want to be on Earth," Bono explains. "But to do so they have to become mortal. That was a great image to play with – the impossibility of wanting something like this, and then the cost of having it."

In Bono's lyrics, it isn't clear where the lines can be drawn between fantasy and reality – if indeed they can be at all in the world of *Zooropa*. It isn't clear whether the girl who stumbles out of a nightclub – *"out of a hole in the ground"* – into the grey morning is a stranger, a friend, a wife or a lover. Or if she's just another image on a screen, a chimera with whom the narrator presumes an intimacy that doesn't exist.

The action happens in a curious dreamscape in which nothing seems certain except uncertainty itself. And yet the performance is full of languorous beauty, a gentle understated kind of emotion that seems at odds with the disorientation in the lyrics.

It ends with a start, Larry Mullen emphasizing the downbeat on the cymbal as the dreamer suddenly sits up, staring into the black night, the image of a fallen angel burning in his imagination.

And a curious bang and clatter ringing in his ears.

That faraway look:
A still of movie director
Wim Wenders.

117

There's a suspicion that *Zooropa* is largely about nightlife, and the obscure and often empty liaisons that fertilize in that artificial universe. 'Daddy's Gonna Pay For Your Crashed Car' is about a woman who's protected from the consequences of her own actions by an indulgent sugar daddy.

bono originally conceived it as a blues. "John Lee Hooker is the person I'd love to sing that," he says and launches into a slower, rootsier version of the song. *"You're out on your own/You know everyone in the world/But you feel alone/Daddy's gonna pay/for your crashed car/Daddy's gonna pay…"* You can hear Hooker hollerin' it out alright.

"God is a sugar daddy, as well," Bono muses. "Is it God or is it the Devil? Who's gonna get you out of the mess? It's a song about being strung out. You can be strung out on a lot of things, not just smack. The thing you need is the thing you're a slave to. How much do you need this? How much do I need to be in a band? How much do you need anything?"

The fanfare which introduces the song is taken from the album *Lenin's Favourite Songs*, on what was formerly the state-owned Soviet label, Melodia. There's a sample in there too from the song 'The City Sleeps' by MC 900ft Jesus. But hey, why this sudden interested in crashed cars, Bono?

"They're Berlin images," he explains. "There's a piece of waste ground outside Hansa that's inhabited – or was inhabited – by a bunch of gypsies and crusties. When we were there it was like a surreal junkyard. They'd collected bits of F11s and tanks from Russia and wrecked cars. There's dogs and ducks flying around there, in what had been the centre of Berlin when Berlin was one of the great cities of Europe. It was the Trafalgar Square of Berlin, and these travellers were living there almost in holes in the ground. I used to love that area.

"Of course, now that Berlin has been reunited, they want to rebuild the centre but these gypsies had been given this place to live. They owned Trafalgar Square! That's where the crashed car imagery came from, the wheels spinning in 'Stay' and all that.

"I think Mercedes Benz has bought them out now, but it was one of those great stories, while it lasted."

daddy's gonna pay for your crashed car

Is it a bird? Is it a plane?
No, it's a super-Trabant.

Zooropa is probably U2's least emotional record. It's something that Bono observes unprompted about 'Babyface', about 'Daddy's Gonna Pay For Your Crashed Car', about 'Numb'. And 'Some Days Are Better Than Others'? "They sure are," he says mischievously. "I think that's just one of those songs. It's like a summer song. It's just fun."

Between Bono, MacPhisto and The Fly, the main man was becoming an increasingly split personality. Bono felt that he needed some privacy, a way of keeping something for himself.

"Depending on the person I wake up as, one day I can verbose, the next unable to speak, quite shy," he says. "But with this thing, it was great. Whether it was The Fly or MacPhisto, it was like put the batteries in and off he goes! I got through the whole tour like that. Also people thought we were just mocking rock 'n' roll stardom and all that, but I was actually owning up to it. It was owning up to the side of yourself that is an egomaniac. I mean, why did you want to be in a band in the first place? Why did you want to play electric guitar? There's all kinds of reasons you join a band and up until then, people were just getting one side of me – and it was getting smaller. It was turning me into a certain kind of character who was set up to take a fall. And I knew that any minute that bell-jar was going to come down.

"So then we put out a whole bunch of characters from the preachers in the travelling show, through MacPhisto to the silver suit, The Fly. Suddenly there was a lot of versions of the singer in the band. Now which one is for real? And of course they're all for real. It's not such a stereotype anymore.

> "Bono sends himself up royally in a track that reflects some of the turmoil that surrounded the making of the album"

some days
are better than others

in fact Bono sends himself up royally in a track that reflects some of the turmoil that surrounded the making of the album. "It was mad," Bono laughs. "You can't imagine what it was like. We would fly out to Rome, play to 60,000 people and I'd still be dressed as MacPhisto with the make-up running, and we'd get into the cars, out to the airport, onto Zoo Airlines and all that.

"We'd get back to Dublin at 4 o'clock in the morning, work till eight, sleep till noon and then go back on tour. So a few things suffered, but the record has a nice kinetic energy to it, I think."

It's a load of stereotypes."

There's a bit of owning up on 'Some Days Are Better Than Others' too. *"Some days I feel like a bit of a baby,"* Bono confesses, and you can imagine Ali nodding in agreement. And then there's the line about bouncers that won't let you in. "I think The Kitchen might have to take credit for that," he laughs. "But it's just throwaway."

And I thought it was a profound statement about the human condition...

"One of the things I have to deal with every day is the fact that I'm very moody, so I'm just having fun with that."

Left: MacPhisto: please allow me to introduce myself.

The Rev. Al Green.

This was one that Bono heard in his head first. He'd been listening a lot to Al Green and it had influenced his singing: the Fat Lady was his version

of Green's sweet high-pitched tone pushed a notch further.

Sometimes the inspiration sneaks up on you like that: you hear the chorus in someone else's voice.

It can be easier to write if you come at a song in that way. The self-editing, the self-censorship that frequently comes into play when you imagine the words coming out of your

own mouth, doesn't happen. You're free of baggage. People aren't going to be

listening to Al Green and thinking that it's some kind of confession on your part, some kind of soul-baring.

it was intended to be an "up" song. Bono gives a demonstration of how the chorus might have sounded, and you can hear the soul backbeat and the swirl of imaginary strings.

It's hard to avoid the impression that the song was written in two separate bursts. It almost certainly began as a straightforward testifying song, but became something quite different in the third verse. Here, 'The First Time' abandons its symmetry and offers a new twist on an old parable.

"We decided to keep it for ourselves," Bono says. "Brian really loved it. But instead of doing an 'up' version, we just emptied it out, deconstructed the song and ended on this line about throwing away the key, and the prodigal son doesn't go back. He sees all this stuff there for him and he doesn't want it and he goes off again. That's a really interesting take on that story.

"There are many rooms to see/But I left by the back door/And threw away the key." It's a line that captures Bono's own wanderlust, the urge that's always there to light out, leaving all the obligations and responsibilities of his role behind.

"It's about losing your faith," Bono adds. "I haven't lost my faith. I've a great deal of faith. But that song expresses that moment a lot of people feel."

Always someone looking at you.

In some ways *Zooropa* was taking U2 right back. The imaginary city of the future had long been abandoned as a theme, hopefully to be revisited at a later date. Now, it was down to finishing an album that hadn't been planned, in the middle of the most demanding tour the band had ever undertaken. There was a touch of the desperation that had marked the recording of *Boy*, *October* and *War* about it all.

form, laughing and joking. "I've got someone here wants to talk to you," he quipped. "It's my wife, Linda. And, by the way, she really wants to fuck you." It turned out she was a U2 fan who'd been to every concert the band had played in LA. She was also the backbone of this great writer.

The next time the band were in town, Bukowski came down to the gig and had a great time. Larry got up to sing 'Dirty Old Town', which was dedicated to him. It meant a lot, even to a hard-ass like Charles Bukowski.

Bono describes him as one of those guys who was working in the basement. "Dirty day" was a phrase Bono's own father would use but it had a certain relevance to Charles Bukowski too. "Essentially 'Dirty Day' is a father and son song," Bono says. "It's all the little things my dad would say like 'dirty day'. 'It's a dirty day'."

Co-written by The Edge, it's also a song about passing the torch. About taking on responsibilities you don't know if you're cut out for. The days run away like horses over the hills, it ends, borrowing a phrase from Bukowski. Bono had a feeling it was out of control.

The other kind of fly: Charles Bukowski relaxes at the bar.

dirty Day' was born out of a band improvisation. It was one of those murky numbers, with the band reflecting the tiredness they felt and the pressure they were under in a sulky, brooding performance that had an undeniable dark intensity. Imagining his way into the lyrics, Bono felt a crushing sense of sadness in the music. Every time he went to improvise, an idea kept flashing up in front of him of a father giving surreal advice to his son.

On the mike, it was back to the influence of Iggy Pop and the way he'd make up songs in performance. He kept seeing Charles Bukowski in his head, and remembering the kind of advice he'd give, like "Always give a false name". He had the sense that there was some blackness at the heart of all this, some small tragedy. Maybe the father had disappeared and left the son and the mother behind. That idea was preying on his mind. It was like a guilt thing about having been away from his own children so much when the band were on the road. It had become a bit of an obsession.

Things gel in funny ways. Sean Penn had come out to the house one night and they were talking bullshit about poetry and God knows what else until six o'clock in the morning. Bono told him he was a fan of Charles Bukowski and Penn said hang on a minute. Dialled Los Angeles on the spot and got the author on the line. Bukowski was in good

dirty day

> "Bono felt a crushing sense of sadness in the music. Every time he went to improvise, an idea kept flashing up in front of him of a father giving surreal advice to his son."

Zooropa was a trip. It took you into this strange terrain where nothing seemed quite to add up. Perspectives were constantly changing. Voices kept shifting. Gradually you realized that there was nothing you could rely on. Nothing you could believe in. Not even fantasy itself.

the wanderer

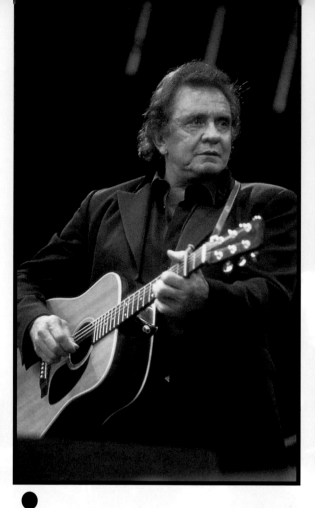

Johnny Cash; the man in black.

U2 had plunged you into this moonscape. Now they had to get you out. Bono thought he'd found the way. He'd made Johnny Cash's acquaintance a few years previously. They'd been promising to write a song together and had worked on something tentatively entitled 'Ellis Island'. It would be familiar Cash country, when it happened. If it happened.

In the meantime, Bono had another scam in mind. At first Eno and Flood opposed the idea, but he pushed it through…

In the middle of recording *Zooropa*, Bono spotted that Cash would be arriving in Dublin for a gig. This is how it would work with Willie Nelson later: hook up with him in the studio while he's in town. No harm in seeing if the man in black could spare a few hours.

"If you imagine the album being set in this place, Zooropa," Flood reflects, "just when you're expecting the norm to finish the album, you get somebody who's outside the whole thing, wandering through, discussing it. It's like the perfect full stop. It throws a whole different light on the conceptualization of the record."

The working title was 'Johnny Cash on the Moon'. But Bono knew where he wanted to go lyrically. He was thinking of The Book of Ecclesiastes, which translates as The Preacher. That was the first real title. The Edge suggested that it would connect better with the rest of the album to call it 'The Wanderer'. Bono had no problem with that. Wanderlust was still on his mind.

The band wanted to end the album on a musical joke. They took on the identity of the ultimate Holiday Inn band from hell and produced an anachronistic noise to match. The Edge had the musical ideas. Eno made a few suggestions along the way to help it flow. But the track is dominated by Adam's wonderfully absurd arcade-game bass that sounds like some mutant cordovox programme on a cheap Casio. It is diabolically effective.

It might sound potentially like a thin joke – until Johnny Cash opens his mouth, that is. The result is awesome and eerie at once, the contrast between the cheap throwaway backing and Cash's monumental delivery lending the whole a thoroughly skewed power that's entirely appropriate.

It's the story of a preacher who embarks on an epic journey and experiments on himself at every level: knowledge, sex, gold, whatever's going, he's taking it. The setting is a kind of surreal, post-nuclear *Paris, Texas* world in which loyalty, faith and honour have become virtually extinct. Bono had Flannery O'Connor in mind – the way she writes about the strangest American characters and their do-it-yourself religion with humour, sympathy and love.

"I suppose, in our picture, I want to have that kind of crackpot in there," Bono told John Waters, "who's off to save the world and, at the same time, he's just up for the ride."

Bono knows when he says that kind of thing that he could be describing a song about himself. In a way, that's the whole point. But Johnny Cash had reservations. He wouldn't have appreciated The Fly's phone-call on the run to his poor neglected partner at home, on *Achtung Baby*. He wouldn't have been too keen either on the shyster falling off the sidewalk at six in the morning at the risk of losing his way back home in 'Trying to Throw Your Arms Around the World'. Or the guy in 'Ultraviolet (Light My Way)' who sometimes feels like checking out, who wants to get it wrong – the bastard! Not at this stage of his life. And he never liked singing the line in 'The Wanderer', *"I went out for the papers/told her I'd be back by noon."* The jokey line: it was Bono through and through. The same old restlessness. The desire to cut and run. The need to be irresponsible.

"He used to leave that verse out because he liked it much heavier," Bono recounts. "I always liked that, you know, bottle of milk, newspapers and he's off. He's got God's work to do. He's looking for knowledge as well, and experience. He's on tour [laughs]."

There's a kind of freak energy that follows a band home after a spell on the road. It can take weeks to come down from it, months even. During the break in the *Zoo TV* expedition, U2 hadn't wanted to come down. "We have all this energy," they'd agreed. "Why not use it? Why not go into the studio and see what happens?"

Now they knew.

> "I always liked that, you know, bottle of milk, newspapers and he's off. He's got God's work to do."
>
> – BONO

Adam: a journey into outer bass.

pop

backstage at some celebrity charity bash, a plum-accented classical conductor is talking at Bono. "You're involved in a pop group," he says, one eyebrow arched like an accusation. It isn't what he says, it's the way that he says it. There's a pause and then it comes out like...*pop* group. His contempt for the very thought of it is palpable. A lower form: *pop music.*

Pop(Island U2 10)

Produced by **Flood.**

Recorded at **Hanover, Dublin; Windmill Lane Recording Studios, Dublin; South Beach Studios, Miami and The Works, Dublin.**

Released **March 1997.**

The encounter plays on Bono's mind. The condescension rankles. *Who* the *fuck* do these guys think they are, talking down to the practitioners of such a noble calling? The implicit assumption seems to be that there's something unworthy, something unclean, something to be ashamed of, in being in a rock 'n' roll band. In a successful rock 'n' roll band.

Pop music. A term of abuse.

It crystallises something for the U2 singer. *Pop.* Your man thinks it's an insult. Well, fuck him. It's time to reclaim the word. Turn it into a badge of honour.

What do you do?

"I'm a member of a pop group."

What sort of music do you play?

"*Pop music.*"

They had thought of calling the album *Pop For Men* or *Pop Pour Hommes*. In the end they simply called it *Pop*. You can interpret it as defiant or ironic – or simply as a statement of fact. But it's not a bad title for an album destined to chart at No.1 in 21 territories around the world in the week of its release. Not a bad title at all. *Pop.*

So let's talk about – pop music...

If Howie B had known how it would end, he might never have started it. 'Discothèque' originated in a jam between himself and Edge, 15 minutes of rhythmic surfing that would provide a launching-pad for the opening single from *Pop*; the first, cleverly-pitched trailer to what was to become U2's most widely acclaimed album ever.

With 'Discothèque', U2 took the art of disguise to a new level of sophistication. It's a conjuror's trick. If it is tactically desirable to use an idiom, use it. While you're using it, learn how to use it well. Use it well and you'll enjoy it. Enjoy it but don't let it absorb you. Discover how to stamp your own authority on it. And, in case all else fails, make sure that your tongue is somewhere in the vicinity of your collective cheek. Now, have fun!

And so they did. Howie had programmed up a selection of beats on his deck and at the end of a gruelling evening he began to mess around with one of his favourites. Edge was hanging nearby and on impulse picked up the bass and began to riff along. Never one to be left out, Bono joined in on improvised vocals. "Virtually nothing remains from that original jam," producer Flood says, "but it was the inspiration, and provided a context for the track."

"It was going to be the first public statement."

— ADAM

To get the vibe right while they were recording, they dressed the studio up in mirror balls and disco lights – and gave it loads. Long before the final shape of the album had been decided, everyone knew 'Discothèque' was going to be the first single. That made it harder to finish. "It was going to be the first public statement, the first track that people were going to hear," Adam Clayton says, "so there was a lot of double-checking yourself to be certain that it was going to stand up as such."

'Discothèque' is an earnest little riddle about love, disguised as trash. *"You know you're chewing bubblegum,"* Bono sings, *"You know what that is but you still want some."* Yes, there is an addictive quality about living for the moment. Yes, there is an undeniable pleasure in

surrendering to the hedonistic buzz of the dancefloor. Yes, yes, yes!

Musically, the trick was to acknowledge those parts of your record collection you wouldn't normally own up to: "KC and the Sunshine Band, Boyz 2 Men, Donna Summer, Los Sex Pistoles," Bono lists them off. Village fucking People! The boys got to dress up like tarts for the video – and, mmm, they enjoyed that too. There's a soupçon of camp in all of us, girls.

'Discothèque' doesn't quite know what its chorus is. It mixes metal and dance in a cheesy hybrid. It is self-consciously kitsch. But it also undeniably rocks like a monster, particularly with the volume turned up to eleven on the Howie B or Steve Osborne mix, when a club is jumping at 2 or 3 o'clock in the morning. BOOM CHA BOOM CHA DISCOTHÈQUE. The implicit message to humourless U2 fans was "You didn't think you'd like this, now did ya?"

discothèque

Meantime, the style counsellors were goin' "Well, hello! U2 are far cuter than we thought. U2 are far fucking hipper than we thought."

If it was going to be the first single, it had to be the first track on the album. The whole shebang in the bag, the entire entourage of band and producers set out for New York, further behind schedule than ever, to finally master the album. Even then, the job wasn't done. Even then, Bono couldn't let Howie be...

"It was outrageous," Howie says. "It had gotten to the stage where I couldn't speak, I was that ill. I was run down, my chest was caving in, everything was caving in. It was Saoirse's birthday and she was in New York as well and I had to meet her and then at about 10.30 Bono turns

125

Village People: masters of the disco universe.

around and goes 'listen, it'd be magic if you could get a new intro together for 'Discothèque'. And it was just like... (groans).

"I got into a cab, went up the road to the Hit Factory. I was kicking things like you wouldn't believe, going 'Fuck! Fuck!' Like, we were in the middle of mastering an album and they wanted to change the intro! It was like, 'any ideas?' And swirl was the idea. That was what they came up with, a 'swirl' sound. For fuck's sake!"

Howie had a bash, thought he'd cracked it, phoned Flood at Master Disc and played it down the phone to him. Flood said nothing and Howie got the message. Fuck! Fuck! He threw down the phone, turned up the speakers, pushed all the faders up – and BAM! Blew the fuck out of them: two £30,000 speakers gone for a burton.

"After I'd got all that aggression out of me, I got what is now the intro to 'Discothèque' about ten minutes later. So I phoned them up and I went 'come on 'round, ye

fuckers, I'm ready'. So they all trooped around and I couldn't play it to them properly 'cos I'd blown the fucking speakers! I'm still annoyed about that evening – but I got a good piece of work out of it anyway."

There were rumours that 'Discothèque' was about drugs. Well, no one's going to deny that but actually it's about something much simpler, and much more complicated too. It's about the pleasures of the flesh. And it's about the heart's yearning. In a way you could say it's as earnest as you can get. "U2 are just better at disguising it now," Bono says.

And he laughs.

▌ "And swirl was the idea."

– HOWIE B

How does a monstrously successful rock band, around for the best part of 20 years, get to grips with a whole new area of musical expression? When you've learned your chops in one creative school, making the transition into a different idiom can be potentially traumatic. If it doesn't work, the result can be an awful, career-threatening embarrassment.

U2 were facing that dilemma – so they did the smart thing, not just immersing themselves in the new music, but getting a couple of its most live-wire exponents involved. In particular there was Howie B, who'd worked on the Passengers record with them. With that test run under their collective belt they knew they could work together on the big one, and so Howie became a central cog in the making of *Pop*.

Part of his role was to act as a catalyst. He'd take records into the studio – vinyl records! – and play them for the band to see if they sparked any ideas. It might simply be a case of picking up on a rhythm. Or, if the emotion of a track caught the group's imagination, they'd set themselves the task of translating that into their own special brand of noise. 'Do You Feel Loved' was a case in point, growing out of a Naked Funk track that Howie opened his set with one night in The Kitchen when the band were on the town. That Naked Funk were mates of his was beside the point: everyone got off on 'Groove Sensation' because it was a blast. With Larry's back acting up, they needed a rhythm presence to create a foundation, so they got Howie to do his DJ *thang* with the track in the studio and the band jammed along. It was like a trapeze act, jumping off that groove into their own tune, but there was no need for a safety net: the spin held. Howie spent a lot of time working with Adam on getting an extraordinary bass sound that, in the jargon of the studio at the time, seemed to vibe everyone up. "It was like, 'hello, where the fuck did that come from?'," Howie laughs.

It was one of the first cuts to get close to its final shape, but there was still work to be done. Steve Osborne, who made his reputation producing the Happy Mondays' *Pills, Thrills And Bellyaches* album, and who'd been involved with Paul Oakenfold in remixing a number of U2 tracks, including 'Even Better Than The Real Thing', 'Mysterious Ways', 'Numb', 'Daddy's Gonna Pay For Your Crashed Car' and 'Lemon', came in for the final push. He worked across the canal from the band's own HQ in Windmill Lane Studios, on a series of final mixes – the role that had often been filled in the past by Steve Lilywhite.

When he got his hands on 'Do You Feel Loved' he felt that it needed a new groove and Larry came in to get that down. "Then I got Edge over, and we worked on the guitar line that comes in over the chorus – we suddenly came up with that one," Steve says. "The core of the tune was there but we added a fair bit."

Bono talks about the lyrics as if they're playful and in a way they may be. But to someone coming at it fresh, they sound remarkably confessional. 'Do You Feel Loved' is nothing more or less than a love song, that strays into the erotic boudoir first mentioned by Bono in 'Your Blue Room', with its references to conversations and prayers amid the tangle of the senses.

'Do You Feel Loved' may be a smart thing to say to a lover – but it's an even smarter one to put to 50,000 people in an open-air arena. It's a track that has all the hall-marks of a likely centre-piece of the band's live set – and yet there was still one final adjustment to make.

"It's quite a question," Bono says, "but there's no question mark on it. We took the question mark out because we thought it was a bit heavy with the question mark." Clearly a case for the grammar police to get working on.

Bono: shampoo, haircut and a rave.

do you feel loved

mofo

It began as a conversation with Simon Carmody, a master of the art of rock 'n' roll argot. Bono picked Simon up on his use of the term "motherfucker" and a philosophical debate ensued about the origins of the word in black slang and the way it was being turned from a term of abuse into one of praise. "It's such a dumb cliché, you wanna have a good reason to use it," Bono smiles. And so they set about finding one, settling on 'Mofo' as a likely title and building from there.

Salmon Rushdie: knows a God-shaped hole when he sees one.

edge and Bono were in Nice on a song-writing expedition, away together to fish for ideas. They got a structure down, with Bono playing wah wah guitar. It had a blues feel until they took it into the studio and Adam added a Motown-style bass part. It was shaping up but as the lyrical ideas began to crystallize, they felt that it needed to become tougher – to capture a kind of rage as well as the inherent sexiness of rock 'n' roll. "We spent months, probably, farting around with it," Adam Clayton confesses, "and then Bono said 'let's give it one more night'. So we said to Flood 'let's hip-hop it, let's strip it back, let's get a beat together, let's see where it goes'. And it rose from those ashes."

It rose from those ashes and transformed itself into the hardest cut on the record, a techno assault reminiscent of Underworld or The Prodigy, powered by a towering

double-tracked drum attack from Larry Mullen. It's the track Flood singles out as the one he had most influence on. "It had started as a traditional-esque R&B type of song," he remembers, "and there was actually a finished version that people were quite happy with. But I always felt that there was more to it than that and I was the one who was pushing them to go further. So one weekend me and Howie set about de-constructing it and it sort of mutated on from there. Howie was acting the maverick, playing different ideas to them for feel and rhythm and they had to take it on from there."

Steve Osborne did his bit by throwing in a blaring Moog line, against which Larry could work his rhythm magic. "That changed the feel a bit," Steve said – and everyone was happy with the result. Yes indeed, 'MOFO' had transformed itself – into a techno carnival, a record of quite staggering sonic muscle, man. Meanwhile, with Howie B acting as critic and catalyst, Bono had gone for broke lyrically, throwing references to Salman Rushdie ("lookin' for to fill that God-shaped hole") and William Butler Yeats ("Still lookin' for the face I had before the world was made") into a song that otherwise trades in rock jargon.

"I was reading in a book on Jack Kerouac," he says, "about him smoking a bag of grass and praying, literally, for a vision of a language, or a way of writing that would be both precious and trashy. That's what I'm aiming for," Bono reveals – and nowhere does he come closer than on 'MOFO', a song about identity in which he wrestles with some distinctly personal demons. "There's no question about it, 'MOFO' is one of my favourite tracks," says Gavin Friday, who is credited on the Pop sleeve as consultant poptician. "To me it sounds like Led Zeppelin after taking an E (laughs). But it's got real heart to it. I just love Bono's plea to his mother in it."

In a way it takes him back to where he started, to the oedipal pull of 'I Will Follow'. "Yes, but any time he made a reference to his mother in earlier songs, it was quite obscure," Gavin observes. "But the middle eight in this just sends a chill down your spine. Like, that's the whole reason he's in a band – because his mammy died when he was a young fellow."

'MOFO' is about the fact that very basic things often make you what you are, that go back to the way you got on with your brothers, sisters, father, and – in this case most emphatically – your mother. It's about being an abandoned child, an experience that goes to the heart of the blues. *"Mother, am I still your son,"* Bono sings. *"You know I've waited for so long/To hear you say so/Mother you left and made me someone/Now I'm still a child/But no one tells me no."*

It's a song of which Bono is clearly and justifiably proud, oscillating as it does between the throwaway and the profound with consummate craft, and amounting, in the end, to his best shot yet at capturing the demon spirit that drives him. "In the middle of it, when you go into that conversation piece, it's like WHAT?," he says. "It's the most exposed moment, in the hardest tune on the record. It was as if my whole life was in that song. I think it was the first thing mixed on the album and when we were finished, as the fella says, we couldn't get over ourselves. I had a deck in the car and we were playing it, going on a kind of club-crawl – but we wouldn't go into the club because we just had to hear it one more time. At one point it felt like I had 17 people in my car, and I can't drive, so you can imagine what that was like. Crazy!"

They survived.

> "To me it sounds like Led Zeppelin after taking an E."
>
> – GAVIN FRIDAY

The award-winning Irish band, U2.

The same songwriting expedition to the South of France that had produced 'MOFO' also yielded another gem. 'If God Will Send His Angels' had existed as a title at the time of the making of *Zooropa*. 'Stay (Faraway So Close)', on that album, had been inspired by a Wim Wenders film, which was about angels who wanted to be human and to live on Earth. The seed of an idea had been sown, and it lurked until the songwriting sessions for *Pop* began in earnest.

if god will send his angels

Flood bunks down for the night.

> "I thought – this is like pure pop. Now drop acid onto that."
>
> – BONO

it was one that was written on an acoustic guitar, with Bono and Edge strumming away like latter-day Simon and Garfunkels. The tune reminded Bono of The Fugees, or even Boyzone, and he became fiercely excited about its potential. "I thought – this is like pure pop. Now drop acid onto that."

What emerged is a classic U2 ballad in the mould of 'One', a song with a very subtle emotional tug that's brilliantly highlighted by the superb arrangement. Rhythmically, Adam Clayton and Larry Mullen supplied a light, lazy skank groove and then Howie B got to work. "He came on board about half-way through that song's life," Flood recalls, "and he was involved mostly from an engineering and a mixing point of view. He took all the elements that were on tape and over a period of time he managed to refine them. Then more overdubs were put on and he took a break from it, but he came back on board right at the end and tied it all together. I think it's one of the tracks that's closest to his heart."

Howie B's imprint is there throughout in the subterranean trancey noises and the unexpected spaces – but there is one sublime and quintessentially Howie moment. Having taken a sample of Larry's hi-hat, and lowered it a couple of octaves, he unleashed the resulting whoosh to magnificent dramatic effect. Similarly, the chorus of children – or angels – with which the track finishes could be a direct

lift from the *Music For Babies* album. And yet in many ways this is the track that is most unrepentant in its U2-ness. The links back to *Zooropa* are obvious in Bono's reference to the track as a kind of science-fiction gospel. Edge describes it as country hip-hop. Gavin Friday thinks about country too – gone science fiction. "It's a classic song," he believes, "a ballad you can space out to." But what's it all about, then, eh?

Most U2 albums had been conceived with an imaginative location of one kind or another in mind. *Pop* was different. "The record doesn't seem to have any physical place that it's centred in," Bono explains. "Instead, to me the songs feel like conversations. Overheard conversations. Or conversations you're having with yourself. It's like a movie that opens in the middle of a scene. You're brought immediately into the action and there's lot of little arguments going on. It's like being in a band, really (laughs)."

That's certainly what's going on in 'If God Will Send His Angels', but there's an essential bleakness in the pictures being painted: loosely about a guy beating up his girlfriend. Bono describes it as being a sour song, "But you can still hear her somewhere in there, through the music," he adds. "You can feel there's light there."

Asked what the themes of the album are, Edge was humorous. "Love, desire and the crisis of faith," he said, "The usual stuff." On 'If God Will Send His Angels', the crisis reaches epidemic proportions. In a world where love has taken a train heading south, the blind are leading the blond and God has got his phone off the hook, there isn't much left to hang on to. *"So where is the hope and the faith and the love?"* Bono asks. The eternal questions.

An album can be like a diary of what was going on in an artist's life during a particular period. The same is true of a song – only more so. "That's the great thing about songs," Bono says. "If you open your eyes they're all around you." That was the kind of thinking that gave rise to 'Staring At The Sun'.

it came together almost by accident. The band were working on another song entirely but they got stuck in an unproductive groove. A couple of bizarre loops were introduced, Larry got a really sweet pattern going against them and Edge made a significant call, out of the blue. It was familiar territory for U2: "Oh, I know another song that will work over this." It was a completely different speed and a completely different feel but the potential was immediately apparent. They spent a couple of days on the new creation and then put it to one side. A little later Edge and Howie B got to work together, bringing a few vital new pieces to the sonic jigsaw.

"I had a great time with Edge on 'Staring At The Sun'. I got a mad wee sound out of his guitar," Howie recalls. "After we broke our first deadline, Edge and I spent a week playing around with the tune. We put his guitar through a Leslie and it was a nice little thing. What you think is an organ on 'Staring At The Sun' is actually Edge playing the guitar. And it's a mad sound. It shimmers."

It's an appropriate verb in the context of the song as a whole, a classic tune about lazing on a sunny afternoon that's reminiscent in other ways too of The Kinks, but which is so magnificently potent and hummable that it transcends any hint of influences.

Curiously, in that light, there's a Zen-like aspect to the lyrics of the song, a sense of being totally immersed in the moment and experiencing a feeling of weightlessness that's perfectly articulated through the euphoric music. Even after Howie was finished, however, there was work to do. Steve Osborne and Mark Grant got involved in the mixing

and they did a lot of searching through tapes looking for different guitar parts. When Edge gets going he produces a lot of ideas and they found some discarded stuff that worked, enhancing the arrangement considerably.

The Something Happens album *Stuck Together With God's Glue* had been left lying around in the green room – it went into the song. Howie B developed an abscess in his ear – it went into the song. The television was running in the background, newspaper headlines had been pinned on the walls, the marching season was in full swing – it all went into the song. The British presence in Northern Ireland is alluded to ("*Intransigence is all around/Military still in town/Armour plated suits and ties/Daddy just won't say goodbye*"), as is the European Cup, which was in full swing while the song was being recorded. And there's a modicum of self-mockery, too, in the line "*Those who can't do often have to preach.*" Or could that be a veiled reference to priests and sex?

"If you're going to have a dig at someone, it might as well be yourself," Bono laughs. "But there are other things in there too. All these references are quite personal – but they wouldn't be in there if they were just personal."

It may well be that 'Staring At The Sun' is one of the most personal songs on the record. There's no doubt that Ali Hewson had a tremendous influences on the lyrics of *Pop*, and not just because of the fact that she's the focus for Bono's ongoing affair of the heart. She is also a woman of great courage, who has been placed directly at risk, through her involvement in the Children Of Chernobyl charity. There is a sense in which 'Staring At The Sun' may be a reference to Ali's experiences. An attempt to reassure in the face of all the odds, it's a blast of defiant optimism, underscored inevitably by a sense of creeping paranoia.

But what a blast!

staring at the sun

Irish band Something Happens: together they stand.

Appropriately enough, it was like a reprise of the final night of recording *War*. Then, U2 had had to lock out the next group who'd booked into Windmill Lane Studios, to finish '40' – a song that was destined to become a live classic for them. Now things were a little bit more complicated, with a number of mixes still to be finalised, two studios to do 'em in, and 'Last Night On Earth' short not just of a vocal track but of an entire fucking chorus.

last night on earth

George Harrison: The Beatles influence snuck in with the line "and the sun sun, here it comes".

> "Literally, we had people mixing that who hadn't been to bed in a week."
>
> – BONO

there was a team of producers and engineers working flat out, with mixes being ferried back and forth between the two studios for the band's approval. And still, 'Last Night On Earth' was only being finished at the time people were scheduled to check in for their flight to New York, where they were due to begin mastering later that evening.

The song had been in gestation since early on in the recording of *Pop*. The backing tracks done, the search was on for riffs and moods and Howie slid in a couple of Don Cherry pieces that were really atmospheric, pushing things along. The guitar parts were revved up and sampled and slotted into different places in the song. "But we just couldn't crack it fully," Bono ruminates. "The chorus only came into my head at about 4 o'clock in the morning on the final night, and the bit where it goes *'You've got to give it away/You've got to give it away/You've got to give it away'*. I sang a vocal at 7 o'clock in the morning. Literally, we had people mixing that who hadn't been to bed in a week, while our roadies and Paul were waiting outside in the cars for us to go to New York to master the record. My voice was completely shot, which is why we put so much echo on it and Edge sang along with me to cover it up. 'Last Night On Earth' is right."

It's the kind of experience that you get to laugh about – later. By this stage, shuffling back and forth between Hanover Quay and Windmill had become time-consuming, and so Bono had acquired a speed-boat for the purpose. On the final push, the ferry service, of necessity, had become particularly frantic. "It got so busy that we had to pull in Paul McGuinness to drive the boat," Gavin Friday

recalls. "I don't drive, everybody else was either busy or tired, so McGuinness ended up bringing people from Windmill to Hanover and back."

They had planned to have a big breakfast fry-up when they finished: sausages, rashers, eggs, fried bread. The food was all cooked and ready, but there wasn't time to sit down and demolish it. "It ended up with people eating rasher sandwiches in the speedboat while Paul McGuinness was driving them across the basin," Gavin laughs. "It was all very intense and serious. I think champagne got involved in the last hour, so it was rashers, sausages and champagne in a speedboat on the Grand Canal at 8 o'clock in the morning. It was surreal."

There were some serious disagreements about the lyrics too, which didn't make matters any easier. "I had a row with Bono and Edge," Howie B confesses. "Right up till the last night we were still arguing about that one. But that's what's so great about music. You feel like expressing yourself. And with these guys anyway, they weren't looking for yes-men. They actually want to know what you think. But I had really strong opinions about that – and I still do (laughs)."

It isn't a subject on which Howie B will say any more. "I know that that track's based around a certain kind of woman that we've all met," Gavin Friday adds. "You're at a party or a club and you just don't know where this 23-year-old is getting her energy from. And we're not talking drugs or alcohol here. It's just a vibe, a wild woman who gives you a charge of energy."

Maybe Howie felt so strongly about it because he saw a reflection of someone close to him in the lyrics. Someone for whom freedom is not just a by-word but a name, perhaps?

It's one of the things that makes Bono most visibly angry. The basic premise seems to be that once you're successful, you've sold out. Automatically. It doesn't apply in sport. It doesn't apply in the movies. It doesn't apply in poetry, for fuck's sake. And yet in rock 'n' roll, it's a common assumption that amounts almost to an article of faith among those who claim the ideological high ground: the very fact that an act has become successful means that they must have lost touch with the street.

U2: real, real gone.

U2's success may have turned the group into a corporation, but does that mean they're capable of producing nothing except corporate rock? Bono is contemptuous of the notion, dismissing the posturings of the guardians of the indie ethic as vainglorious lies.

"Right through the '80s this is what we had to put up with," he remarked, early on in the recording of *Pop*, "the idea that there was something morally superior in being in one of these shoe-gazing bands, these indie bands. I've written a song now that's like a two-finger salute to the people who tried to foist a sense of guilt on us because we were successful. The thing is, we always wanted to be one of the biggest bands in the world. And this song is celebrating that. It's saying that we enjoy being up here in space. It's like: goodbye! We're having a great time. We're out here in the ether and it feels good."

The longer you're at it, the more you realise that songs have a life of their own. You can know what you want them to be about, but they have a way of sneaking up on you in the dark and taking you by surprise. They have a way of writing themselves – and of turning into something entirely different in the process.

'Gone' was one of the first tracks that the crew knew would make it to the album, but it went through many personalities before it finally made the cut. "At one stage," Gavin Friday says, "it was a hard rock thing, then a punk thing, then a hard rock thing again." But they still couldn't seem to get to the core of it.

The indecision may have had something to do with the death of Bill Graham, the *Hot Press* writer who'd been a friend and inspiration to the band from their earliest days. It was towards the end of May and they'd just been working on the song in Miami, where they'd gone to do a photo shoot or two and to record, when they heard the news of his

death. The connection sounded an eerie resonance that fed back into the sinews of the song. Rather than being the fuck-you to the begrudgers whom it had originally been intended for, it became instead a meditation on the superficiality and transience of success itself, over which the spectre of death hangs like a stark premonition. "*Closer to you every day*," Bono sings, "*I didn't want it that much anyway*" – and the echo is unmistakably of the hymn 'Nearer My God To Thee'.

Sometimes you have to be brutal. Two broken deadlines on, so much had been put into 'Gone' that it had reached supersaturation point. It needed to be stripped back and Flood and Howie went at it with a vengeance, paring it down to its essence. And then Steve Osborne came in to finish it. "It was fantastic to mix," he observes. "Flood had it right down to just a few parts but they were the right ones. They were all pitched at exactly the right spot, so it was a really good vibe."

Vibe. It's a word that's bandied about a bit but one that's useful all the same in understanding the power of U2's music. It's not what the songs are saying literally that matters, it's the truths they touch on – and the light in which the music reveals them. 'Gone' is full of those little explosions.

"The background is so atmospheric and disturbing," Gavin Friday reflects. "It's weird. The track conjures up all the things that make U2 what they are. You can't properly put your finger on it. A vocal line here, a riff there, a lyric – it just gets you."

Bono puts it in context. "The bridge, which was put in to make it more of a pop song for me – and for Edge too – ended up having this incredible emotional weight," he says. "It's almost like Gavin's 'The Last Song I'll Ever Sing'. That's what it felt like to me. It felt like the last song I'd ever sing."

> "The track conjures up all the things that make U2 what they are…"
>
> – GAVIN FRIDAY

gone

pop

Recording for *Pop* had started in November of 1996. The Christmas break was followed by a period of down-time as Larry Mullen struggled with a bad back. Howie B took up some of the rhythm duties and by March they were on full alert again, sticking down the backing tracks and making worthwhile progress. But they still lacked any real sense of what was going to give the record the sense of continuity they'd always striven for in the past. It needed a location – or so they thought.

miami

> "We came, we saw, we conquered –it's in the lyric."
>
> – ADAM

f or a while they toyed with the idea of heading for Cuba and inviting the spirit of Havana to infiltrate the grooves, but the cynicism they'd almost certainly have been confronted with as a result dissuaded them. As April turned into May, they upped camp and split for Miami instead.

There were a dozen reasons why it might have made a good location for the record. It's a crossroads between North and South. It has a glamorous side, a humorous side, a dark side – and the strangest underbelly. It's a melting pot of cultures, religion and sex. But in the end, the idea was more enthralling than the experience. Instead of leading them to the heart of the record, their sojourn there produced a small movie of a song that Edge wryly describes as a kind of "creative tourism". It's an experience that no-one regrets.

"We'd been in the studio, slugging it out with the direction of the record," Adam explains. "It's a nice place to be for six months or so, but I think we all needed a bit of fresh air. So we went to Miami and we had a very good time! We went out. We met a lot of very serious people and some very superficial people and enjoyed both. We were introduced to the art of smoking cigars. We went to this kind of Mafia late-night place – none of your old spit 'n' sawdust here, this was shag-pile carpet all the way. And generally we had a good time. We came, we saw, we conquered – it's in the lyric. It was all there and our eyes were wide open. Some of the time (laughs)."

Lyrically, 'Miami' exhibits a kind of holiday snap-book gaudiness, coming on like a handy-cam diary that slips into the themes of consumerism and violence with remarkable ease. There's a strongly visual, impressionistic quality to the writing that goes back to 'Promenade' on *The Unforgettable Fire* – only here there are hints too of the voyeurism that underscores 'Babyface' on Zooropa. Everybody likes to look. Snap!

Bono's sense of humour comes across on the oedipal pun of the chorus, a reference that briefly brings the ghost of Al Jolson to life: "*Miami! My mammy!*" But the whole thing hangs together as finely as it does because it was a labour of love for Howie B. "That was very much Howie's bag," Flood explains. "After it had been recorded, he locked himself into a room for three days and he arranged everything – not just the way things were treated but where they come in, and things like that."

It was by far the quickest track to complete as a result of Howie's special interest. Picking up in different ways from where 'God Part II' on Rattle And Hum and 'Elvis' on the *Passengers* album had left off, it's a thoroughly modern exercise in studio magic that features another monster drum part from the modest Mullen, entwined with subterranean trip-hop rumblings that border on the avant-garde.

But as Mullen himself asserts, the genres and reference points mean nothing. It's got to be a U2 groove to be on a U2 record – and there's no doubts about 'Miami' on that score.

Roy Orbison was a master of form. He never felt constrained by conventional song structures, instead producing mini-symphonies in two or three movements that built to unexpected and often brilliant climaxes. Anyone who's heard the magnificent 'Running Scared' – all two minutes and 30 seconds of it – or 'In Dreams' will know.

the playboy mansion

having befriended Orbison before his death, and written 'She's A Mystery To Me' for his 1989 comeback album *Mystery Girl*, Bono and Edge had learned something from the master. "He was always way ahead of the pack," Bono reflects, acknowledging the musical lineage into which 'The Playboy Mansion' taps.

It started life as 'Hymn To Mr Universe', beginning with a jam, back in the early stages of making the record. It popped out and everyone felt confident about it – so much so that it was one of the last tracks completed. Howie had a clear sense of how he wanted the rhythm to feel and Flood handled the atmospherics, pushing Edge's slide guitar effects right to the fore at the end of the verses. Over a slow-burning looped trip-hop backdrop Bono is back on familiar turf, playing with clichés, truisms and advertising slogans. His voice is way out front, intimate and warm, as the song's central character completely unselfconsciously parades the ultimate in consumer envy, planning for the moment when his numbers come up in the Lottery. It's a powerful image of the spiritual collapse of a world where everybody wants more, and your worth is ultimately measured according to your ability to spend... on yourself. Having been alluded to briefly in 'Miami', plastic surgery gets another mention here; Michael Jackson is also on the guest-list in an opening verse that recalls 'Even Better Than The Real Thing' before moving on: "*If coke is a mystery/And Michael Jackson...history/If beauty is truth/And surgery the fountain of youth/What am I do to/Have I got the gifts to get me through/The gates of that mansion*."

"That's the thing about plastic surgery," Adam responds. "You start with the nose and pretty soon you're into big money (laughs). I heard a story about this rich lady recently, who decided she was going to look after her hairdresser, who was a young girl, by paying for her to have a new nose. So the girl goes off and she has the new nose and she comes back and the woman says: 'Darling, I think now we've done the nose, we need to do a bit to the eyes'. The thing about plastic surgery is once you start, where do you stop? I think that's what happened to Michael Jackson."

"I think surgery with Michael Jackson might have something to do with editing," Bono theorizes. "If you're in the studio and you're in control of what you hear – you can up the bass, down the snare, you know, 'louder, boys, less horns' – I think Michael Jackson started to do that to himself in some way. It's the critical eye that makes him such a genius being turned on himself – the knife turned around."

Its wry humour notwithstanding, 'The Playboy Mansion' is not intended to be smart. For all the warped values in evidence, the song is infused with a real sense of spiritual yearning, as if at some deep level the covetous protagonist knows that it's all fake, that far from being even better than the real thing, his desires are but a pale shadow of the heart's need for a more fulfilling kind of truth. Or perhaps that's just Bono's real voice coming through when he confesses "*And though I can't say why/I've got to believe*".

"People in America say 'if you don't have cash it's hard to believe in yourself'," Bono explains. "It's almost like prosperity as a religion." That's the territory we're in here. 'The Playboy Mansion' is a gospel song for American white trash. It's about how people demean the idea of heaven by seeing it as a Rolex watch, or a picture in *Hello* magazine, or a day out at the Playboy Mansion. But it ends in a sublime slice of gospel-verité, a la Al Green, which enables us to see the grace that is to be found in even the more mundane things - if you look hard enough.

It's a bunny old world: Hugh Hefner forgets to put on his playgirl uniform.

"It's almost like prosperity as a religion"

– BONO

if you wear that velvet dress

When the news first emerged that U2 were in the studios the word was that they were making a trip-hop album. The assumption was based not just on the soundings they'd taken about Howie B's availability. After all, the first producer on board was Nellie Hooper, one of the lynchpins of the thriving Bristol scene and a man with a proven feel for a good groove.

> "To me that's the most sexual thing they've ever recorded."
>
> – GAVIN FRIDAY

Bono: changing the fabric of our society.

they got together with him in London and stuck a number of backing tracks down. Among them was 'If You Wear That Velvet Dress', a song that comes from the same place as 'Your Blue Room', but which also dips into territory mapped out by Massive Attack and Tricky, the masters of spaced-out dance.

Lyrically, it is reminiscent of 'Until The End Of The World', dealing with a shadowy encounter where the protagonist is torn between two women, represented by our contrary tendencies to worship the Sun and the Moon. No one who worked on it is in any doubt about the song's lascivious intent. "To me that's the most sexual thing they've ever recorded," Gavin Friday observes.

Having worked with Hooper during November, U2 slipped back to Dublin. If there was any disagreement between them, it doesn't show now. Though he isn't listed in the credits on the album, his involvement is openly discussed. "He started things off on 'Velvet Dress' but because of time constraints he couldn't stick with it," Flood says. "And because the band were only half-way through the

track, or whatever, when he left it just went off in a completely different direction. There were things running around in the version he was working on that they didn't use.

"Actually what happened," he adds, "is that I sat down for a day and did my usual sort of fascist number: 'I don't like this, this or this. Now, how about trying this? And then Howie came in and did the same kind of thing, and the track began to take its final shape."

Bono reflects ruefully on the need for such strong-arm tactics. "We gave Flood a spiky helmet at one stage," he laughs, "because he had to become quite the gaffer. There are four of us and while we love starting songs we hate finishing them and democracy is a pain in the hole to be around. But Flood was amazing at pushing things through. I don't know how anyone can be so anarchistic and yet so organised. Howie on the other hand is like music itself. There's no difference between him and the music he makes." Which may explain what he brought to 'If You Wear That Velvet Dress'. "For me my main input was sexual," he says. "There was a lot of sex put into that one. Again, it was like a little bit of a throwdown from the band to me. 'OK, Howie, we want this to be on the album. Make this be on the album'. So I put a lot of jazz into it. Jazz and sex." A familiar combination.

"It's great to be able to get away with it," Bono says. "We can write sexy songs and spiritual songs – and songs that are both. We can write anything we want, and get away with it. This is the place we've made for ourselves after 15 years of making albums."

And Adam always thought the song was addressed to him!

Gerry Adams of Sinn Féin: the political stuff bleeds through.

Anyone who thought that *Pop* was going to be a dance album was entirely wrong. "I'm sceptical about these genres or reference points," Larry Mullen states emphatically. "I just like the idea of taking what's out there and fucking with it."

please

and so that's what U2 did, using techno, trip-hop and hip-hop as jumping off points for the different tracks. Ultimately they had to pass the Larry Mullen test: if what the band produced was unmistakably a U2 song it could go on the record. The examiner had his own reasons for marking hard. Larry had been concerned about elements of *Zooropa,* which had been rushed. And he had been downright disgusted with what he saw as the self-indulgence of parts of the *Passengers* album. He was determined that *Pop* wouldn't suffer from the same problem. 'Please' was an example of how the synergy could work.

Howie B had been doing one of his sessions as musical *agent provocateur,* playing stuff to the band. It was like musical tag, with everyone following the leader – Howie would change decks, play something else he'd lined up and they'd all re-group around that. Over one shimmering rhythm, Bono came up with an idea for a melody and everything flowed from there. "Once Bono got it – boom!" Howie reflects. "Once the band got it – boom! The actual backing track is the first take. It was the first time the band went through the song."

On the face of it, 'Please' sounds like a bitter song of personal disillusionment, set against an unsettling wider backdrop, where things are falling apart and the centre cannot hold. Bono acknowledges that it is the heaviest song on the album, and that it is hard, almost spiteful.

'Please' was written with someone specific in mind but you get the distinct impression that there was much more at stake than the satisfaction of a well-crafted put-down.

"I think we all know the type of person anyway," Bono comments. "Somebody who really needs to have their face in the mud before they feel they have a licence to dress up in the garb of rhetoric and all that."

It is a song about victimhood, self-indulgence and hypocrisy. Written against a backdrop of the collapse of the ceasefire in Northern Ireland and the summer of conflict that ensued, with the siege of Drumcree as its tribal nadir, it could be addressed, in different verses, to people on either side of the sectarian divide. It could be addressed to individual citizens of the North. It could even be addressed to the Ulster Unionist leader David Trimble.

"It's a mad prayer of a tune," Bono attests. " 'Please... Please...' Just think what that will be like live, in front of 50,000 people."

The lyric device that gives the song its form – a series of lines beginning 'you never' – was Edge's, linking back to the 'Numb' lyric and its use of lists. And the guitarist must also take considerable credit for the song's astonishing arrangement which builds from a relatively contained opening into one of U2's most molten – and moving – statements ever. "It's one of our most intricate pieces," he argues. And yet it was done relatively quickly, with Bono also settling on a vocal that was captured in one take.

It isn't a song 'about' the North, but the political stuff bleeds through.

"Songwriting is more like painting than people think," Bono reflects. "Pictures, feelings in your head – you're instinctively led to them. You intellectually check yourself but you're led by instincts first. And they're not necessarily autobiographical. You've got the arm of one person and the leg of another. In a way that's what makes them hard to talk about.

"The lyrics for this album were written quite quickly in the end. I intended to make it more of a record about words but the way things panned out they weren't over-worked and that's what's fresh about it."

It's an observation which rings particularly true of the penultimate track on *Pop.* 'Please' may be steeped in ambiguity but the finished painting is magnificent.

> "It's a mad prayer of a tune. 'Please... Please...' Just think what that will be like live, in front of 50,000 people."
> – BONO

Pop begins on a high. 'Discotheque' is bright, contemporary and in your face. At least on the surface, it is a hedonistic celebration of the ephemeral, built around a big, 'phat' upful beat. But from that acknowledgement of worldly addictions on, the record journeys down – from dance to despair. It may have been planned differently, but in the final analysis *Pop* presents us with a bleak picture indeed, portraying a world devoid of sense or values, teetering on the brink of collapse.

Edge: echoing Ennio Morricone.

wake up
dead man

as a lyricist, Bono emerges as a kind of Everyman desperately searching for something to hang onto amid the escalating din we're surrounded with: a hellish combination of political mayhem, consumerism gone crazy and the culture of the soundbite that is in the process of divesting language of its meaning.

"*Jesus, Jesus help me,*" the final song on *Pop* begins, "*I'm alone in this world and a fucked-up world it is too.*" Bono has never sounded quite so hopeless before. If *Pop* begins with dance, it ends with a slow *danse macabre*.

The song was started during the *Zooropa* sessions under the title 'The Dead Man'. It had been a big rock song with distinct gothic leanings, but no one was too enthusiastic about that anymore. They did some work on it with Nellie Hooper in London and came up with what you might call a trip-hop version – but it still wasn't right.

"You know, you can write a tune in any style," Bono says, " but when you bring it back to the band, it takes on a new life. I guess we always knew this, but what happens when we play together – as they say in New Orleans, some other kind of shit happens. That's what we found on this whole album. Things would go into one area, what you could call a genre, and we'd have to pull them back out. We'd find out that the band version, in the end, would be more interesting than anything we'd produced along the way."

It took shape during a jam, with Howie on the decks. "I think that was the first time I saw the band go 'wait a minute, something interesting can happen here with these decks!'," Howie laughs. " 'How come he's playing a record on top of our record and it sounds OK? Not only does it sound alright, it sounds ho-ho'. So that was an interesting adventure for them."

It came together quickly. Recorded live for a B-side, it was finished in two days and everyone loved it. "I really pushed for it to go on the album," Gavin Friday recalls. In the final analysis it was unanimous. It made sense to tie the album up with an end of the millennium psychosis blues-song.

Neither protestant nor catholic, neither working-class nor middle-class, U2 had started out as a band who would have to forge an identity without much of the familiar ballast of Irish cultural life – or its baggage. As a result, they could wrap rock'n'roll and religion up together in a way very few other bands would even have contemplated. All things considered, it was inconceivable that an album as ambitious and searching as *Pop* would go out on any other note.

"This is the end of the century when God is supposed to be dead," Bono observes. And so 'Wake Up Dead Man' comes on like a call to arms, a plea for Jesus or God to reveal himself. But the strength of Bono's faith notwithstanding, there is something eerie and forlorn about the call, even amid the epic beauty of the music. Edge's ringing guitar is to the fore, echoing Ennio Morricone or Peter Green in its authority, but this is truly a great,

dynamic band performance where Adam and Larry climax what is undoubtedly the U2 rhythm section's finest record to date.

"People want to believe but they're angry," Bono says. "If God is not dead, there's some questions we want to ask him."

'Wake Up Dead Man' doesn't attempt to offer any answers.

> "People want to believe but they're angry. If God is not dead, there's some questions we want to ask him."
>
> – BONO

Larry puts the rest of the fab four in the shades.

the million dollar hotel

(Island/Universal)

Produced by **Hal Wilner**

Recorded at **HQ Dublin.**

Released **March 2000**

it was in 1987 that Bono first laid eyes on The Million Dollar Hotel. The band did a photo-shoot there, and the setting haunted him. There was something other-worldly about the place and its inhabitants, and not long afterwards he set to sketching out the story-line for a movie based there.

Having spent the guts of quarter of a century on the road, Bono knows all about the kind of places where a musician can lay his hat (or even Edge's). "I think it is sad but true that I know a lot about hotels. And having spent most of my life in them, now the final chapter in the Spinal Tap episode is owning one," he laughs, referring to the Clarence Hotel in Dublin, which he co-owns with Edge. "The guy comes back from touring and actually builds his own Holiday Inn room! But my experience in hotels has, for the large part, been the plate glass window to separate you from the storms outside – whereas the experience of the people in the Million Dollar Hotel is rather the opposite."

It's a place where misfits of various stripes congregate. Here they come up with a plan of Baldrick-like cunning: to turn the hotel's rich – and recently deceased – benefactor Izzy into an art martyr, and in the process to make a bank-full of money, selling his work. Bono has described the movie as a dark fable about the redemptive power of love, but – as Peter Murphy observed in *Hot Press* – there are also elements of murder mystery, art-farce and even hints of science fiction in it too. Directed by the renowned German director Wim Wenders and starring Milla Jovovich as the bewitching Eloise, the film, for the most part, eschews action in favour of atmosphere. Described with marvellous wit and not a little insight by the trumpet player on the soundtrack, Jon Hassell, as 'a screwball tragedy', *The Million Dollar Hotel* is a tone poem of haunting resonance that benefits greatly from Bono and U2's involvement in the soundtrack.

The film begins and ends with a suicidal leap. "After I jumped I discovered, life is perfect... life is the best," the film's oddball hero, Tom Tom, intones. In a sense it is the ultimate metaphor for what Bono and U2 have been up to for almost 25 years. Every album, every performance, every song constitutes a kind of leap in the dark – a leap of faith. It may have taken 12 years to make from its conception, but The Million Dollar Hotel sees Bono flying blind – one more time with feeling.

Stateless

'Stateless' came out of a soundcheck jam. U2 were in Australia and felt comfortable enough before the upcoming show to let the music flow through them. The band's sound engineer, Joe O'Herlihy, routinely stored the raw material on a DAT. They came back to it during the recording of *All That You Can't Leave Behind*. "There was always this beautiful seed rendition," Daniel Lanois says. "To this day it's very, very uplifting. It's mostly Bono – he picked up Edge's guitar, with those huge sounds, and came up with this thing on the spot. We tried to get this on the U2 record."

but it didn't quite fit. Besides, Bono had other fish to fry. He started to hear it over the scene in Million Dollar Hotel where Tom Tom jumps off the roof. It would have made a certain amount of sense. *"I ain't got no home in this world,"* Bono sings, echoing the bluegrass spiritual 'This World Is Not My Home', *"just gravity, luck and time/I ain't got no home in this world/Just you and you're not mine/stateless/weightless."*

In the end they had to find a home for it elsewhere in the movie but it still provides one of the magic moments where music and visuals elide with a quiet power. It's a classic U2 idea, conjuring the spectre of the itinerant spirit that haunts *Zooropa*, on 'Stay (Faraway So Close)' and 'The Wanderer' in particular. "It's like a Robert Johnson blues," Bono reflects. "It's sort of a sci-fi blues." A different kind of blues, you might say.

Bono with Million Dollar Hotel star, Milla Jovovich

Dancin' Shoes

Some of the things that ended up on the *Million Dollar Hotel* soundtrack were U2 out-takes.

Shining light: Milla Jovovich with Jeremy Davies as Tom Tom

Others were recorded specially, with Bono and Lanois working more closely together. "Happening right in the middle of recording the album, the fact that Bono was involved in the film *The Million Dollar Hotel* was not appreciated. It was just very, very bad timing," Lanois suggests.

"Bono asked me to do the soundtrack with him and I did. I largely did it so we could finish the U2 record. What could I say? You do it on your own and call me when you're done? So I had to do the soundtrack for *Million Dollar Hotel* in the name of finishing the U2 record."

To speed things up they reversed some of the normal processes. 'Dancin' Shoes' was a chord sequence Lanois had lying around and Bono responded to it. "I co-wrote some songs with Bono, so that was great," Lanois says. "But I think the U2 record would have been finished much more quickly if we hadn't had that project in the wings."

Screenwriter Nicholas Klein helped with the lyrics and Bono introduced a new vocal character into the repertoire of styles. "Yeah, it's like the fat lady's cousin," he says, referring to the falsetto-ed character in 'Lemon'. *'And you hurt someone, you won't find a bruise/Learning to walk in those dancin' shoes.'* It's a sort of a record really about feet! It's foot fetishism."

Call the psychiatrist, quick.

The Ground Beneath Her Feet

When a fatwa was declared on Salman Rushdie by the Ayatollah Ruhollah Khomeini of Iran in 1989, following the publication of his book *The Satanic Verses*, the celebrated author went to ground. The impression was that he lived like a character in one of Bono's songs – under constant protection, in a twilight zone of not knowing either the week, or the day. Or the hour. He must have figured it was good prep for writing a book about a rock star!

along the way Rushdie turned up in Dublin. He stayed out at Bono's place in Killiney and experienced there a feeling of release, breathing in the sea air, and a sense of – admittedly qualified – freedom. Rushdie was toying with the idea of writing the book that would become *The Ground Beneath Her Feet*. He developed the lyrics for a song of the same name and gave them to Bono. "Salman asked me to put a tune to them," Bono says, "and I thought 'if a song comes into my head that fits them, they'll be there'. And literally the first time I looked at them, that's what happened."

It was during a dinner break, in the recording of *All That You Can't Leave Behind*. The rest of the outfit had gone up for a bite to eat and Bono and Lanois hung around and turned on the tape recorder. "I sang the melody and it was all there," Bono recalls.

"It's a lovely song to sing with just an acoustic guitar," Lanois adds. "That's the mark of a good song, isn't it? That's probably the way the song should have been presented."

For good measure, Lanois conjured up some cosmic pedal steel magic on the recording, and Edge came in with a beautiful riff. For a moment, it might even have been considered strong enough for the band to claim it for their record. But not quite. "When I played it to everyone afterwards," Bono recounts, "they thought 'ah, y'know...'. In U2 they called ballads 'salads' and it's like 'Ah, that's another salad!' And I'm thinking 'OK, I'll take it for *The Million Dollar Hotel*.' As soon as I finish it off, everyone comes up to me and is going 'Why are you giving this to the movie?' And I'm saying 'You didn't fuckin' bat an eyelid, no-one was jumping up and down, you all thought it was a nice tune, but it was another "salad"'. And they were looking for some steak or something. I don't know what they were looking for. Sushi maybe. Raw meat!" The movie it was, then.

"I think the song that really defines the movie is 'The Ground Beneath Her Feet'," director Wim Wenders says. "When I heard it I thought he had so perfectly grasped the spirit of the film, I couldn't believe it. I fought hard to get it in the film because I thought it was just too good to be true for us. That song really defines the attitude of the film towards Eloise."

Brought to record!: Salman Rushdie author of The Ground Beneath Her Feet

143

million dollar hotel

Falling At Your Feet

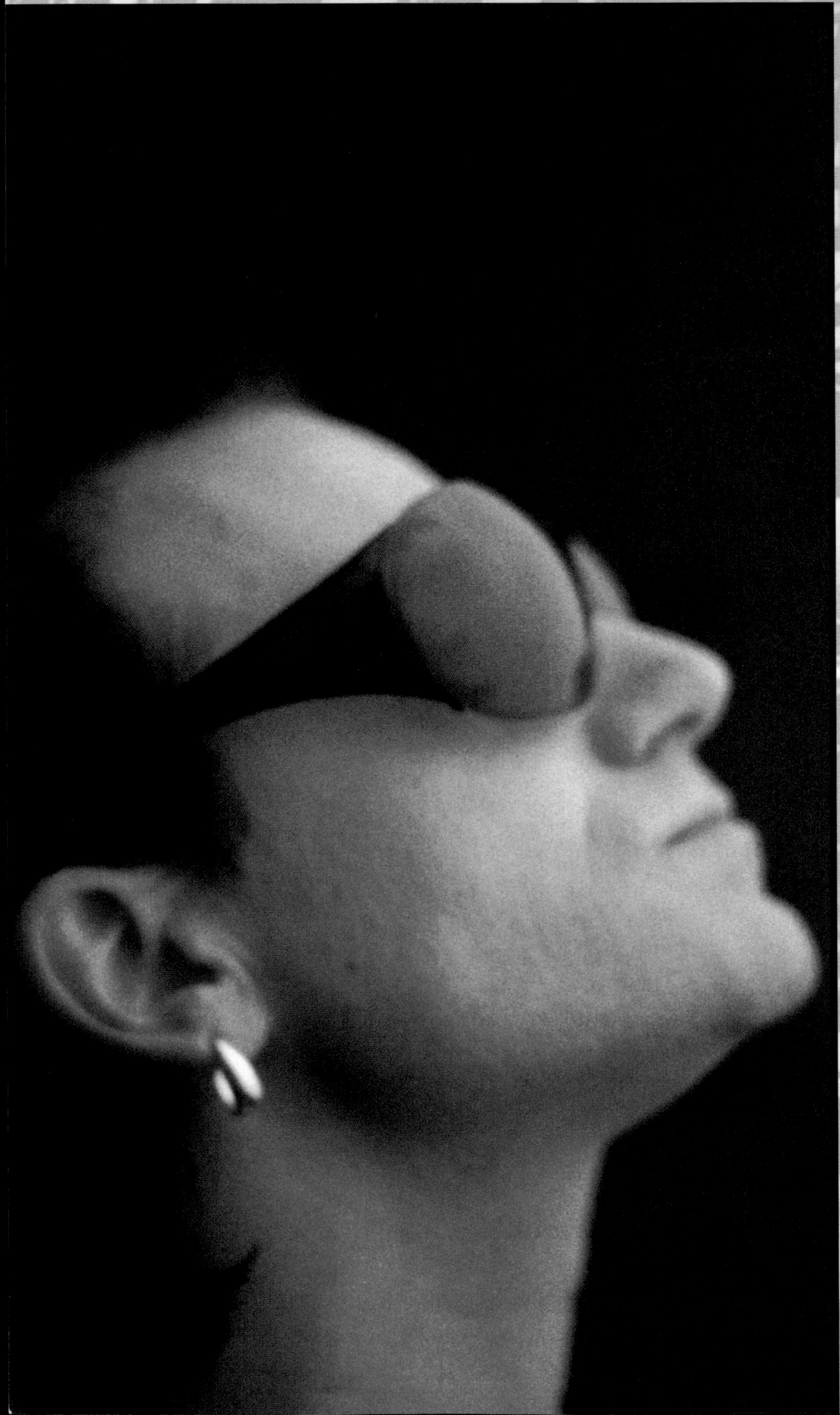

Bob Dylan is the master of the litany song. No middle eights. No bridges. No fucking choruses even. Just a list of stuff that wants to be signposted, that needs to be written.

that's my favourite to write," Bono confesses. "It's like you build up a rhythm when you're writing and it doesn't have to stop and I could write a hundred verses. It's like a Bob Dylan talking blues – he just keeps going, whereas if you're working in a tight pop or rock'n'roll context, you can't really break into a stride, y'know? You only get a couple of couplets and then you have to move off."

'Falling At Your Feet' is a beautiful song that finds Bono re-entering familiar terrain, echoing the adoration – the abasement, even – of 'Mysterious Ways'. Written for the movie, it was constructed around a chord sequence that Lanois had already sketched out. "In the case of the soundtrack," Lanois reports, "it was more one-on-one with Bono. He'd sing a melody or I'd start playing something and he'd jump on it. He's very good that way, very spontaneous. And then we'd rummage through his lyric book. I think some very nice lyrics ended up in 'Falling At Your Feet' that potentially could have gone into the U2 record."

But it fitted *The Million Dollar Hotel*. "I like love songs that are bittersweet," Bono says. "I don't wanna write a song that reddens my face when I hear it on the radio."

Better dead than red, eh?

Bono: Please help me,

I'm falling...

Bono describes Wim Wenders as a jazzman, an old hand at flying blind without instruments. That's often what U2 do writing songs – except they do it *with* instruments.

the *Million Dollar Hotel* soundtrack came a little bit easier – or that's how Bono remembers it, at any rate. "I think it's the first time in a while where songs are used as a score," he speculates, "where the scenes were actually cut with the songs in mind, as opposed to songs just coming in to provide music. Recording the soundtrack was a piece of piss. We did it in ten days. [Where a song didn't already exist] we just put up the pictures. We got three giant monitors in the studio, and everyone just responded to the picture. It was a thrill. And John Hassell is really the sort of keeper of the flame at the moment, there's no-one who plays trumpet like him."

Hassell gets a writing credit on 'Never Let Me Go'. It began with a jam, over which Bono improvised a lyric that was later refined. "This is the first U2 song that sounds explicitly influenced by Gavin Friday," *Hot Press* writer Peter Murphy observed. "I wouldn't rule it out," Bono says, "he's influenced pretty much everything else. He certainly lent me the big shoes."

Curiously, the dysfunctional cast of *The Million Dollar Hotel* recall the characters adopted by Bono, Gavin, Edge and all the rest of the inhabitants of Lypton Village, the imaginary place where the

entire U2 saga began in earnest, all those years ago – with the hero, Tom Tom, being eerily reminiscent of the strangest Lypton Villager of them all, Dave Id. "They all have to co-operate in a lie to discover their true potential," Bono reflects.

Maybe there's a lesson there for everyone. He moves in mysterious ways!

Goggle-eyed: Bono (left) and 'jazz-man', Wim Wenders

Never Let Me Go

a fter *Rattle and Hum*, U2 started playing their own kind of mind games. Dressing up. Wearing masks. Wrapping their songs up in hip threads. Throwing shapes. Doing their best to confound those people who figured they had the band sussed. From *Achtung Baby* through to *Pop*, subversion was the order of the day.

You could say that this strategy worked not wisely but too well: they succeeded in confounding legions of their own fans too, while failing to pick up enough hip young gunslingers to compensate. U2 were still huge. But ticket sales for their live shows were disappointing. Album sales were down.

You could take the pessimistic view and conclude that U2 was a brand – and a band – in decline, and that it would be better to bow out gracefully. Or you could go for the big one again.

U2 decided to go for it. On *All That You Can't Leave Behind*, they ditched the dance gurus and went back to their roots. The trip-hop techniques of *Pop* were abandoned. Instead, they called in Eno and Daniel Lanois, with whom they'd made their biggest-selling record, *The Joshua Tree*. This was a time for big hearts. This was a time for soul.

According to Lanois, it was a hell of a record to make – almost as black as *Achtung Baby* at times. With Bono's voice badly frayed around the edges, the approach had to be different: the conductor could no longer afford to bawl his heart out in the studio. Lacking this, the collective were plunged into uncharted territory and the strain was palpable. Making *The Million Dollar Hotel* exacerbated it. And, noble as it may have been, Jubilee 2000 turned the screw even further.

But U2 are made of stern stuff. It was fraught – and, hey, when has it not been? – but they battled through and made it to the finishing line. And released a wonderful, exhilarating, triumphant and, above all, accessible record. Like as if it couldn't have happened any other way.

No couch potato: Brian Eno

Beautiful Day

(Island U2 12)

Produced by **Daniel Lanois and Brian Eno, with Steve Lillywhite, Mike Hedges, Richard Stannard and Julian Gallagher.**

Recorded at **HQ Windmill Lane Recording Studios, Westland Studios and Totally Wired, Dublin.**

Released **21 October 2000**

When Jimmy Iovine landed in Dublin, he was given a preview of what was going down in the studio.

O ne of the great rock producers, Iovine had worked with the band on *Rattle and Hum* and so he knew the U2 methodology, the burrowing that goes on, the prospecting, the frequently exhausting search for something precious amid the profusion of musical sketches and ideas that are laid down during the opening phase of studio work by the boys in the band and their co-conspirators – in this case Brian Eno and Daniel Lanois.

It wasn't finished at the time: the lyrics were only half-crafted when Iovine heard the track – but he was still overwhelmed by the power of the music when he listened to 'Beautiful Day' in its formative stages. It surged and sparkled and rose in a crescendo of exaltation. This was where U2 had come in all those years ago, going back as far as *Boy* and even further, on a silvery glistening guitar ride that spoke of exhilaration and of rapture, in the face of rampant uncertainty and chaos. "It's a beautiful day a-a-a-a-a-a"! There wasn't an iota of doubt in Iovine's mind. "You've landed a big bass," he told them, applying an angling metaphor. Now all they had to do was to reel it in.

In fact, they'd been fishing for a long time: 'Beautiful Day' had started as another song entirely. It was Brian Eno who got the show on the road, coming up with the beat, a kind of contemporary twist on a Bo Diddley classic. Edge found a guitar sequence that went with it, and Eno did about ten different renditions of that, meticulously searching for the magic. The bits were good and they were pushing on through, not knowing where the track might take them, but sensing that there was something in it, if only it could be uncovered. On one of the takes they kept going, doing what musicians do when they get hooked on the groove, jamming for two minutes, three minutes, even longer. And in a moment of spontaneous invention, Bono yelled out the declaration that would take the song into another dimension. It was one he'd used before as the opening line in 'I'm Not Your Baby', a minor song that had finally appeared as an instrumental on the CD single of 'Please' – but what the hell! "It's a beautiful dayeeeeeee", he ejaculated, because the feeling was good, and he had that sense that they were cooking up something special.

Daniel Lanois, sitting in the control room also had that feeling. "The track at that point was really pumping," he remembers, "and the mix that we did had the power of shattered metal. You don't know where it comes from – I think it was a lot of processing. And I had this image of Bono, singing about beauty in the midst of flying pieces of metal and mayhem. It was only a glimmer at the end of the jam version." But it was enough. Lanois had seen the light and he began to proselytise for it, kindling the spark that had been lit in that moment of spontaneity, pushing Bono to consider what had been a throwaway interjection, a mere coda, as the chorus. "And so he did that," Lanois says.

U2 had the scent for it now, but it was still an elusive one. Lanois constructed the melody line for the chorus, a kind of a '50s thing, two parts do-wop to one part spiritual. Edge came up with a harmony line and when they put the pair of them together and processed it they sounded almost like angels. "It's like a hymn," Lanois reflects. "I believe that song

has that in its backbone. So I did an even more transcending mix of it. The verse had never really been established lyrically but we just knew we had something special in the chorus. It wasn't an easy one to pull into the boat, but it was worth fighting for."

The Jubilee 2000 campaign that Bono got involved in was just another distraction in the course of making *All That You Can't Leave Behind*. There was frustration in the air, as this typical Bono crusade followed the indulgence of making *The Million Dollar Hotel* movie in the middle of doing a U2 record. When the Jubilee 2000 ship came in, however, Bono experienced a surge of optimism. He'd sat down with arch-conservative Congressman Jesse Helmes in Washington and hit some kind of emotional nerve. Now the US had come on board, to the extent of $435 million in cancelled debts. Maybe the world wasn't such a bad place after all. There was hope. It's a beautiful day – it was a feeling rather than a thought. But when he went in to the studio, that's the way it came out, the sensation of "connectedness", of well-being, of... vindication. It's a beautiful day! Edge reached for the Explorer – the Gibson guitar he'd used during U2's formative years – and the sound was complete. "Because we were coming up with some interesting and innovative music, I felt I had a licence to use some signature guitar tones," Edge says. "It was a real talking point. Bono was particularly uncertain about it. But it really stood up. And it was inarguable, in a way."

Good call. When Steve Lillywhite arrived in at the death and polished it up even more with a sparkling final mix, they had the opening track, the lead single – and a monumental U2 anthem that would run and run, delivering them back to the top spot in singles charts all over the world. It would eventually be awarded a Grammy for Single of the Year. As Daniel Lanois joined the band on stage at the awards ceremony, and held the prize aloft, you could look back over the history of the song and think of a hundred ways in which it might have turned out very differently – or how it might not have happened at all.

But there it was. A shimmering triumph.

Daniel Lanois picks up U2's Grammy Award for 'Beautiful Day'

> "It's like a hymn – I believe that song has that in its backbone."
> **Daniel Lanois**

147

Stuck In a Moment
You Can't Get Out Of

> "The greatest respect I could pay him was not to write some stupid, sentimental, soppy fucking song." **Bono**

Bono first bumped into Paula Yates when she was just 17.

Yates was an extravagant doll at the time, hanging out with Bob Geldof during the prime of the Boomtown Rats and making like a particularly chintzy rock moll. Bono was chalk to her cheese. "I ducked her for years," he says, "'cos I just thought 'Whoa, where's she coming from?' And then years later, I really discovered this thing that people who've had a lot of pain in their lives are not in pubs talking about it. It's people who haven't – but are in the queue for some! (laughs) – that you meet in pubs talking about it."

Yates was wild in the strangest of ways. Smart and feisty, she spent her whole life trying to come across as a dizzy blonde. But there was substance there, and as Paula's life moved on through her own brand of celebrity, presenting 'The Tube' and 'The Big Breakfast' on British television, in the course of which she fell in love with Michael Hutchence of INXS, her path crossed Bono's with increasing frequency. Both the breakdown of her marriage to Bob Geldof and the

In the Rats prime: Richard Jobson of The Skids, Paula Yates and Bob Geldof

ensuing battle for custody of their children were played out in the full glare of the tabloid spotlight. So was her romance with the glamorous and flawed INXS frontman, a story that would itself take on an even more tragic complexion.

Excess was the defining quality in their lives. Drink and drugs were about the place and they indulged, often at the expense of stability and reliability. What traumas and insecurities may have haunted Hutchence and his partner, we can only speculate. Yet it still came as a shock, even to those closest to him, when Hutchence was found dead in his bedroom in the Ritz Carlton Hotel in Double Bay, Sydney, in his home country of Australia. Paula clung desperately to the belief – which she found comforting – that he had died accidentally, strangled and asphyxiated in the course of an auto-erotic experience of some kind. But Bono read it differently. He had spoken to Hutchence along the way about suicide, and they had agreed how pathetic it was. Now Bono felt angry at the probability that Hutchence had chosen what from one angle can be seen as an easy way out. In the heat of his anger, not long after he heard the news, he wrote the guts of 'Stuck In a Moment You Can't Get Out Of', a song he describes as being a row between mates. "The greatest respect I could pay him," Bono reflects, "was not to write some stupid, sentimental, soppy fucking song." And so he wrote instead what he describes as a tough, nasty, little number which, in Bono's account, slaps his old, lost friend around the head for having had the gall – or the weakness – to do himself in. "It's like somebody's in a stupor and you're trying to wake them up," he says, "cause the cops are coming and they're sitting at the wheel and you're trying to get them out of the car 'cause they're gonna crash it."

But the song doesn't quite bear out that explanation all

the way, sounding at times more like a plea written from the vantage point of Paula Yates, as she attempts to wrestle with the loss of her lover of lovers.

The opening verse is clearly Bono's voice and it offers an opportunity for a statement of intent about the whole of *All That You Can't Leave Behind*, that defines the crucial difference between it and its predecessor, *Pop*. *"I'm not afraid of anything in the world/There's nothing you can throw at me that I haven't already heard,"* Bono sings, *"I'm just trying to find a decent melody/A song that I can sing in my own company."* It didn't start out so confidently. "The original opening line was *'I'm not afraid of anything in this world/But when I see what it's done to you, then I'm scared,'"* Bono explains. "Imagine making pop music out of all this (laughs). There's a thing."

Beyond that the perspective gets trickier, sounding more like a lover engaged in a bout of long-distance morale-boosting that finally fails. And in the bridge, the spectre of Yates' reaction to Hutchence's death – and, finally, of her own demise – looms large. *"I was unconscious, half asleep/the water is warm till you discover how deep..."*, it runs, *"I wasn't jumping... for me it was a fall/It's a long way down to nothing at all."*

Whoever's voice is being implied, and whether Bono or Edge – who gets a co-writing credit – conjured up particular lines, between them, they did Hutchence and Paula the justice of creating one of U2's finest pop songs. This is a track of epic grandeur that finds some of its persuasive power in the use of the familiar language of pop – the throwaway Beatle-ish 'my oh my' at the conclusion of the second verse, and the easy 'baby' in the first. But everyone knew what the song was about, and there was a feeling that it needed a gospel end to give it a sense of resolution – of acceptance and release. Edge came up with the lyrics and bingo! "It's something that we always wanted to do," Daniel Lanois recalls, "to have a sort of choral chant. We tried a few variations on it and we ended up with what we got. It's the kind of thing that you could easily bring in the choir for – you can imagine the singers that would be happy to sing on a U2 record – but we didn't want to do that. Bono just says – 'no it's just going to be Edge, Eno and big bad Danny Lanois'. We're good singers but, you know, there's better singers in the world! But if you want it to sound like a U2 record, then you use the team."

That way it remains a song that they all can sing, in their own company. And so it is.

Paula Yates and Michael Hutchence (R.I.P.)

149

all that you can't leave behind

Elevation

Bob Dylan once said that he never heard a good song that had a middle eight. Which just goes to show that even Bob Dylan can be wrong. It was also where Eno and Lanois parted company with 'Elevation'. The song had started out with a sound from Edge, fashioned on an effects pedal that Lanois describes as his secret weapon. "It's like a distortion pedal that has a warp, or a tone control, built on," he explains. "As you push the pedal down, you get the high frequency. It's a great little pedal. It has a lovely, specific personality to it."

S ometimes when you're engaged in a spot of sound-painting, a sonic like that will act as a springboard. Eno conjured up an electronic beat as an undertow and Adam and Larry played on top of it. Edge came through with a riff and they were halfway there. But the song still needed a bit of contrast to open it up – or so the band thought. When Eno and Lanois were slow to play ball, reinforcements were called in. The masters were taken across the river from U2's Hanover St. HQ to Windmill Lane

Bob Dylan

studios. There the boys joined forces with ace pop producer Richard 'Biff' Stannard and his cohort Julian Gallagher to conjure up a kind of science-fiction middle-eight that provides a tender interlude, amid the onslaught of 'Elevation'.

A distant cousin of Sly and the Family Stone's 'Higher and Higher' and The Pixies' 'Levitate Me', 'Elevation' is scarcely the album's most original moment. The mole livin' in a hole diggin' up his soul in the fourth verse is reminiscent of the central character in 'The Fly' from *Achtung Baby* and there's a hint of the climax to 'Mysterious Ways' in here too. But from Adam Clayton's engorged opening bass figure onwards, the song captures well the murky terrain inhabited by a writer struggling with the attempt to make art of his or her experience. "Adam really came into his own on 'Elevation'," Edge reflects. "He's the hip hop man in the band, and there's a hip hop attitude in the rhythm section on that one."

'Elevation' achieves a quality that's reminiscent of the Rolling Stones, and their capacity to create epic muck. But there is an exhilaration to it that is uniquely U2 – a combination of primordial lasciviousness, ecstatic spirituality and soulful need – that renders analysis virtually redundant.

Bono howls like a priapic dervish who's just successfully stormed the palace and stolen the sultan's harem, Larry and Adam mix up the medicine in the basement and Edge slams menacingly onto the low E – and the inescapable conclusion, as the temperature continues to rise and the voodoo magic takes over, is that the best way to get high is to get low down and very, very dirty.

In March 2000, U2 were given the freedom of Dublin city.

Walk On

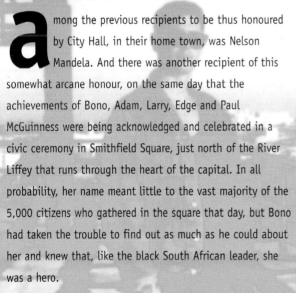

Edge and Bono: a big chorus is on the way

among the previous recipients to be thus honoured by City Hall, in their home town, was Nelson Mandela. And there was another recipient of this somewhat arcane honour, on the same day that the achievements of Bono, Adam, Larry, Edge and Paul McGuinness were being acknowledged and celebrated in a civic ceremony in Smithfield Square, just north of the River Liffey that runs through the heart of the capital. In all probability, her name meant little to the vast majority of the 5,000 citizens who gathered in the square that day, but Bono had taken the trouble to find out as much as he could about her and knew that, like the black South African leader, she was a hero.

A Burmese academic based at Oxford University, Aung San Suu Kyi took her courage in her hands and returned to Burma. She knew that she was going back to a country controlled by a brutal and oppressive regime and that inevitably her life and her freedom would be under threat. But inspired by the belief that only by fighting – and defeating – fear can you be truly free, she became leader of the National League for Democracy and spearheaded the campaign against the corrupt controlling military junta. "It was just one of the great acts of courage of the twentieth century," Bono reflects, "and it continues into the twenty-first."

Aung San Suu Kyi was placed under house arrest in 1989. She was unable to receive visitors or communicate freely. But neither her spirit nor her convictions could be broken and she has struggled on, and in the process has become a powerful and enduring symbol of the fight for democratic rights in the face of totalitarianism. Following international pressure, democratic elections were held in Burma in 1990, and over 80% of those eligible voted for the National League for Democracy. In the wake of that rebuke, the military tightened their grip, imprisoning newly-elected MPs and forcing others into exile. Awarded the Nobel Peace Prize in 1991, Aung San Suu Kyi remained under house arrest until 1995, and her movements have subsequently been severely restricted.

It was the human dimension of the story that captured Bono's imagination. As someone who has demonstrated his own sense of outrage at inequality and injustice, and taken some flak for it along the way, the empathy that he felt was in part at least political. But Aung San Suu Kyi's experience had a particular poignancy, leaving as she did not just the comfort and security of academic life in Oxford but also her husband, her son and the home they had built together to go back to the place that she grew up in, the place she truly thought of as home.

At first Bono tried to write the song from the point of

all that you can't leave behind

view of the husband and son left behind – dreaming of what might have been and living through the pain of not knowing how Aung San Suu Kyi was, or even if she was still alive. But it seemed presumptuous. "So I kept it a little abstract," he explains, "and just let it be a love song about somebody having to leave a relationship for all the right reasons."

But of course it becomes much more than that, as Bono explores some of his own obsessions on what is clearly perceived by the band as one of the major songs on the record, giving *All That You Can't Leave Behind* its title and inspiring the sleeve artwork of a band in transit, apparently travelling light through an otherwise sparsely populated Charles de Gaulle Airport in Paris. You can sense a touch of envy on Bono's part in the shifting refrain, especially the second time around. *"Walk on, walk on,"* he proclaims, *"What you've got they can't deny it/Walk on, walk on/Can't sell it, can't buy it"* – and you know that he knows that the same can never quite be said of his own contribution to making the world a better place, heartfelt and immense as it might be.

And Aung San Suu Kyi's journey becomes a point of departure in itself, a springboard towards the realisation that in the end we're all going to have to leave the baggage that we create or accumulate behind, as we undertake the final journey to whatever home awaits us in the beyond.

The obsession with the meaning of the word home, and the way it impacts on our lives, is a familiar one for U2. It's also understandable in a man who has spent a substantial part of the last 25 years living in hotels. But Bono finds a new twist here with a freshly-minted aphorism

There's always someone looking at you - Edge and Bono perform for 'Top of the Pops', on the roof of the Clarence Hotel

of the kind that has been engaging him since *Achtung Baby*. "Home," he sings, "Hard to know if you've never had one/Home... I can't say where it is but I know I'm going home/That's where the hurt is." That's what they say, isn't it – that home is where the hurt is? The song, appropriately, echoes the great Liverpool football anthem – originally a hit for Gerry and the Pacemakers – 'You'll Never Walk Alone' (*Walk on, walk on, with hope in your heart...*). But for all the layers of 'Walk On' and the uplifting spiritual reverie with which it ends, Daniel Lanois was dissatisfied with the final cut. Along the way both he and Brian Eno had advised that it was not one to chase – but it meant too much to Bono to let it go. There was a more low-key version that Danny preferred, but the determination to turn it into a big track – an epic even – was there. So they played a familiar card, bringing in Steve Lillywhite to listen to it with fresh ears and to spruce it up. "He's got such an amazing personality, and such optimism in his genetic make-up that you just can't help but respond to it," Lanois says. But he remains sceptical about the end result, and in particular it's dramatic, bristling intro, Edge's heraldic prototype shadings immediately suggesting that this is one for the live arenas.

"When it gets to that stage of making a record, people are looking for songs that the record company can proudly go to radio with," Lanois ruminates. "And the ultimate version comes along with a bang, you know. The Edge sounds amazing and it holds so much promise in its first 30 seconds that it's hard to say no to. But the version I preferred did not have such a slam-bam beginning. So that one got welded and bolted together."

In the end it's an argument about aesthetics and if you weren't there for the prep work and you aren't familiar with the detail of the ingredients, the end result works, with the added spice of low melody lines, and lingering feedback on the guitar counter-pointing Edge's jangling intro superbly.

For those familiar with the musical geography of north Dublin, there's a curious note in the coda as for fifteen seconds U2 sound uncannily like their Finglas/Ballymun near-contemporaries Aslan, with Bono searching for and not quite finding a couple of notes in a way that sounds like he's been taking singing lessons from Aslan frontman Christy Dignam. And you're left wondering: how did that happen?

all that you can't leave behind

Write about what you know. It's the oldest one in the book and it makes a whole lot of sense. But of course it should never be taken literally. Great art requires a leap of the imagination, an ability to see the world through eyes other than our own.

It happens to most of us at some stage in our lives. The cards fall in a certain order, and suddenly people around us seem to be dropping like flies. And others are threatening to. That's the way it was during the recording of *All That You Can't Leave Behind*.

Death was in the air and Bono was confronted afresh with a visceral sense of his own mortality. Death had shaped him since his teens, when his mother was lost in tragic circumstances. Now, having himself passed the big four-oh, he saw his father in serious decline for the first time.

Tributes to his mother – and rage at the fact that he lost her prematurely – litter U2's repertoire. Bono's relationship with his father is more sparingly evoked but now that there was cause for serious concern, it was a subject that could no longer be circumvented. It gnawed away at him, demanding that a song be written. But it needed something to give it lift-off, to get it airborne. It needed a metaphor to make it fly.

The rock star's life is a dislocated, disorientated one. Locked in the studio for months on end, and then – gone. For Bono's children – now he's here, now he disappears. The scarlet pimpernel. And the minstrel feels guilty, he wants to be a dad and to do all the daddy-like things that he remembers from when he was a kid. Or the things that other daddies did at any rate. And so he troops down to the beach at Killiney with Jordan and Eve to fly a kite.

The expedition could hardly have been deemed a successful one. The kite went up, and it came down with a phhht, embedding itself in the strand. "Daddy, can we go home and play with the Playstation?" one of the kids asked, and suddenly dicking around with the console didn't seem like such a bad idea, after all. But when the kite hit the sand, a seed was sown. There was a song in it.

'Kite' begins with a portent of doom. *"Something is about to give,"* Bono ruminates. *"I can feel it coming... I'm not afraid to die/I'm not afraid to live/And when I'm flat on my back/I hope to feel like I did."*

He's seeing the world through the eyes of his father, and imagining how he himself will assess his own life, his own contribution, from the edge of the abyss. He's talking to his father, talking to his children, seeing himself through their eyes, seeing them through his. And seeing himself through everyone else's – and through his own.

That sense of foreboding has been part of U2's arsenal since 'Out of Control'. Watching the flying machine go up and go down, Bono feels it again. *"Who's to say where the wind will take you?/Who's to know what it is will break you?"* he asks.

He's looking at his children and thinking about his father – who could be spirited away at any time. The voice could be his or his old man's, or any father's for that matter: *"In summer I can taste the salt in the sea/There's a kite blowing out of control on a breeze/I wonder what's gonna happen to you/You wonder what has happened to me."*

It's a big subject – fatherhood, responsibility, mortality, time and our capacity to blow it. Life: writing about it didn't come easy. Bono struggled with the verses, determined not to leave himself too vulnerable. Edge got stuck in and gave him a hand, pushing the vehicle across the finishing line. "It seemed I knew what he was writing about and he didn't," Edge laughs. "It was one of those weird scenes. I was throwing in lines and he didn't like them at the time, but we went through this circular process where he was thinking, 'Oh yeah, that was a good line,' and so they went back in."

The weightiness of the ruminations notwithstanding, someone's sense of humour was still intact: *"Did I waste it?/Not so much I couldn't taste it... The last of the rock stars/When hip hop drove the big cars."*

A dying breed, maybe. But not entirely extinct. Yet.

Dad's place: the house in Dublin's Cedarwood Road, where the Hewson family lived

Kite

In a Little While

'In a Little While' was one of those songs that started with a phrase.

Sometimes that's merely a launching pad and gradually the notion metamorphoses into another creature entirely – and before you know it you've written a song called 'Right Here, Right Now'. Not this time.

It was an Eno line, one that he'd been playing with for some time. It's the measure of a hook with potential – it nags at you, and refuses to go away, till you just know that you have to do something with it. Without an obvious outlet himself, Eno gave it to U2, to see where they could take it, and in one of those strange twists it fitted the moment.

It's part of the pattern when U2 record, the Thursday night drink. Bono may insist he's abstaining for Lent, but come St Patrick's Day, or someone's birthday or even any old Thursday night, he'll be slamming 'em down till five in the morning, better than the best. "Come Friday he'll pretend it never happened, but everybody knows it has," Lanois laughs.

It was one of those Thursday nights and the age-old ritual was being enacted. The gang were there, but Bono bumped into someone he hadn't seen in 15 years, maybe even 20. Sometimes chance encounters of that kind can be a pain in the ass, especially for someone who's got the profile of the U2 singer, and there's nothing that you want more than to be transported out of harm's reach – but politeness forbids. This was different, however, stirring up old ghosts that whispered about how *other* things might have been. The conversation was an awakening, ricocheting into the morning. Full of the mystery of life and the strange way in which the cards can be shuffled one more time just before they're dealt – and one person's loss becomes another person's gain. It was a long night, and the next day Bono arrived in the studio and blurted out most of the lyrics of 'In a Little While' – a spiritual song that draws on the legacy of Al Green, mating it with a high, lonesome keening figure that gives the track its special haunting power.

Bono: always in transit

In fact, a few things came together in the song. Around the turn of the year, Bono had been thinking Millennium thoughts, watching old clips of the Apollo moon landing on TV and experiencing again the sense of awe that he'd felt when he saw those pictures for the first time as a kid, the ecstatic realisation of how tiny and insignificant we are as individuals – and as a race – in the grand scheme of things. It was a mood that fed into 'Beautiful Day' with its vision of Bedouin fires, the Great Wall of China, the Grand Canyon and other earthly phenomena, as seen from above, the narrator cocooned in the bosom of a space ship orbiting the globe. It slipped in here too, in a metaphor for the restless spirit that's so often denied but that nestles dangerously even in the warmest embrace of the most committed relationships. *"A man dreams one day to fly,"* Bono sings and you can tell that it's the Wanderer in him talking.

When the track was done there was a concern that it might be a bit pedestrian and needed a stickier groove, so U2 took it to Windmill Lane Studios, for 'Biff' Stannard to work on. Biff stripped the layers right down, found a chunk of rhythm track that felt good and rebuilt the entire edifice from there. "He found a Larry Mullen hair follicle in the shower," Lanois jokes, "and built the track up from it! I still don't know how he did it. But he did some nice work."

'In A Little While' drew a great vocal performance from Bono, aching, tender and full of longing and guilt. *"In a little while/I won't be blown by every breeze,"* he promises. And he's got so much soul, you almost believe him.

We came, we saw, we conquered –it's in the lyric.

154

There's a sub-text to any album – the story of what might have been.

there were two or three big rock songs that everyone was committed to getting onto *All That You Can't Leave Behind*. A lot of work went in. They were going to make it. They had to. But there's something in the dynamic of making a U2 record that defies logic. You're operating on instinct, poking around in the entrails of ideas, impulses, snatches of inspiration, with only a vague sense of what the objective really is. "We reckoned people aren't buying rock records any more," Bono explains, about the genesis of *All That You Can't Leave Behind*, "because of this progressive rock lurgy, where the single has been forgotten. In our heads we've written eleven singles for this record."

At the same time, there was another key complementary impulse: a desire to take a step sideways from the kind of dance-stances that U2 had experimented with on *Pop*. "It just felt right for now," Bono says. "That din of choices in dance music, and just the very democracy of that music, had kind of worn people down a bit." Including the band. And so they asked themselves the question that they have tried, consistently, to ask themselves each time it comes to making a new U2 record: what is it that you want to hear? And if you can get four people to answer that question in the same way, then maybe you're onto something. "We just wanted to hear songs," Bono adds. "Songs that made you want to get out of bed, as opposed to songs that made you wanna get under the bed."

The din of dance and the indulgence of progressive rock were to be avoided. And there was another foil that they identified, in the music that has dominated charts the world over these past five years and more. Pop!

There was something in the air in 1977, in the summer of punk, and U2 inhaled it: it wasn't really new, but the energy and passion that exploded on the streets of Britain and Ireland in that brief heyday of punk rock was shot through with an anti-establishment spirit, and a sense of wanting to put the world to rights that was particularly strong and infectious. Bono talks about the defiance in rock, something that's designed to wake you up and get you motivated. On the other hand, pop is an anaesthetic – in

Marxian terms an opiate of the people Its social role is to make you feel everything is alright when patently it isn't.

But those first principles, the parameters that are sketched out at the outset of recording, can be bent and twisted out of shape by the time that everyone has to accept that there's no further pushing the deadline back, that whatever is done will have to do. The record is finished.

The changes of direction that occur along the way are often about balance. Everything is too dark – Jesus, we need to let a little light in. Everything is too slow – was there an uptempo idea that we could work on now to get us out of this slump? Everything is too heavy – what we need is a love song, something sweet and simple!

It's one of the oddest moments on the record, the neat little acoustic guitar intro to 'Wild Honey'. The technology is so sophisticated now that the temptation is there to use it all the time. 'Wild Honey' was captured in its raw state. "It was never monkeyed with," Lanois says. "That's why it sounds like that."

There's so much melancholy elsewhere on the album that it's a vital tangent, slipped in at the last minute to enable people to lift their heads up from the sheer weight of the surrounding sonic and lyrical material. It isn't just the rudimentary sound that makes you think of the Sixties: there's a Beatle-ish flavour to the melody and the harmony lines. And it's impossible not to hear Van Morrison, not just in Bono's voice but also in the pantheistic flavour of the sentiments. "Well, Van sings in major keys a lot," Daniel Lanois speculates. And Bono sounds like Van now and again. They grew up in the same backyard, so he has a licence!"

"We thought it would be fun to include it," Lanois adds, "a nice, simple, clear song with a lovely sentiment. It does have a lightness to it but it's a song of appreciation. I think it's like taking time out to say a little prayer. That's what it is."

Wild Honey

Bono, Van Morrison and Bob Geldof at Van Morrison's induction into the Irish Music Hall of Fame in Dublin

"In our heads we've written eleven singles for this record."
Bono

Peace on Earth

U2 might have felt entitled to believe that they had a stake in the whole thing.

So many Irish musicians had steered clear of the national question: no matter what you said, you were bound to offend someone. It was loaded, far too loaded. Better off saying nothing. Or so the unspoken wisdom ran.

U2 didn't toe the party line. They first addressed the issue glancingly in 'Stranger in a Strange Land'. And then on *War* they gave us 'Sunday Bloody Sunday' – a song that expressed a sense of horror at the atrocities perpetrated in the ongoing war of attrition in Northern Ireland, Bono writing about *"the trenches dug within our hearts/And mothers, children, brothers, sisters torn apart."*

"How long must we sing this song?" they asked. It's a question all of Ireland must have pondered at one stage or another.

It was hardly a surprise, then, that they responded positively to the call they received on the run-in to the Referendum on the Good Friday Agreement – a historic document which set out a way forward for Northern Ireland which held the promise that paramilitary guns might, in the nuanced language of this most intricate of political processes, be placed permanently beyond use. As polling day approached, the Referendum seemed to be in trouble: would they lend their support to the campaign for a 'yes' vote? And so U2 from Dublin travelled North, to join forces with Ash from Downpatrick in Northern Ireland, playing together at a historic rally in Belfast. It was a momentous occasion, widely seen as a turning point in the campaign, during which the nationalist leader John Hume of the SDLP and the Ulster Unionist leader David Trimble joined the musicians on-stage, linking hands to symbolically cement the first major joint unionist and nationalist platform in the troubled history of the Northern conflict. The 'yes' campaign prevailed. The

Belfast Agreement was passed, north and south of the border. The paramilitary guns were silent. Peace, for so long an impossible dream in Northern Ireland, seemed finally to have been given a context in which it might flourish.

That illusion was shattered in the most appalling, heart-breaking and gruesome way when a bomb went off at 2.30 in the afternoon, on 15 August 1998, in the town of Omagh in County Tyrone. There had been an advance warning. But it was inaccurate, and instead of clearing the area around the car containing the bomb, it drove the crowds of people milling around the town on a busy Saturday afternoon towards the danger zone. When the bomb exploded, the resulting carnage was the worst in the bloody history of the Northern troubles with twenty-nine killed and dozens more scarred, maimed and wounded. The bomb had been planted by a new paramilitary grouping styling itself the Real IRA. 'Peace on Earth', an angry and bitter response to what stands as one of the blackest and most loathsome acts of violence ever committed in Ireland by man or beast, was written in the shuddering aftermath of the mass murder of innocent citizens.

"It was written literally on the day the Omagh bomb went off, right then," Bono recounts. "Nobody could actually believe it. In Ireland, when they read out the names of all the people who died on the six o'clock news, the city just came to a complete standstill.... People were just weeping – in cars, on O'Connell Street, all over the place. It was really a trauma for most people – because not only was it the destruction of the lives, it was the destruction of the peace process, which had been put together with sticky tape and glue and tacks and a lot of faith. It seemed to be destroyed. It would be hard to describe to people who are not Irish what that felt like, that day. It was certainly the lowest day of my life, outside of personal losses. I couldn't believe it, that people could do that."

Pop had ended on a note close to despair. 'Please', the penultimate track, had grappled obliquely with the intractability of Northern politics. And in 'Wake Up Dead Man'

all that you can't leave behind

– "Jesus," it begins, "Jesus help me/I'm alone in this world/And a fucked up world it is too" – Bono flirts with the notion that Nietzsche might have been right after all, implicitly acknowledging that if God isn't dead, all the appearances are that he's abandoned us at least. His most agnostic song yet, 'Peace on Earth' takes that sense of abandonment a stage further – "Jesus, can you spare the time/To throw a drowning man a line?" he asks, knowing that the answer must be no. And he reels off some of the names of the Omagh dead: "Sean and Julia, Gareth, Ann and Breda/Their lives are bigger than any big idea."

In 'Wake Up Dead Man' he had paraphrased Seamus Heaney, the Nobel-prize winning poet from Derry, beseeching Jesus to listen as hope and peace try to rhyme. He returns to the same theme, only this time with a deeper sense of betrayal. "Jesus, this song you wrote/The words are sticking in my throat/Peace on earth/Hear it every Christmas time/But

hope and history won't rhyme/So what's it worth/This peace on earth."

"That Christmas, the whole 'peace on earth, goodwill to all men' struck a sour note," Bono observes. "It was very hard to be a believer that Christmas."

It was an essential song – but it was one of those that proved hardest to finish. The sheer protracted process of making the record had taken its toll. Eno who'd done some crucial work shaping the song had flown the coop, burnt out by the whole traumatic process. Lanois was hanging in there but it needed another supportive presence to guide it through its final stages and Mike Hedges was brought in to provide it, his presence helping Bono finally to finish the track to meet the final, final, final deadline. The vocal was the last one down, done the night before the album was finally delivered to the record company.

But at least it was done.

Omagh, after the bomb

When I Look at the World

At the start of the 1990s, U2 had decided that in order to reach people and touch people during a new decade, they had to come in a different guise.

Bono (as MacPhisto) with Salman Rushdie

and so they dressed themselves up for the exotic cover shoot that would adorn *Achtung Baby*. In Bono's fertile imagination the characters were beginning to take shape that would become The Fly and MacPhisto: it was time to don some mad glad rags, to slip behind whatever mask seemed to fit the occasion and to top it off with a pair of shades. Or three. "We played it cool for about ten years," Bono reflects. "And we got quite good at it. I was surprised! Yet we always saw it for what it was. We always knew it was a bit silly."

Now, at the turn of the millennium, a new strategy was called for. How hip can you be when you've been around for nearly twenty-five years? The band realised that there wasn't much point in going up against the latest grooves, or battling for a slot on the turntable when the coolest DJ in town is trying to fill the dance floor at the hottest club. Instead they wanted an album of big songs that would be strong enough lyrically and subtle enough melodically to reach into millions of hearts world-wide. "We're going up against *Bridge Over Troubled Water*," Bono jokes, "and we have our work cut out." The hard front could be peeled away. This was a time for empathy, for tenderness – for love. It was a time for homage to the muse. It was a time for humility.

Bono has been accused of putting women on a pedestal: it's something that Ali, his partner, has protested about on occasion. But she is a remarkable woman who strikes anyone who meets her as being special, as having an inner glow. Ali has done extraordinary work, with Adi Roche, on the Children from Chernobyl project that assists the children of a region that will remain infamous as the location

> "I still think that the world is a really unfair and often wicked place."
>
> **Bono**

of the worst ever peacetime nuclear catastrophe.

Since the nuclear accident took place there in April of 1986, the most terrible consequences have been seen in the Ukraine and in Belarus, where a quarter of the annual budget is still being spent, even fifteen years on, attempting to cope with the aftermath of the accident: in this benighted place, the land has been blighted, agriculture has been decimated, people have been uprooted, sickness stalks the terrain. But amid all this wanton devastation, there is nothing quite as emotionally overpowering as the impact of the catastrophe on the children of the region, many of whom have suffered the most terrible cancers, physical deformities and illness as a result. At great risk to her own health, Ali and her co-workers have gone to Chernobyl and Belarus and spent time there working with people who are the victims of this nightmare occurrence, and with their children, in an attempt to alleviate the suffering, isolation and neglect, which is part of their shocking legacy.

Written by Bono and Edge, 'When I Look at the World' acknowledges the special qualities that this kind of commitment takes. It isn't just the capacity that Bono's muse has to light up any room that she enters – it's the empathy of which she's capable, the composure that she shows, and the example that she gives to someone who by comparison feels flawed and impatient. "I am not in any way at peace," Bono states. "I still think that the world is a really unfair and often wicked place and beauty is a consolation prize. And it's not enough for me. It just isn't. There's always been a kind of rage in me and it does still bubble up." But rage doesn't help the lame to walk. *"So I try to be like you,"* Bono sings. *"Try to feel it like you do/But without you it's no use/I can't see what you see/When I look at the world."* Even having ditched the shades.

It's one of the cards that every writer plays. It isn't autobiographical! There are bits of you in there alright.

New York

there may even be lots of you. But when a song or poem or novel is written in the first person, and it's littered with "I"s, there's still no reason to assume that it's the literal truth about what the author has been up to. It's the old "what if?" conundrum. It's a good starting point for any plot: I just missed that cat who raced across the road, and now I'm home, and nobody knows that I had too much to drink. But what if I'd hit it?

Bono didn't even start it. There was a Larry drumbeat that everyone loved – but it was proving tricky to find a home for it. No matter how many different angles they came at it from, it didn't seem to explode into life.

Friday is meeting day. The boys in the band sit down and wait for the bad news! We've been asked to do this. Yes. We've been asked to do that. No. We've got to find a way around this. Oh! It was a phenomenon throughout the making of *All That You Can't Leave Behind* that became a distraction first, and then a right royal pain in the ass for anyone outside the most inner of inner circles. It wasn't just Fridays anymore, it was every second fucking day.

Passionately as they might have felt like railing against it, Eno and Lanois had to live with it. The Friday meeting is on? Fine, we'll work away. Can we dig up that Larry rhythm thing? We might get something out of that.

Frequently, Eno does his best work when he gets the hell out of the studio. "We're always glad when he goes away," Larry smiles, "because we know that when he comes back, he'll be back with some more goodies! Danny just stays in there and brings a different touch to it. So we're pushing one way, they're pushing others – and the results are always interesting. A lot of tension."

On other occasions, it happens in the room, where the smell of the conflict and the frustration is fresh in everyone's nostrils. "Brian brings a very different thing to U2," Larry adds. "He gets onto those keyboards and he just takes songs in directions you wouldn't expect."

The meeting was a long one, but in the meantime

Brian was in inspired form. He got a kind of a foghorn sound going over Larry's drumbeat. He conjured another chordal thing out of his bag of tricks and Lanois snuck in on guitar and they had a groove happening.

The band came down from the meeting feeling itchy

U2 take to the streets of New York

159

and scratchy. They grabbed their instruments and whaled into it. The chemistry worked. Eureka! "It all happened very, very quickly," Lanois remembers. "Bono thought 'this is going to be the home for my New York idea'! I think we work best like that: Eno and I provide the sonics for the band, they come in and respond to the invitation." A song was born."

That was a case where a great piece of work by Larry

'I just got a car in New York' - Bono plays back seat driver

got everyone inspired," Edge says. "Brian loved this particular drum performance and when he hit on this foghorn sound, everyone got really excited about it. It pretty much came together there and then, with everybody playing on it." Hearing it, it's impossible not to think of Lou Reed, of Frank Sinatra, of Ian Curtis and of P.J. Harvey, a Principle stable mate whose *Stories from the City, Stories from the Sea* is in part at least a paean to the city that never sleeps. Originally the song ended with a free-form conversation about Frank Sinatra, with whom Bono had the privilege of sharing a duet on 'I've Got You Under My Skin' before he died. Old blue eyes! "It's a true story," Bono says: "I was at dinner once with Frank and he took a blue paper napkin from the table and he was just staring at it and he said, to no-one in particular, 'I remember when my eyes were this blue'. He put

it, and kept it, in an inside pocket. It was very cool."

For the most part 'New York' is just that, the cool pulsing groove acting as a backdrop as the narrator confesses quietly to the terms of the mid-life crisis afflicting him, while all around 9 million other, fascinating stories are being written. New York! New York! But halfway through it explodes in a grungy mess that's impressively appropriate to the theme of the song. That sonic thunderstorm was there in the track's infant state but Edge got to work on it and bent it into a different shape. "That's an overdub. It's very effective," Lanois comments. "He was right."

But was Bono? There's a line in it that's inclined to rankle, that sounds almost boastful: *"I just got a place in New York,"* Bono declares. Interviewing Bono, Neil McCormick – an old school mate and music journalist – told the singer he found it really irritating. "I was gonna change the line to something less consumerist," Bono responded, "but why I left it in was... I had just got a place in New York! And it kinda made me smile. Even though the song is not autobiographical. Now you're thinking 'the bastard's got a nice place on Central Park' – but for the character in the song it could be a shoe box."

Obviously there are a bits of Bono in there. But only bits, he insists. No mid-life crisis here. "If anything I'm at the other end of that," he says. "I'm trying to calm down. I had a mid-life crisis much earlier, about age 27, for all the classic reasons. I just went downtown in Los Angeles, drank a lot of whiskey and made up for all the years pushing a rock up a hill. Or a rock band up the hill! I got quite good at being silly and that, in a way, prepared us for the silliness of the '90s – which I've thoroughly enjoyed."

Oddly, it ends on a glancing reference to 'The Stolen Child', a poem by William Butler Yeats. *"In the stillness of the evening/When the sun has had its day/I heard your voice a-whispering/Come away child/New York, New York."*

Unconscious. Maybe.

all that you can't leave behind

The mood starting out had been relaxed and positive. They went into the studio without a fixed agenda. The plan was to jam, to see what would come out of it without the pressure of actually making an album. It had worked well for U2, and for Eno and Lanois as their producers, in particular with *The Joshua Tree*. So they tried it again. It was kind of a fun time, but a fruitful one.

Grace

grace was minted in that first loose flush of creativity. It was put on the shelf in embryonic form: one to come back to later. They did about mid-way through, but nothing gave. Bono hadn't linked it with any lyrical cue yet, and they had a frustrating time trying to move it along. It went into cold storage.

It's the way they work, proceeding crab-wise. On one of his retreats to London, Eno took it with him. He was looking for a melody to open it out and help it take flight. Nothing. It went into storage for a third time. They were on the final countdown, with paranoia playing havoc all around, when the lightbulb went on. "Pretty much at the end of the record," Lanois recalls, "we pulled it out and Bono wrote something very beautiful for it. I came up with the guitar part and that sparked another keyboard part from Brian and Larry put some drums on it – it was kind of layered. And Bono just had this idea that we should approach the subject matter of 'grace'. It was lovely."

It's a tribute to womankind. You can sense the spirit of Ali informing it, but 'Grace' is not just about an individual, or about women – it's about a way of dealing with the world that offers intimations of another, better place.

Earlier U2 albums ended like this. No matter how many doubts were raised along the way, no matter how many bloody dramas unfolded, they led us back to a place of acceptance, of resignation, of serenity even.

On *War* it was '40'. On *The Unforgettable Fire* it was 'MLK'. 'Grace' continues in that tradition. An album that exploded into life on a wave of barely-founded optimism – the sky is falling but hey, it's a beautiful day! – ends on a deeper note. 'Grace' finds beauty in everything. It's a state we can aspire to. Not easily attained when you're trying to

finish a U2 album, and the world is collapsing all around you. But worth chasing nonetheless.

how to dismantle an atomic bomb

(Island/Universal)

Produced by **Steve Lillywhite**

Recorded at **HQ and South of France**

Released **November 2004**

the band came off the Elevation Tour – the tour to promote the hugely successful *All That You Can't Leave Behind* – on a high.

They were back at the top of their game, over ten million sales – and rising – racked up, and the coveted title of Biggest Rock Band in the world successfully defended against all-comers. And they had a whole batch of new songs brewing, or at least that was the way it felt. Bring 'em on!

They began a new phase of recording in the South of France and got enough stuff down to feel that they were on the way. Then it was into the longer haul. With a ballsy rock'n'roll record in mind, they picked Chris Thomas to produce the album and, after Edge had completed the initial composing, sorting and assembling stage, the band ensconced themselves in their Dublin HQ to get the job finished. Well, started...

As the recording progressed, all the noises emanating from the studio were encouragingly positive and upbeat. The best U2 record ever was on the way, we were told. It was a return to the band's rock'n'roll roots that would blow everyone away – a guitar album, with Edge leading the way, in coruscating form. But those in the know sensed that all was not right down in Hanover Quay. The record – as yet untitled – had been scheduled to hit the racks in time for the Christmas rush, 2003, but the deadline for the delivery of the finished masters came... and went.

The band decamped to the South of France again, and there was the by now almost *de rigeur* security scare when a CD of rough mixes was lost or stolen. What had started out in high expectation had become a long and tortuous process. Chris Thomas gave up the ghost and departed in ambiguous circumstances, the band later acknowledging that they had probably driven him mad. Steve Lillywhite was drafted in, and was still there as the finishing tape came into view, but by the time the album was fully done and dusted, no less than eight producers in all had been involved.

Sometimes it's necessary to do things the hard way. Over 25 years on, no one knows this better than U2. After a colossal and at times painful two years in the studios, the record was finished and put to bed. Someone joked that next time maybe someone should put a bomb under them.

Now, as the discs were pouring off the production line, and the printing presses doing the cover artwork rolled, they could finally afford to laugh...

It began with a riff, concocted at Edge's house in Malibu. He played it to Bono – *Da da da da da da da dahn* – and it registered. When you get a good one, it plays itself back to you when you're least expecting it, slipping in and out of your consciousness, until it claims its place in a song. *Da da da da da da da dahn*. This felt like a classic, one that might have been purloined from the Stones, the Pistols or even Led Zeppelin. but it was where Edge was leaning in the early stages of making what was to become *How To Dismantle An Atomic Bomb*.

vertigo

i t's only rock'n'roll but I like it. The Vines, the Hives, the Strokes and outfits like Black Rebel Motorcycle Club had thrust the guitar back to the centre of things. U2, ever aware of the zeitgeist, wanted to see any new pretenders off by coming up with an even bigger riff, a harder one – something that would blast out of the radio like a calling card. Edge thought of the working title 'Full Metal Jacket' and that was how it started to take shape. There'd be blood on this track alright. Blood and guts.

Bono got enthused, thinking MC5 and the Stooges and deciding that the riff alone, and the rock'n'roll energy that blazed through it, was reason enough to make a new album before Larry and Adam had even heard it. He came up with an agit-prop set of lyrics about the plight of the native American Leonard Peltier, wrongly jailed for aiding and abetting in the killing of two FBI agents. He called it 'Native Son' and the song took shape in that guise. Thinking that a blazing punky record was on the cards, they'd hired Chris Thomas to produce. Not only had Thomas worked with Roxy Music – an unacknowledged influence on U2 throughout their career – but he was the man at the control desk for the recording of the Sex Pistols' landmark album *Never Mind The Bollocks*, a record notable for its snarling guitars. With Thomas in the production seat, they recorded 'Native Son', and the band loved it so much they sent it to their American label Interscope to get them equally fired up. It worked and everyone was buzzing about it, thinking they had a winner on their hands.

The Vines: guitars are back in fashion.

how to dismantle an atomic bomb

He came up with an agit-prop set of lyrics about the plight of the native American Leonard Peltier, wrongly jailed for aiding and abetting in the killing of two FBI agents.

It was a fling that was destined to come to an end. The recording went into a slump and the band decided to bring in Steve Lillywhite to act as, in footballing parlance, the fresh pair of legs that was needed to get them through the second half. He immediately decided to change things around, to set the band a different kind of challenge. To take them out of the comfort zone, he turned the studio inside out, pushing them into the bigger of the Hanover Quay rooms to play. He found a more ambient room for Larry, to get closer to the early U2 sound and in the process to bring something fresh to the rhythm department. The track was still called 'Native Son' when they whacked down some great new parts in the re-organised set-up. Lillywhite asked Bono for a guide vocal and the frontman started to sing it – and something odd happened. "After thirty

seconds he stopped," Steve Lillywhite recalls. "All of a sudden I realised 'he's imagining this as a stage and he's up there in front of 20,000 people singing this – and he doesn't want to'."

It's an ever-present consideration now for U2, and for Bono in particular. He writes a U2 song, especially one with a big stonking riff that's potentially an album opener and the first single, knowing that he's going to have to go out and play it live. 'Native Son', he had just figured out, wasn't one that he would feel comfortable doing that with.

Going back to the drawing board was hard. Larry talks about the fact that the song had to be deconstructed and put together again – and that's what they did. They changed the chords around, tried a variety of different lyrics and titles. It became 'Shark Soup' and then 'Viva La Ramone', a tribute to the great Joey Ramone. There was even a Spanish version that gave the track the mathematically challenged intro – "*Unos, dos, tres, catorces*" (One, two three, fourteen!) – bellowed by Bono at the start of the record. Eventually it transmuted into 'Vertigo', and even then they struggled to choose between a number of different potential choruses. They weren't sure which was the one, until a few outsiders had heard it and support for the "*Hello, hello...*" variation gathered momentum. "It's a club and you're supposed to be having the time of your life," Bono said in an interview on the U2achtung.com website, "but you want to kill yourself. Vertigo is a dizzy feeling, when you get to the top of something and there's only one way to go.

"In my head I created a club called Vertigo with all these people in it," he added (though there's a Club Vertigo in Boston and rumours of a place in Germany called Vertigo too), "and the music is not the music you want to hear and the people are not the people you want to be with and then you see somebody and she's got a cross around her neck, and you focus on it. Because you can't focus on anything else. You find a tiny little fragment of salvation there."

Whatever the origin of the imaginary club, they had found the fragment of salvation necessary to realize the full potential of the track. Steve Lillywhite took the unusual initiative of double-tracking Bono's voice on the chorus, which gave it added impact. Finally, after more heartache, indecision and grief than Edge could possibly have imagined when he came up with that first killer riff, they knew that this was the one. And the riff had survived. *Da da da da da da da dahn.*

"'Vertigo' refers back to their past," according to Neil McCormick, who conducted interviews for the album's accompanying DVD. "Bono sings at one point, 'Hello, hello' and I said, 'You've used that line before' and he said, 'Have I? Where?' and I said, 'Well you used to use it all the time, basically when you ran out of words! And it's on 'Stories For Boys'. And that's on their first single, on U23.

"So 'Vertigo', the first single off the new album refers back to their first. It's like the early U2 pumped up in the 21st century, a really exciting record. It actually includes my name in it, so I definitely voted for that as the first single! At the end, Bono's singing 'Your love is teaching me how to kneel'. And then he goes: 'Kneee-heel!' He and Edge were playing this in the studio and at that exact moment they both looked up and saw me standing there and Bono went, 'Hey Neil!'"

But the break in the song also directly references the guitar part in 'I Will Follow'. Thus 'Vertigo' takes them back and forward at the same time, reclaiming their heritage and putting it in a modern rock context. According to producer Trevor Horn, the first overdub on the record doesn't appear until over two minutes into the song, making it essentially a live recording by the band – an incredible thought given that they were a full two years in the studio making *How To Dismantle An Atomic Bomb.*

"Adam is fantastic on that song," Steve Lillywhite says, "because on the verse there's nothing but bass and drums and vocals. Edge just does a couple of clicks, so Adam and Larry have to carry it. It's a really big song, as big as any of their songs actually."

The ideal electric shock treatment, you might say, with which to open the record.

Bono: NYC, November 2004.

how to dismantle an atomic bomb

When the first glow of the pounding rock'n'roll of the Chris Thomas sessions had dimmed and the hard labour they'd put in subsequently had worn thin, there was a feeling of uncertainty, bordering on depression, in the air.

there was a lot of stuff there, a lot of sweat in the tracks, but nothing was getting finished, no one was coming up trumps. Larry, who'd had his foot off the gas, listened to the material, and decided that what had been done didn't add up to the record he wanted to make. Exhaustion was beginning to take its toll, the band were feeling down, individually and collectively, and there was no guaranteeing that they'd get back up off the floor. There never is: the way U2 work, they're a catastrophe waiting to happen. The band had a creeping feeling now, that they might have been barking up the wrong tree all along. Originally scheduled to hit the shops late in 2003, the release of the record had to be put back. When Steve Lillywhite was drafted in, he had a good listen and tended to share the downbeat assessment: this gig wasn't going to be about mixing and fixing. A radical change of tack was needed.

Too often, what was there didn't have the spark; it was like, Lillywhite mused to himself, not-great versions of things U2 had done before. He girded his loins and said what nobody wanted to hear. "I think you need a few new

miracle drug

songs," he announced, to the dismay of all concerned. But in a way it was liberating. Adam, for one, recognised that he was right. Rather than kicking the same balls around the same pitch, going for something fresh might provide a platform for badly needed inspiration. Realising that they had a chance of rescuing the record, everyone was on their best behaviour. Having been so down, the only way was up. So they went away and wrote. 'Miracle Drug' was one of the first pieces under the new dispensation and it felt like another big song in the making.

The chord sequence was one Adam came up with, the band improvising their way to a song shape from there. Bono'd long had an idea in his head to write a song about Christopher Nolan, who went to Mount Temple, the school in north Dublin, at which the band originally formed. The working assumption had been that Christopher, in a wheelchair as a result of cerebral palsy, and unable to communicate, was just a spectator. But with the support of his mother, a woman of great dedication and love, and the help of a new drug – a miracle drug – he was able to move his head. At the age of 13 he began to write, using a unicorn on a band around his head to type. And when he did, hard as the tortuous process made it, the words began to flow. In 1981, his first book of poetry was published, and he called it *Damburst Of Dreams*, capturing with beautiful eloquence the sensation of finally being able to express the thoughts and feelings that had forever been racing through his mind – but which had remained trapped inside until that extraordinary time. At 21, Nolan produced a powerful autobiographical novel, *Under The Eye Of The Clock,* that won the Whitbread Prize. Hard to believe! Such an unprecedented outpouring of intelligence and emotion from someone who hadn't been able to speak or walk or even move independently. Yes, there was a song in it alright.

"*I want to trip inside your head,*" Bono wrote, the image of Christopher Nolan in his mind's eye, "*Spend the day there/ To hear the things you haven't said/ And see what you might see...*"

Without the familiar presence of either Brian Eno or Daniel Lanois in the studio for any extended period, the band felt that they would benefit from having another

> 'Miracle Drug' was one of the first pieces under the new dispensation and it felt like another big song in the making.

Adam, performing on the first night of U2's 2005 world tour, San Diego, March, 2005.

musician involved in the production and brought in Garrett 'Jacknife' Lee to fill the role. A keyboard player, and a former member of Dublin bands Thee Amazing Colossal Men and Compulsion, as a producer Lee had hit paydirt with Snow Patrol's *Final Straw*, and the feeling was that he might now bring a bit of left-field sonic experimentation to the high table. He got involved, helping to push 'Miracle Drug' along. But, as it evolved, in Bono's mind it wasn't just going to be about Christopher Nolan. There was something else working its way through, something to do with AIDS and the drugs that have been developed to contain it.

There was a line he wanted to use, and it fitted. He'd had a conversation with Sean Lennon about Tibet, in which the younger Lennon asked him what freedom smelled like. "Like the top of a new-born baby's head," he'd said at the time. And he'd carried that around with him since. He'd tried it in a different context, but now, definitively, he'd found a home for it. "*Freedom has a scent/ Like the top of a new born babies head...*" he sang. And the melody and the mood took on an anthemic purpose, allowing the track to grow until it became a kind of prayer of hope about the miracles that can be wrought through science and medicine.

"Some people think it's a great lyric and some people think it's terrible," Steve Lillywhite reflects. "I think it's great. I think Bono does the things that make people question themselves and their responses. In a strange way, though, it works. It's a special song.

sometimes you can't make it on your own

As far back as the recording of *All That You Can't Leave Behind*, Bono had known that his father was dying of cancer. It was a tough time for him, the hardest since his mother had died when he was a teenager. And so he wrote a song for Bob, and called it 'Tough' because that was what his father had always seemed to him. "A tough old boot of a guy," in Bono's own words, "Irish, Dub, north side Dubliner, very cynical about the world and the people in it, but very charming and funny with it."

they worked on the song for *All That You Can't Leave Behind*, and it turned into 'Sometimes You Can't Make It On Your Own' during those sessions – but it wasn't ready, didn't get finished, went into cold storage. Well, not for that long, in truth. Bob died the week before the band's Slane Castle appearance, one of the highlights of the Elevation tour. Bono took the song out and dusted it down and sang it at the funeral, a portrait of the artist as an old man – a working class guy who loved opera, and who had bequeathed something of his beautiful tenor voice to his son.

"He never talked about any of the music," Bono recalled of his father talking to Stuart Clark of *Hot Press*. "Oh, I do remember he liked 'The Unforgettable Fire'. Not the album but the song. He thought we were getting quite good around the time of *Rattle And Hum* – 'When Love Comes To Town' was a bit of a favourite. But he didn't know where we were going in the '90s!"

He had never really been a fan of the band, but no matter. They came back to the song for *How To Dismantle An Atomic Bomb* and it felt good – but there was something bothering Edge about the chords. It was built on a traditional rock sequence that felt too obvious. He tried sticking in an augmented, but that made it sound more Beatles-ish and it didn't do for the melody what was needed. It was a tough one. Hah! It was a great song, it was important to Bono, but they'd been at it for years, and still hadn't cracked it. Daniel Lanois popped in and worked on it briefly, unlocking the beginning of the song. But it was Bono who delivered the breakthrough, when he suggested dropping the bass down a tone on the verse before hitting the relative minor, lifting the song away from the likely 'Stand By Me' comparisons. Everyone felt that they had it nailed. Except Steve Lillywhite. When he came in, he gave it a critical appraisal that was to prove, well, critical.

"My contribution to that song is that I was listening to it with Edge – and Bono was there as well – and I said

> Bono took the song out and dusted it down and sang it at the funeral

how to dismantle an atomic bomb

> It was written in two seconds. Sometimes that's how it goes. Nothing. Nothing. Nothing. And then a great idea in the blink of an eye

'Edge, this song doesn't have a chorus'. And they said 'What do you mean?' And I said, well, it just finishes the verse and then goes 'Sometimes you can't make it on your own'. And Bono immediately went 'Give me a guitar'. So he picked up a guitar and went *'And it's you when I look na na na na'* – he didn't have the lyrics yet – *'And it's you du du du du du du du/ Sometimes you can't make it on your own'*. And all of a sudden the song was finished. That song had been around for the best part of five years and no one had ever said to them that it didn't have a chorus."

It wasn't just that they had added a chorus. There had also introduced a falsetto section that contributed something fresh and memorable to the character of the track; and, given the long gestation of the song, perversely, as Bono says himself, it was written in two seconds. Sometimes that's how it goes. Nothing. Nothing. Nothing. And then a great idea in the blink of an eye. It's those lines too that give the song its universal resonance, picking up on that eerie feeling we all get at that moment we catch ourselves unawares, looking or sounding just like our father or mother before us.

"My voice is the best it's ever been on this record," Bono confided around the time of the launch of the album. "And I believe that it's my father's gift to me. He was a great tenor, and when he died he passed that on to me."

Or maybe it's just that his death, and the closeness to him that Bono worked to establish in those hard days as the clock wound down to his father's final exit, opened up afresh emotional pathways that had been closed by the ravages of the years.

Sometimes you can't make it on your own...

Daniel Lanois.

how to dismantle an atomic bomb

How To Dismantle An Atomic Bomb was made against the backdrop of the invasion of Iraq, as well as Bono's own involvement in the Drop The Debt campaign. That there was no modern day equivalent of 'Bullet The Blue Sky' on it may have struck some fans and critics as odd, but the album wasn't bereft of political resonance.

there was a song hanging over from *All That You Can't Leave Behind*, the bones of which everyone loved. It was built around a distorted bass part Brian Eno had come up – a real gut-wrencher – to which Larry had added a '70s Glitter Band drum beat. But good as they all felt it was, the track didn't come together for *ATYCLB* and was shelved. Now, every time they listened to the out-takes from those earlier sessions, it clamoured for attention. Bono had the melodies and the vocal more or less mapped out, but it needed something to glue it together. This time it was Edge who supplied the sought-after magic ingredient, with a killer guitar part. "Once that guitar was

'Love And Peace Or Else' is set against the backdrop of military conflict in Iraq.

down, the song was there," Adam reflected .

Lyrically, inspired by Eno's end-of-the-world, subterranean guitar sound, Bono had in mind a preacher-type character, cracked but making sense. "It's like The Fly went to the seminary and became a priest," he revealed to u2achtung.com. Around the time of the album launch Bono enjoyed quoting couplets that he was especially pleased with to anyone who was writing about the record. In 'Love and Peace Or Else' it was this one; *"When you enter this life I pray you depart/ With a wrinkled face and a brand new heart."*

But this isn't a personal song as such. Politics are at the heart of it, with the imaginary preacher – an alter ego

love and peace or else

for Bono, needless to say – throwing down a challenge. *"Lay down, lay down you guns/ All you daughters of Zion/ All ye Abraham's sons."*

In the middle of a song that's about the state of the world we're in, there's a digression to a kind of lover's row, but even this is set against the backdrop of military conflict. *"The TV is still on/ But the sound is turned down/ And the troops on the ground/ Are about to dig in,"* Bono sings and, briefly at least, we are close to the heart of darkness. We are in the war zone. In truth, Bono had set out to write a political record, in part at least with Iraq as a backdrop, but you can only write the songs that flow through you.

"I very much sat down to address it, hence the title of the album," Bono reflects. "It's worth reminding ourselves of those days after 9/11, and what they felt like. At no other point in history had there been a sense that people would commit that sort of mass murder as a terrorist act. You'd had mass murder before in Hiroshima as part of a fully declared war – which I don't think is any excuse, by the way – but no one knew whether we were going to wake up and a quarter of London, maybe Kilburn, would be gone.

"That's no excuse for prosecuting a war in Iraq, but it puts it all into context. Because – apart from what happened in Madrid – we haven't had that same level of atrocity in Europe. We may have forgotten the fear and paranoia that was going around at that time. Of course I was going to address this – and yet the opposite came out.

"I told Thom Yorke two years ago, 'I know what the album's about and what it's going to be called, which is *How To Build An Atomic Bomb*'. That was the original title because the toothpaste was out of the tube. There was an article in the *Guardian* newspaper with two college students discussing how easy it is to get your hands on this kind of weaponry.

"A private arms company in the US has developed this GPS-guided system made out of papier-mache and plastic, which for less than a million dollars can fly 2,500 miles with anything you want attached to it. Somebody asked their CEO, 'Are you not worried about these getting into terrorist hands?' to which he replied, 'We've offered them to the Pentagon if they're prepared to buy in bulk, but the knowledge to make these things exists everywhere. We're just packaging it commercially'."

This was getting to him, as the record was being shaped, watching the news and reading the runes.

"Someone who's paranoid, in my opinion, is a person in full possession of the facts," he says. "These are nervous times. After Bikini Atoll, after Mexico, after indeed Enola Gay was dropped in Japan, everything has changed – and the idea that the human race can destroy everything and remove all traces of itself is now in the air. What does it mean? Two things – you party hard, and you hold on to your loved ones a little tighter. I kind of enjoy forgetting I'm in a band."

> "It's worth reminding ourselves of those days after 9/11, and what they felt like. At no other point in history had there been a sense that people would commit that sort of mass murder as a terrorist act."
>
> **Bono**

171

There are love affairs that never end. When U2 first went to the United States, they were wide-eyed kids, open to what the world had to offer them. A lot of the other British and Irish bands of the time were deeply cynical and condescending about America. Almost alone among their contemporaries, U2 crossed the Atlantic knowing that they had a lot to learn, conscious that they needed

city of
blinding lights

to establish a foundation there in order to further their ambition to become the biggest rock band in the world. Their first trip to New York was a magical experience, and one they'd never forget. They have paid tribute to the city in many, and different ways since, notably in 'Angel of Harlem' on *Rattle and Hum* and 'New York' on *All That You Can't Leave Behind*, but the allure remains as strong as ever. 'City Of Blinding Lights' is just the latest manifestation of an enduring crush. It's one of Steve Lillywhite's favourite tracks on the album.

they came up with the idea as far back as the recording of *Pop*. The way they work is at once sprawling and instinctive. If something feels right for the time, it gets done. If it doesn't, it's filed away. The skeleton of 'City Of Blinding Lights' didn't have the necessary flesh put on it for *Pop* and it wasn't revived successfully for *All That You Can't Leave Behind* either. But it was one in reserve that they could turn to when the hits failed to do whatever they do to the fans. They plugged back into it for *How To Dismantle An Atomic Bomb*, and listening to it now, it's hard to believe that it could have waited so long to come good.

Talking about it, Bono name-checks Scott Walker but there's a hint of Blue Nile in here too, in the restrained visual evocation of the world, and the spirituality that's to be found in every sparkle of light. "You can hear that in our music," Bono attests, "that painterly side of the lyrics, that

It is an Ali song too, a love song to Bono's muse, that's shot through with a sense of the ravages of time

kind of melodrama." But it is an Ali song too, a love song to Bono's muse, that's shot through with a sense of the ravages of time.

"*I've seen you walk unafraid*," he sings, "*I've seen you in the clothes you've made/ Can you see the beauty inside of me?/ What happened to the beauty I had inside of me?*"

"It's a New York song," Bono told *Q* magazine. "About going there for the first time. We were the first band to play Madison Square Gardens after 9/11. During 'Where The Streets Have No Name', the house lights came up, and there were 20,000 people in tears. It was beautiful."

'City Of Blinding Lights' indeed.

They plugged back into it for *How To Dismantle An Atomic Bomb*, and listening to it now, it's hard to believe that it could have waited so long to come good.

More shades of Scott Walker, in 'City Of Blinding Lights'.

At times, it seems that momentum is the key. The Elevation tour was a triumph for U2, not least because in the dark days after 9/11 they decided to keep the show on the road. It would have been natural for people – the band included – to retreat into their shells. Instead, U2 upped their collective game. What America, in particular, needed was a return to some semblance of normality.

all because
of you

not in any shallow or illusory way, but via pathways that mapped out a recognition of what the country had been through. Among bands that were on the road at the time, U2 were uniquely well positioned to realize that, and to meet the need.

The adrenalin from the tour was irresistible. They felt good about what they were doing, so good that they pressed ahead almost immediately into recording. They were on a high, and blasting into the sessions in the south of France they believed they were really onto something. They wrote 'Electrical Storm', a new track recorded for *Best Of 1990-2000*, and 'The Hands That Built America' for *Gangs of*

relating to the Drop The Debt campaign and AIDS in Africa. In that milieu, the singer brings a sense of organization and purpose to his work that is sometimes missing from his rock'n'roll adventures. "He is, as he says of himself in 'All Because Of You', an intellectual tortoise," Adam reflects. "He is a unique character. He is organized intellectually, but he wouldn't know where his car keys are. And to say he is disorganized is kind of derogatory. That stuff isn't important to him and it never was. As long as he could borrow money off someone, he didn't care if he had any. And likewise, as long as he had money, he would lend it to someone else."

'All Because Of You' is another mother song, in a line from 'I Will Follow' and 'Tomorrow' through 'MOFO'. It could be addressed to his mother Iris, it could be to Ali, it could even be to God the Mother. But it is, without doubt, about the debt that man owes to woman, one that can never be dropped. "*I'm alive/ I'm being born / I just arrived/ I'm at the door/ Of the place I started from/ And I want back inside.*"

Don't we all.

> "That tour, playing indoors, doing the material from *All That You Can't Leave Behind*, we really seemed to connect with people. But the one survivor from that session was 'All Because Of You'."

Adam Clayton

New York there, and lashed some other stuff down too, full of punky energy, that gave them a lift at the time. It seemed like maybe they were on their way to a new album already, but the initial buzz tailed off. In a way, in retrospect, that was inevitable. "That tour, playing indoors, doing the material from *All That You Can't Leave Behind*, we really seemed to connect with people'" Adam Clayton recalled. "But the one survivor from that session was 'All Because Of You'."

It survived, but had to be revived. Steve Lillywhite took over the production. Jacknife Lee tossed in some keyboards. They changed the melody in the chorus, did some tinkering with the lyrics, changing a verse, and gave the lot to Flood to mix. They were in business.

One of the things that delayed the making of *How To Dismantle An Atomic Bomb* was Bono's involvement in issues

All because of you – hand
on heart.

> "He is, as he says of himself in 'All Because Of You', an intellectual tortoise, He is a unique character. He is organized intellectually, but he wouldn't know where his car keys are. And to say he is disorganized is kind of derogatory. That stuff isn't important to him and it never was. As long as he could borrow money off someone, he didn't care if he had any. And likewise, as long as he had money, he would lend it to someone else."

Adam Clayton

Phil Lynott.

It's a couple of weeks before the album is due to hit the shops and Bono is conducting another gathering of notables through *How To Dismantle An Atomic Bomb*. As the playback progresses, he's like a man possessed. He draws you in and takes you

a man

and a woman

through the songs like an especially expressive conductor, in charge of a wild and wonderful orchestra.

We're on 'A Man And A Woman' and he makes like a magician about to pull off his ultimate party piece, a conjuring trick to end all conjuring tricks. "Wait till you hear this," he yells again. "No one would know it, but I'm about to show you where this song came from – where it was stolen from. I'm going to sing it in a Phil Lynott voice and you'll get it. This is Thin Lizzy. Listen."

The languorous guitar strum and Latinised feel of 'A Man And A Woman' pour from the speakers, redolent of Burt Bacherach in its romantic pop-ishness. It is impossible not to think of Anouk Aimee in Claud Lelouch's 1966 movie of the same name. Bono starts singing. Through his nose, just a little bit, and in a Dublin accent. And you recognise the antecedents of the song, you see them perfectly. Caramba! Elsewhere he would talk about 'A Man And A Woman' as a song that rolled up The Clash and Marvin Gaye into one. But that was for the rest of the world. This one is for Ireland.

"People won't see where it comes from. They won't get it. But that's it. It's Thin Lizzy," he says. And he goes back into character, in a way that is both funny and lovely and moving. The original Dublin rocker's presence fills the room. And a wonderfully beautiful song about "the mysterious distance between a man and a woman" – how come no one ever expressed that idea so perfectly before? – becomes even more mysterious and beautiful in the re-telling.

As far back as 2000, interviewing Bono for the *Saturday Telegraph* magazine, Neil McCormick asked him if he ever felt constricted in his writing and his interviews by the knowledge that Ali was going to be listening. "Ali doesn't read newspapers." Bono had answered with a laugh. "Or listen to the radio. (Laughs). There's a mysterious distance between us. And that's all I can say. I don't feel in any way constricted, though at times I have. Yeah. I'm as honest as I can be in talking about songs but I'm really honest when I'm singing them. That's just the way it goes."

They'd had a demo of it for a while, but that was just the start of a sketch. It had languished, until Steve Lillywhite came along and demanded some more songs. They threw Jacknife Lee into it and he lent it an extra aura of accessibility. During the recording, Neil McCormick pointed out that the lyric suggested somewhat melodramatically, and probably unintentionally, that the eponymous woman of the title was dead and Bono rearranged verses and altered a line to fix it. This was one of the new ones that would light up the second half of recording, that everyone could imagine wafting from the radio, in cars or in shops, from Manorhamilton to Miami to Melbourne, the sun shining endlessly in the imagination.

"It's a song for adults, for people who have been together for a long time and who are still together," Bono reflects. You know what he means when he sings: *I could never take a chance/ Of losing love to find romance/ In the mysterious distance/ Between a man and a woman.*"

Bono and Ali.

crumbs from your table

Bono's initial intentions notwithstanding, *How To Dismantle An Atomic Bomb* isn't a political record. The more personal it got, the more often Bono would refer to it as 'How To Dismantle An Atomic Bob', the reference to his father reflecting the band's growing understanding that – more than anything else – it was a record about the ties that bind us to what we are.

about birth, death, family, relationships. But Bono's personal politics seep through it. There may be nothing on the record as virulently hostile to US hegemony as 'Bullet The Blue Sky'. But Bono insists that this is not down to having to do business with George Bush and his aides in the cause of Drop The Debt.

"It's a real question and one that I can honestly answer with a 'No'," he says. "As I've said before, the songs that you want and the songs that you get are often very different. I don't really have much control over it – and if there are lyrics that offend some of the people I work with, so be it. 'Crumbs From Your Table' is one of the most vicious songs ever. It's full of spleen about the church and its refusal to hear God's voice on the AIDS emergency."

He describes the recording, the band in full flow in the studio, when a call comes through from a friend. She's full of good humour and heart. Hard to believe that she's in a hospital in Africa, taking care of AIDS patients, where they're packed in, three-to-a-bed. It's Sister Annie, an Irish nun, and she's looking for a favour. Actually, by calling just then, she's done him one. "You're going into the song," he tells her. And so she does, a symbol of those who give generously and don't count the cost to themselves. Unlike the Catholic Church, or fundamentalist Christian groups in the US, who, says Bono, have failed the AIDS challenge.

"I went to to speak to Christian groups in America to convince them to give money to fight AIDS in Africa. It was like getting blood from a stone," he recalled. "I told them about a hospice in Uganda, where so many people were dying they had to sleep three to a bed. Sister Anne, who I mention in the song, works at that hospice. Her office is a sewer."

The last thing U2 need is a return to the self-consciousness of the *Joshua Tree* era – or that's the unspoken consensus, at least. But there are different ways to skin this particular cat.

"Whenever U2 gets specifically agitprop," Bono says, "the band here starts nodding off and Brian Eno or Daniel

Lanois or Steve Lillywhite will start making people dance. 'Bullet The Blue Sky' is like U2 doing The Bad Seeds, it's biblical much more so than it's a polemic. We didn't make those kind of anti-personnel type songs to suddenly stop. There are moments when I keep my opinions out of the press – but not out of songs."

'Crumbs From Your Table' came out of a late night session, Bono and Edge drinking and free-wheeling into the wee small hours. It was one of those scenes where two

> "As I've said before, the songs that you want and the songs that you get are often very different. I don't really have much control over it – and if there are lyrics that offend some of the people I work with, so be it. 'Crumbs From Your Table' is one of the most vicious songs ever. It's full of spleen about the church and its refusal to hear God's voice on the AIDS emergency."
>
> **Bono**

mates have stopped making sense, but the further into it they get the greater it, to use Bono's word, coagulates. Instruments were to hand and when they started into 'Crumbs', it fell into place they way songs seldom do for U2: a melody, chords, words...a song. As Bono told Neil McCormick, it's the only song they ever wrote while drinking.

"No, I never mull over every word, which is one of the reasons for the uneven set of lyrics," Bono says. "For me, there's something about the moment when you put the first mark on the canvas – you don't want to overwork it. The paintings I love are the ones where you can see the first brushstroke. It doesn't have to be the most inspired to begin with; it just has to add up to something inspiring in the end."

A graveyard in Africa – the dead and buried are all victims of AIDS.

Edge had been doing the prep work, burrowing away in the kitchen in Zen mode, coming up with some melodic structures, getting the possible recipe for a song down. There comes a time when you have to put it into the pan and see what the others think, if it sparks something. He produced the chord sequence with everyone in the studio and the band began to jam it. It's the most distinctive element in the creative process for U2, the stage where they all get to toss in different ingredients and see if they can come up with a signature dish. It's why the song credits run: "Music U2".

The Blue Nile.

this one smelled good. Early on, it felt like a Velvet Underground song, with Bono delivering a melody that Edge loved, and the rest of the band responding in kind. Everyone knew that it had potential, but they still had to unlock it fully. "There are very clear rules of engagement," Larry explained to U2achtung.com. "And one of them is, unless everyone agrees that this is something special, there must be something not right with it." It still had to pass that test.

"The U2 working process is utterly unique to them and quite frustrating for everyone else," Steve Lillywhite observed. "It involves working tracks over and over and over again, dismissing every possible thing they don't like and ultimately ending up with the thing they like."

The theme was a big one. In the early days, U2's music was full of ringing certainty, but by the time of *Achtung Baby*, doubt crept through every crevice. Faith is still of the essence, but acknowledging that, in truth we

> "Unless everyone agrees that this is something special, there must be something not right with it."
>
> **Larry**

one step closer

don't really know, has become part of the art. 'One Step Closer' ponders the meaning of death, shades of Blue Nile again in the picture of the tail lights glowing and the imminence of our inevitable tangle with the grim reaper captured in a plaintive question – *'Can you hear the drummer slowing?'* – that sounds like it might have been tossed in first as a studio in-joke, but rises way above that:.

They almost nailed this with Chris Thomas in the driving seat, aided first by Daniel Lanois, who put some extra guitars into the mix. Jacknife Lee added synthesizers, giving a stately backdrop to the throbbing heartbeat evoked by the band. But it is the beautiful simplicity of the idea around which the song is built that gives it its special resonance. Bono had been talking to Noel Gallagher of Oasis about the fact that his father, dying at the time, seemed to have lost his faith – that he no longer believed he knew where he was going in the after life, if indeed there was one. "Well, he's one step closer to knowing," Gallagher had drawled.

"He's on a pint of Guinness and a packet of crisps for coming up with the title," Bono laughs.

> Bono had been talking to Noel Gallagher of Oasis about the fact that his father, dying at the time, seemed to have lost his faith – that he didn't seem to know where he was going in the after life, if indeed there was one. "Well, he's one step closer to knowing," Gallagher had drawled.

Noel Gallagher.

original of the species

The Edge, San Diego, March 2005.

Adam Clayton talks about the thematic threads that run through *How To Dismantle An Atomic Bomb*.

it deals with questions about how you fit into the world, about the power and strength of family relationships. Larry Mullen makes similar observations. That the world U2 are in now is one in which people recognize the value of family. That it's a dangerous world out there. That we are, to one degree or another, collectively living in a state of fear.

Sometimes what we have to fear most are the ghosts inside, the things that haunt us about who we are, about what we should do and be – and about how we fit into and around the images of ourselves that have been ingrained into us.

Bono was thinking about Edge's daughter Holly when 'Original Of The Species' took shape first, during the making of *All That You Can't Leave Behind*. Bono is her Godfather, and so he feels a special, different kind of closeness. Edge loved the lyrics when he heard them: it was a song that made him cry. "It started about Holly," he told *Q*. "He's her Godfather. The lyric became more universal, about being young and full of doubt about yourself." Edge speculates that there is, in the song, an element of Bono looking back to when he was 20, and remembering his own insecurities: you have to have been there to know what it feels like, to identify with the confusion over self and worth.

Bono sees it as a melodic journey. There is something of Roy Orbison's mini-operas here, with Edge's piano adding to the orchestral flavour. "It's about seeing some people who are ashamed about their bodies," Bono explained, "in particular teenagers with eating disorders, not feeling comfortable with themselves and their sexuality. I'm just saying to them 'you are one of a kind, you're an original of the species'. So it's a 'Be who you are' song. I can't wait to play it live."

"It just formed in my mouth, as a lot of U2 songs do," Bono explains. "There's the sound, and then trying to figure out what that sound is – and it was this word, 'Yahweh'."

It's one of the biggest songs on *How To Dismantle An Atomic Bomb*. Edge had the music, but even he wasn't prepared for the dramatic new direction in which Bono took it when he got involved. The first vocal take was inspiring, the melodies soaring and brilliant. Most of what went down on that initial run survived the picking and unpicking – the mantling and dismantling – that inevitably goes on with a U2 song. Almost immediately, he came up with the Yahweh line – and the band accepted that it was one of those songs that had to be written. "I had this idea that no one can own Jerusalem," Bono explained, "but everybody wants to put flags on it."

"Yahweh is the name for the Most High," Edge elaborates, "which Jewish people do not utter. It is written, not spoken. It's a sacred name for God, and in this song it's a prayer."

"It's not meant to be spoken," Bono confirms, "but I got around it by singing it. I hope I don't offend anyone."

They recorded it with Chris Thomas, Daniel Lanois came in and added mandolin and they kicked it around with Steve Lillywhite – but eventually went back to the original. As Flood explains, sometimes you have to chop a song's head off to see if it springs back to life, in its original form. This one did.

"I played it to Jimmy Iovine of Interscope," Bono recalls, "who loved it up until the point where I told him it's the unspeakable word for God. And he said: 'Call it 'Mozza Balls'. Call it 'Ali'. Call it anything but that!'"

"It's the record company guy," Steve Lillywhite laughs. "It's like the guy who said 'Can you take the bloody out of 'Sunday Bloody Sunday', so that we can get it played on the radio?' That's a true story. The record plugger came in and said 'That's a hit if you get rid of the bloody'. Will they never learn?"

It's a touchy subject all the same, one that arguably could land the band in trouble with either side of the Middle Eastern conflict. Not that it'd stop Bono, who has never been what you might call risk-averse. "A delegation came to see me from the Middle East to talk about the fact that there's no peace movement there," Bono reveals, "They asked would I give them a hand, and I said, 'Look, I'm at the point where the world will find it projectile vomit-inducing if I attach my name to another worthy cause. There are also people in my own native country who'll take it as their cue to brick and bottle me off the stage'."

So he took a rain-check, more or less...

"The only idea I had," he continues, "and one they'll be pursuing, is a Festival Of Abraham, which will celebrate the three traditions that call Abraham their father. Out of that conversation there's another project – to build a sort of cathedral of understanding in Europe, called the Eye Of Abraham, where Jews, Muslims and Christians can watch each other worship. The two very inspirational people who are heading up the initiative were opposing negotiators during the Oslo Peace Accord, but are now friends."

It's an initiative for which the widescreen beauty of 'Yahweh' might yet make an appropriate anthem.

yahweh

how to dismantle an atomic bomb

They needed an extra track in Japan. It's to do with release dates and the dangers of imported copies – and so it's a tradition with U2 to give their Japanese fans something extra as a kind of bonus for waiting. The UK and Ireland generally get the benefit – in this instance with the inclusion of 'Fast Cars' on the album release.

they had a track, 'Xanax and Wine', that everyone had been in agreement should be on the album. They spent weeks on it that turned into months. It gave them the title of the album. "I'm going nowhere," the lyrics ran, *"Where I am it is a lot of fun/ They're in the desert to dismantle an atomic bomb."* That much established, there was a sense of 'fuck it, it has to make the cut' – so they spent some more time on it. And then a little bit more.

They had taken it to a stage where it was ready for release – or not – but in the end the band came to the hard conclusion that, like the narrator of the song itself, it was going nowhere. Reluctantly, they decided to ditch it, though it would be used as part of the Apple iTunes Digital Box Set release of every U2 track.

"U2 albums at the end are always historically mad times," Steve Lillywhite says, "So there we were on the last night, thinking, 'there, we've done it, we've got away with it, we've finished the album and there's no madness' and of course Bono walks in and goes let's re-record 'Xanax and Wine'."

Except now he had a new set of lyrics to work with. "Bono can sometimes use the same lines in different songs," Lillywhite adds. "Like, if it doesn't work in one, it might work in another. He likes the couplet, so he'll try to see how it fits into a few songs. So he had this line that had been the chorus of 'Vertigo' at one stage, when it had a different melody: *'I know these fast cars will do me no good'.* So that came in handy. It was a bit weird calling a song 'Xanax and Wine' anyway, so we re-arranged it at midnight, that final night, as 'Fast Cars'."

The studio lay-out had been dismantled and so the band all set up around Lillywhite. They began recording at 2am and by 3.30am it was done. They came in the next day, did the vocals and mixed it – and ended up with one of the (extended) album's small gems.

"They're in the desert to dismantle an atomic bomb". Chunks were junked, including the Xanax and wine line, but the atomic reference stayed in. The album title rescued! A good job, well done. Thank you very much, ladies and gentlemen. Have a good night.

Nobody even mentioned love.

> "Bono can sometimes use the same lines in different songs. Like, if it doesn't work in one, it might work in another.
> **Steve Lillywhite**

fast
cars

how to dismantle an atomic bomb

> "U2 albums at the end are always historically mad times. So there we were on the last night, thinking, 'there, we've done it, we've got away with it, we've finished the album and there's no madness' and of course Bono walks in and goes let's re-record 'Xanax and Wine'."
> **Steve Lillywhite**

most people are familiar with the big U2 tunes, the kind of things that became live favourites or get consistent radio play even now.

'New Year's Day', 'Pride (In the Name of Love)', '40', 'Bad', 'I Still Haven't Found What I'm Looking For', 'Where the Streets Have No Name', 'Desire', 'Angel of Harlem', 'One', 'Stay (Faraway So Close)' – these and maybe half a dozen others dominated the band's albums, and made them as big as they are in commercial terms now.

But to look at the career of a major band like U2 from that perspective alone is often to miss the most curious and interesting tributaries. It is to miss, in particular, the story of the band that might have been but wasn't. And it is to miss, in addition, the great songs and the great recordings that, in a sense, the band themselves also missed. The ones that didn't fit. The ones that got lost or buried. And the ones that were let go – to other artists, other albums and other projects.

One-off singles, B-sides, film soundtracks and collaborations: these are the slightly less public, marginally less pressurised places in which a band like U2 lets off some steam, and in which the individuals involved get the opportunity to actually relax and enjoy themselves making music. These adventures include some that are consciously throw-away, others, like the Passengers' collaboration with Brian Eno for *Original Soundtracks 1*, that are substantial and ambitious.

Lost classics, crackers, lots of curios and occasional quare things. Would you expect any less?

It is seldom possible for a creative, productive and ambitious musician to fulfil all of his or her potential within the context of a single band unit. Most musicians think across genre barriers. But even if that thinking is intrinsic to the band gestalt, there will still be musical ideas and songs that either don't seem to fit the image or the style of the band at any given time. The question is what to do with them.

In U2, The Edge was the first to set out an independent stall, playing on the Jah Wobble Mini-album *Snake Charmer* with Francois Kevorkian and Holger Czukay, and claiming a co-writing credit on the oddly Steely Dan-esque 'Hold on to Your Dreams'. But it was hardly the stuff of which legends would be created.

With *Unforgettable Fire* and especially their cathartic live performance at Live Aid, U2 had won themselves some vital creative space. For the first time they were financially in the black. The pressure was off the U2 machine. The band sensed that the next record had to be a big one: that only made them all the more determined not to rush it.

Instead they reached a decision, individually and collectively, to use the space they'd gained to take the temperature of what was going on around them, and to make some musical connections.

Bono had initiated the process in 1984, linking up with the Texas songsmith T-Bone Burnett to co-write 'Having a Wonderful Time, Wish You Were Her' for Burnett's *Beyond the Trap Door* album. The connection here had come through Ellen Darst who ran Principle Management's New York office, and also looked after T-Bone's affairs, but they shared a spiritual vision as well as the sense – which was beginning to crystallize in Bono's heart – that you had to sin to be saved. No doubt about it, Burnett was good company for Bono to begin stretching out in.

In 1985, Bono was active again, guesting on Clannad's 'In a Lifetime', connecting – albeit at an angle – into the Irish folk idiom through the great Donegal group, and turning in a stunning vocal performance that marked a new sense of self-confidence in his own singing prowess. It also saw the 'Silver and Gold' collaboration with Keith Richards for Little Steven's *Sun City – Artists Against Apartheid* album, this time looking back into the blues tradition.

The Edge meanwhile was branching out in a different direction. A fan of Ennio Morricone, he was intrigued by the possibilities for original, dramatic and primarily instru-

The Edge: I can't kneel down for tuning up.

mental music offered by film soundtracks. He wrote to his favourite directors, hustled through some Hollywood agents and realised that the doors to movie-land were not going to open easily, even to an ambitious and successful guitar-player from Ireland. Instead, the break came on this side of the Atlantic.

David Puttnam's star was in the ascendant in British film. He took an interest and introduced The Edge to Don Boyd, who was producing a new Paul Mayersberg film, entitled *Captive*, at the time. Boyd was impressed with The Edge's portfolio; he flew the guitarist to Paris to see the rushes before beginning work on the soundtrack.

It was the first time The Edge worked with the composer and arranger Michael Brook, who shared most of the instrumental duties and co-produced the album with him.

Listening to it now, in many ways it seems like a precursor to the Passenger's *Original Soundtracks 1*. There's an emphasis on rhythm patterns, repetitions and atmospheres. For the most part it is an ambient adventure, which is effectively realised, if hardly astonishing. The lyrics of the theme song, 'Heroine', were co-written by The Edge and Sinéad O'Connor, whose vocal performance on the track only hints at her enormous potential – but it's interesting nonetheless, for the ease with which they slipped into the kind of fatalistic religious imagery that Bono had patented in the U2 band context.

It was Daniel Lanois who introduced his fellow Canadian Robbie Robertson, formerly of The Band, to

187

SINGLES, B-SIDES AND EXTRACURRICULAR ACTIVITIES

U2 in 1986. They were in the throes of the early, backing-track stage of recording *The Joshua Tree,* which Lanois was producing, when Robertson landed in Dublin. It was August and the city was being torn apart by Hurricane Charlie, producing the worst floods in Ireland in decades. "There were cars floating down the street," Robertson recalled later.

Robbie had nothing prepared beyond a couple of rough sketches. Neither his lack of preparation nor the inclement weather put a damper on the band's enthusiasm. "Luckily, they were really up for it," Robertson confessed. "They were so great at rising to the occasion." He left Dublin with two songs in the bag, and a feeling of sweet relief. 'Testimony' is the more effective cut, a mighty soul stomper that's powered along by a heavy brass riff. There's a writing credit for the band on 'Sweet Fire Of Love', on which Bono also shares the vocal, but there's no hiding the fact that, on this occasion, the alchemy didn't quite work.

In 1987, Bono was back in partnership with T-Bone Burnett. They wrote 'Purple Heart' together and there's a distinctly U2-ish feel to its opening line as Burnett intones: *"Through the fields of flame I ran with you".* Despite his frequently stated allergy to studios Bono also produced the track, which is on T-Bone's *The Talking Animals* album.

It was Bono's self-confessed ambition to write a truly classic song, in the classic mould. For some time, he'd been talking about having songs recorded by Nina Simone, by Willie Nelson, by Frank Sinatra. Trouble was when he wrote what were the first true U2 classics in that specific sense – 'With Or Without You' and 'Still Haven't Found What I'm Looking For' – he had no hesitation in deciding they should be kept for U2. It was T-Bone Burnett who got him involved in a project which would bear fruit in 1989, and see that ambition at least partially realised outside the framework of the band. Burnett was one of the musicians who was conspiring with Barbara Orbison to relaunch the career of the Big O, Roy Orbison, in a contemporary frame. Bono and the Edge wrote the song 'She's a Mystery to Me', that gave the album its title *Mystery Girl* – and it's a superlative torch song, superbly sung by Orbison.

It is a measure of the increasing maturity and confidence of their songwriting that they could produce

Sinéad O'Connor: On song.

a song that was both so characteristically their own, and yet so beautifully and accurately weighted for Orbison. *"Night falls, I'm cast beneath her spell,"* he sings, *"Daylight comes, our heaven's torn to hell/ Am I left to burn/ And burn eternally/ She's a mystery to me."*

In 1994, Bono became involved in film soundtrack work for the first time, co-writing three tracks with his old Lypton Village mate Gavin Friday and his songwriting partner Maurice Seezer for the Oscar-winning Jim Sheridan film *In The Name Of The Father.* The highlight was undoubtedly 'Thief Of Your Heart', which drew a contemporary dance feel together with Irish melodies to powerful effect. There was a curious resonance from Edge's work on 'Captive' with Sinéad O'Connor again handling lead vocals, and this time her performance is superb. The theme tune 'In The Name Of The Father' and 'Billy Boola' completed an assured hat-trick that added significantly to Bono's stature in Hollywood.

1995 saw another interesting collaboration. During the preparatory sessions for *Achtung Baby,* the band had recorded a piece that slipped into limbo. Both Bono and Edge felt that it had something, and came back to it later when they wanted to produce a song about Dublin. In collaboration with Christy Moore, they wrote 'North And South Of The River', one of just a handful of songs that

they've written about the city of their birth.

"You could ask 'Well, where's Dublin then? You've lived in Dublin. Where is it in your work?'", Bono acknowledges. "Well, most of the time it's there in an abstract way. Most of the time it's not obvious, and that's deliberate. But now and then you've got to break your own rules."

You could say that U2 have made a career of it.

Another prestige commission followed. With a new James Bond movie, Goldeneye, in the making, Bono and Edge got the call. For Bono the resonances were powerful: he had spent his honeymoon in Goldeneye, the house in Jamaica formerly owned by Bond creator Ian Fleming which had given the film its title. "You'll never know how I watched you from the shadows as a child," Bono wrote, recalling the background to 'Stories For Boys'. But this lyric is seductive and knowing, revisiting instead the scene of *Achtung Baby*: "I found his weakness/He'll do what I please/No time for sweetness/A bitter kiss will bring him to his knees." With Tina Turner doing an impressive impression of Shirley Bassey on steroids against Edge's suitably gilt-edged melodic structure, it's close to being as good as these things get.

Tina Turner: Golden voice.

boy-girl

'Boy-Girl' was the third track on *U23*, the band's legendary Ireland-only debut recording, which also included 'Out of Control' and 'Stories for Boys' – both of which reappeared on *Boy*.

"One of the first things that the Virgin Prunes wrote," Gavin Friday recalls, "was something we did with U2, a song called 'Sad'. I don't think it was ever recorded by either band. We had collaborated on that, and we took that forward with 'Boy-Girl'. We took that title and wrote two separate songs. Ours was dealing with bi-sexuality and that gender-bending thing, where they were talking about a more conventional form of love, with a strong boyhood-to-manhood theme going down."

"That was early proto-punk," The Edge adds, "a Buzzcocks-influenced type of thing. The Prunes and the band were almost a unit for a while – we'd share the same rehearsal space. For a long time they were a much better group, I thought *(laughs)*."

A live favourite, though full of zest, the track is certainly the least memorable on *U23*. Produced by CBS A&R man Chas deWhalley and U2, *U23* remains one of the band's most sought-after items.

another day

The tracks on *U23* had been recorded originally as demos. Edge remembers doing 'Another Day' at the same sessions. It was released five months later in February, 1980. "That was the first time that we discovered drone strings," The Edge explains. "In a three-piece it's quite hard sometimes to build up any kind of fullness and complexity. So the drone effect was a way of building up that extra layer."

The theme was one of adolescent angst, with Bono struggling to achieve an optimistic perspective, despite waking up to *"the toll of another dull day."* Not easy, but he tried! An early, demo version of 'Twilight' was on the B-side.

11 o'clock tick tock

Bono is a magpie. He lifts things, carries them around for a while, uses them, loses them, finds them. Sometimes he does it unconsciously, occasionally it's deliberate.

"I called in to his house at 11 o'clock one night," Gavin Friday remembers. "We used to have these meetings. You'd knock on the door, be quiet – you know the way when you're 16 or 17, trying to get a cup of coffee and listen to records, and your parents would be screaming 'Go to bed!' And in the meetings, we used to play certain roles. Believe it or not, he was judge and juror and I was in charge of being in-charge – and so on.

"On this particular night Bono wasn't in and so I stuck a note to the door: '*11 o'clock, tick tock. Gav called.*' A good while afterwards, he says to me, 'Do you remember that note you left? I think I'll take that title'. And I'm there thinking: 'That's my title – 11 o'clock tick tock' *[laughs]*. But that was just one of those little accidents that comes good. A riff can happen or a title can happen – it acts as a springboard, and then you fill in the gaps."

Like 'A Day Without Me', '11 O'Clock Tick Tock' was written in the euphoria of the immediate surge that the acquisition of a Memory Man echo unit gave to The Edge's playing. It is first and foremost a guitar-driven thing, with The Edge revelling in the new power, the new *noise* he'd discovered.

There was some controversy about the riff, with another Dublin band, The Atrix, claiming that they'd got there first. But U2 weren't going to let go. An integral part of the band's live set before they signed to Island, '11 O'Clock Tick Tock' became their second single, recorded in Windmill Lane with Martin Hannett, who was making a name for himself on the British indie scene producing Joy Division.

The chemistry wasn't quite right between Hannett and the band, probably because of the producer's own particular interest in chemical experiments – an ironic penchant given that the song was intended as an attack on prevailing rock values in Britain.

U2 opened a show in the Camden Electric Ballroom in 1979 for Orchestral Manoeuvres in the Dark and Talking Heads, and they were struck by the factionalism that had crept into the post-punk scene. In the first instance, the band had reacted against the pseudo-violence of punk, the laddish aggression that characterized so much of British rock at the time.

"Pretend violence, middle-class kids with safety pins in their noses – of which I was one, for a minute – it just didn't ring true," Bono told John Waters later. Not only that, but in time the beast began to devour itself, the whole charade reaching its nadir in the grotesque spectacle of Sid Vicious lacerating himself publicly, glorying in his own self-loathing, and finally – on the ultimate bum trip – murdering his girlfriend Nancy Spungen and then committing suicide. "The Sex Pistols were a con, a box of tricks sold by Malcolm McLaren. Kids were sold the imagery of violence which turned into the reality of violence," Bono said at the time. U2 wanted nothing to do with it.

It went further than that. The style self-consciousness that was an increasingly dominant feature on the UK scene at the end of the '70s was also anathema to the band. "London is supposed to be permissive. London is supposed to be freedom!

Punk rock – revolt into style?

London is traps. London is boxes. London is chained in bondage," Bono accused, in *NME* in 1980. '11 O'Clock Tick Tock' was written as a reaction to the growing sense Bono felt that, while rock 'n' roll got lost in image games and role-playing, the clock kept ticking away, ticking away. "We are anti-laziness. We are anti-apathy," he said at the time. "I've no time for cynicism with no direction. I've no time for casual rebels."

Not a whole lot of this is captured in Bono's lyrics. "We couldn't play very well," Bono reflects. "The songs weren't very good, and I didn't even know what a couplet was. We certainly hadn't got our *walk* right. We hadn't got our *haircuts* right. We were a very uncool band, at the bottom of the heap. But we knew one thing – at least we sensed one thing – that any artist is as interesting or as important as the new colours he finds."

On '11 O'Clock Tick Tock', Bono was painting. The single had been released in 1980 to a mixed reaction. A couple of years later, the song having become a centrepiece of the band's live set, it was voted No. 1 in their Top 50 favourite tracks of all time by listeners to Dave Fanning's influential *Rock Show* on Ireland's national music channel, 2FM. By the *War* tour, it was a thing of real, robust power.

U2 played the Orpheum Theatre, Boston on 5 and 6 May, 1983. The gigs were recorded for editing and broadcast on the *King Biscuit Flower Hour*, a syndicated concert programme played coast-to-coast in the USA, and when producer Jimmy Iovine was handed a bundle of tapes from the *War* tour to hammer together into *Under a Blood Red Sky*, this was the performance he chose. It is the definitive version of one of U2 fans' favourite songs.

"That was a good steal," one acquaintance of Bono's reflects. "A profitable little larceny. It wasn't the first and it wouldn't be the last. But it was a good one."

touch

When they were working on melodies, the band would often just grab a phrase or a word that sounded musical in the context of the song, to use as the title. 'Touch' was originally called 'Trevor' – possibly after Strongman from the Prunes, whose Christian name was Trevor. But that title was dumped and instead Bono provided an enigmatic lyric that anticipates both 'Fire' and, oddly, 'Surrender' from *October*. Some people felt that it would make a worthy

single in itself but, in the end, 'Touch' appeared on the flip-side of '11 O'Clock Tick Tock'. Like the A-side, it was produced by Martin Hannett.

things to make and do

"That was very much a genre title of the day," The Edge laughs. "There were so many songs with those sort of titles." In the early days, when their backs were against the wall, U2 tended to produce whimsical instrumentals. "No one else was in town and we needed a B-side," Edge recalls, "so I just did that on the 4-track cassette, just me in the rehearsal room. I just sent it up to the studio and away it went." It appeared on the B-side of 'A Day Without Me', which was produced by Steve Lillywhite and released in August 1980.

j. swallow

In the early days, budgets were inevitably small, and U2 were invariably rushed. It was nothin' but the same old story. In these pre-CD days, they needed something for the flip of 'Fire'. "That was done in a mad panic," Edge confesses. "It was a case of two hours to go, let's do it. Johnny Swallow was one of our mates, a guy called Reggie Manuel." There were references to Lypton Village names in the indecipherable lyrics, according to The Edge, but no one listening would have been any the wiser. Still, Reggie must have been pleased.

a celebration

The first secondary school that Bono went to was St Patricks, beside the famous Cathedral in the Liberties area of Dublin. "I used to ring the bells in the Cathedral on a Tuesday. Then I got into trouble in the school – I threw dogshit at the Spanish teacher or something – and I got nudged out. I think I deserved it *(laughs)*. That's how I ended up in Mount Temple."

St. Patrick's is just 100 yards or so from Christ Church Cathedral, which makes a cameo appearance in 'A Celebration'. Inspired by Neil McCormick's review of *October* in *Hot Press* and recorded as a single between *October* and *War*, it was designed to fill a gap created by the relative lack of singles on

the former. Like much of *October*, it reflected U2's Christian commitment, although in this context, the Dublin references to Christ Church and Mountjoy at least give the hint of a social context.

"That was definitely written on paper, as opposed to being improvised on the mic," Bono recalls. "I remember thinking this will do; I don"t remember thinking this is good. I remember being in the studio and writing it down once we had the riff, and trying to paint a picture. I did, but I'm just not sure how interesting a picture it is."

'A Celebration' was conceived and recorded just after the dawning of the video age. Bono brightens up at the thought. "I remember we had itinerant boys, traveller boys, as the four horsemen of the Apocalypse, riding through the back of Sheriff Street, and me in ridiculous red pants in Kilmainham jail. I think I had a badger on my head as well. Some pieces of music are obscured by the haircuts, I think it's fair to say, and the apparel. With 'A Celebration', I just don't think I can see beyond that."

trash trampoline and the party girl

U2 have often been accused of being po-faced and humourless. But, hey, anyone who could wear the kind of check trousers sported by Bono in some of the band's early publicity shots *must* have had a sense of humour. It was just that, in the early days, they weren't sufficiently comfortable on their

The band enjoyed a game of draughts on the road...

instruments and in themselves, perhaps, to allow it to percolate through to the music. They were intense about what they were doing but they were also capable of laughing at themselves.

'(Trash Trampoline and the) Party Girl' was the first inkling of this other dimension on record. The band needed a B-side to the single 'A Celebration', released in October 1982 – and they needed it in a hurry. Without time to agonise over the results they knocked out a throwaway pop tune in little more than half an hour. It stood the test of time far better than the single itself, moving gradually into a prime position in U2's live set: it was frequently used for the band's set-ending champagne ritual, a gesture that was both hedonistic and sexual in its symbolism. As anyone who knew them privately was aware, U2 were well capable of enjoying themselves.

"One of the problems with the earlier records is that there was no sex in them," Bono admits. 'Party Girl' was different. Written, according to one rumour, about The Edge's paramour of the time, Aisling O'Sullivan, it was trashy, throwaway and fun. But who was Trash Trampoline? The smart money seems to be on Adam Clayton, who certainly was out there playing the field in a way that other members of the band weren't inclined to.

The Edge married Aislinn O'Sullivan in July 1983 in Dublin. They subsequently separated but 'Party Girl', which also features on *Under a Blood Red Sky*, sounds as informal and infectious as ever.

Aislinn O'Sullivan and The Edge.

treasure (whatever happened to pete the chop?)

Pete The Chop was a friend of Andrew Whiteway, one of the band's earliest management associates. "Andrew had great fun working with us and avoiding whatever he was supposed to be doing in Trinity College," Edge explains. "He had a couple of friends come over when we played London, and one of them turned out to be Pete The Chop. After the show he came up to us and said I think you should write a song about me. And so we did."

It was the most pop thing that U2 had ever written and when their manager, Paul McGuinness, heard the demo, he thought, "that's a hit single". The people at Island felt the same.

"We said, nobody's ever going to hear it," Bono recalls, "because it would bury the band. And Paul used to get very pissed off that we weren't releasing the song."

"It was very melodic," The Edge adds, "but not really very good."

"So eventually we minced it," Bono laughs. "We turned it around, played it backwards, just sort of fucked it in the ear, and called it 'Whatever Happened To Pete The Chop?'."

That, according to The Edge, was in the days when U2's albums were Top 30 but there was no sign of a hit single. "The new title was a reference to the record company guys who were always saying to Paul McGuinness, 'Whatever happened to "Pete The Chop"? Remember that hit song? *(laughs)*'."

Appropriately, 'Treasure' was the B-side of 'New Year's Day', the band's breakthrough single in the UK, which was produced by Steve Lillywhite and released in January 1983.

endless deep

Adam Clayton didn't often get the credit he deserved as a driving force behind U2's ascent. In the early phase he had spent more time than the others on the business side of the band but by *War* he was really coming into his own as a bass player, displaying a command of styles that was increasingly impressive. 'Endless Deep' reflected this. A bass-driven thing, as Edge puts it, it was released on the B-side of 'Two Hearts Beat as One' in March 1983.

boomerang I and boomerang II

U2 had always liked Talking Heads, so it was almost inevitable that the influence would show when they began to work with the band's producer, Brian Eno. 'Boomerang' came in two mixes, which accompanied different releases of 'Pride (In the Name of Love)' as a single. A rhythmic piece, it was an early manifestation of the interest U2 would later show in dance.

"I think African influences were important there," The Edge says. "That was when the first wave of African music was hitting the West: Fela Kuti, King Sunny Ade and all those people. I was playing a lot of African guitar at the time and there was a bit of that here, in what was basically a jam. Funny, I don't think Brian really liked 'Boomerang'."

the three sunrises

When it comes to putting the finishing touches to an album, a whole other set of criteria come into play. Themes and moods are crucial. There is a need for consistency and flow, so that people will want to listen to the entire record. It's at this stage that a lot of good songs are jettisoned.

'The Three Sunrises' wouldn't have worked on *The Unforgettable Fire* – or that's the conclusion the band came to with Eno and Lanois. But it's an interesting departure, nonetheless, with its combination of Beatles-style pop harmonies and stabbing, almost hard-rock guitar. "One of U2's finest outtakes," Neil McCormick of *Hot Press* concluded.

Originally released on the 'Unforgettable Fire' single, 'The Three Sunrises' also turned up on the US-only *Wide Awake In America* EP, which also featured the definitive version of 'Bad'.

love comes tumbling

This was relatively unfamiliar country for U2 – a simple, gentle, rhythmic love song, with a distinctly romantic feel. It had begun with the kind of exploratory improvisation that characterised the entire *Unforgettable*

191

Fire recording sessions, and the lyrics suffer from the vagueness that was also a hallmark of the band's work in this period. But it's a track which works because of the sweet combination of a fine arrangement and a superb vocal performance from Bono. Again it was released first with 'The Unforgettable Fire' single, with the 'Pride (In the Name of Love)' double 7-inch pack and on *Wide Awake In America*.

bass trap

When 'The Unforgettable Fire' was released as a 12-inch single, 'Bass Trap' was included as a bonus track. Produced by Eno and Daniel Lanois, it is an ambient, atmospheric piece.

"At that stage, we were trying lots of different approaches to songwriting," The Edge explains. "Brian was into that, and 'Bass Trap' was a good example. He used this really cheap electric harmonics device – I think that describes what it was – to trap a bass figure that Adam had played.

"It was sort of like what Phillip Glass does with his work. You start with a very simple sequence of notes which keeps repeating, then you work other melodies on top of it. It can be quite effective."

sixty seconds in kingdom come

A great title but the noise hardly matches its grandeur. An extra track on the double 7-inch single of 'The Unforgettable Fire' released in April, 1985, The Edge dismisses it as just another piece of music that never went anywhere.

luminous times (hold onto love)

The band were in prolific form during the run-up to *The Joshua Tree*. It wasn't just that they were producing a lot of new songs: the quality count was high and as a result some superb tracks didn't make it to the album. 'Luminous Times' was one, a piano-driven piece that surfaced on the 'With Or Without You' single, which went to No.1 in the US. The lyrics on *The Joshua Tree* itself are generally more finely-wrought.

'Luminous Times' sounds improvised, but there's a quality of emotional honesty running through it that is hugely impressive. "I remember at the time," The Edge explains, "saying 'Look, Brian, I think this is as good as anything on the album. I think we should work on it.' And Brian said, 'I think you're probably right but I don't think we can.' So, reluctantly, we didn't finish it at the time."

Neither Eno nor Daniel Lanois were there when U2 completed 'Luminous Times', but it made a hell of a B-side all the same, as Bono struggled to come to terms with the contradictions and complexities of love.

"Around that time Bono was fascinated with blues imagery and American mythology," The Edge asserts, "but there was something else going on in these twisted love songs he was writing, like 'With Or Without You' and 'Luminous Times', that was more European."

"She is the avalanche/She is the thunder/She is the waves/And she pulls me under," Bono sings. The drowning man is back!

walk to the water

If 'Luminous Times' was strong enough to have made it to *The Joshua Tree* album, so too was 'Walk To The Water'. "I thought that came out so well," The Edge says, "but we just didn't have the time to get it ready before *The Joshua Tree* was finished." The mood of the song has been compared by Bill Graham of *Hot Press* to that on *Astral Weeks*, but my own sense is that Philip Lynott's influence is discernible here, in the gentle evocation of some past, more romantic Dublin. Lynott had died in January of 1986.

And rather than being about his own experience, might Bono have been attempting to describe the courtship between his own father and mother on Dublin's north side? Either way, it was an impressive first flirtation with rap.

spanish eyes

U2 hadn't written many songs of sheer sexual need before *Achtung Baby*. 'Spanish Eyes' was one of them, ranking up there alongside 'Desire' and 'Hawkmoon 269' as statements of intense, primal lust.

It began as a jam, with the lyrics and the vocals coming later. *"I love the way you talk to me/ And I love the way you walk on me,"* Bono confesses

in a line that looks ahead to the sexual humiliation explored more fully on *Achtung Baby*.

"I think 'Spanish Eyes' is Ali, to be honest," The Edge offers. "I think that's what Bono was on about."

'Spanish Eyes' made an intriguing companion to 'I Still Haven't Found What I'm Looking For' when the latter was released on 7-inch in April 1987.

deep in the heart

A combination of factors ensured that love and sex and the whole damn business wouldn't be too heavily represented on *The Joshua Tree*. 'With Or Without You' aside, it was left to the B-sides and bonus tracks on the album's various singles to cover this terrain. Like 'Spanish Eyes', the ominous 'Deep in the Heart' does it powerfully, depicting a *Lolita*-style scene with an almost disquieting sense of detachment.

The bass part was the key. Once Adam had that down, The Edge could improvise over it and – in his own words – it started to sound really interesting. All it needed now was powerful vocals...

sweetest thing

Sometimes you take a left turn. You seem to be heading off into the unknown before the road swings back towards the main artery.

There's a spine that runs through U2's work. They can zoom off into the ozone but the link to that spine has got to be strong enough to hold. Now and then, the connection can seem frazzled or stretched: there was a lot of resistance from within the band to 'Still Haven't Found What I'm Looking For' but Bono pushed it through. He didn't feel quite so convinced about 'Sweetest Thing'.

It would have made a powerful, radio-friendly single for sure – but might it have tilted the perception of the band in a way that would ultimately have been unhelpful? Agree or otherwise, that was the call the band made; 'Sweetest Thing' was omitted from *The Joshua Tree* and turned up on the flip of the 'Where The Streets Have No Name' 7-inch.

"Bono came up with that on the piano," The Edge recalls. Adam supplies a massive, rumbling, bass attack to give musical root to what is another intense, besotted ode to Ali that combines sweet surrender with hints of the desperation that would take hold by *Achtung Baby*. "It's a soul-pop song,"

The Edge adds with characteristic economy. "It's actually a good tune." There's quite a few critics who think it's one of U2's finest.

race against time

It doesn't take a genius to recognise that U2's recent immersion in the possibilities of dance has its precedents. From the urban funk of parts of *War* onwards, there's always been an interest in the groove. 'Race Against Time' was cut from that cloth.

"That was a kind of Afro-rhythmic piece I put together," The Edge says. "We did a bit of work on it and then realised it wasn't going to make the album, so we left it to one side."

Like 'The Sweetest Thing', 'Race Against Time' is interesting as an indicator of the album U2 *might* have made instead of *The Joshua Tree*! It appeared on the 'Where The Streets Have No Name' 12-inch single in August 1987.

hallelujah (here she comes)

Another song that The Edge and Bono came up with in John Heather's house in Connemara, 'Hallelujah (Here She Comes)' is a piece of upful gospel rock. That productive songwriting session yielded 'Hawkmoon 269', 'Desire' and the beginning of 'Angel Of Harlem'. "'Hallelujah' just didn't seem to fit the album," The Edge says. It was the B-side to 'Desire', released in September 1988.

a room at the heartbreak hotel

If there's one thing U2 know about, it's hotels. For the best part of 20 years they've been living out of suitcases. Bono has written a film script entitled *The Million Dollar Hotel*. And now they've bought the Clarence Hotel in Dublin, bringing the road home with them. But this is not about the Clarence.

Bono explores his fascination with Elvis Presley to reflect on the themes of love, lust, fidelity and betrayal without ever achieving the condensed poetic power that *Achtung Baby* would reveal. As on 'God Part II', Jimmy Iovine's production is dense and claustrophobic but the band whip up a powerful

Anthony Burgess, author of *A Clockwork Orange*.

noise. "Gospel meets Suicide," The Edge says succinctly. Gospel could do worse. 'A Room at the Heartbreak Hotel' made a murky companion to 'Angel Of Harlem' on the 12-inch single released in December 1988.

alex descends into hell for a bottle of milk

When the British Royal Shakespeare Company were planning a theatrical production of *A Clockwork Orange*, they decided that an original score would be a good idea. Director Ron Daniels approached U2. "He wanted a hit musical," The Edge says. "We cautioned him that we weren't very good at 'hits' and that we were more into experimenting."

The Edge isn't convinced that the story suited a theatrical production. And from a musical point of view, the snatches allotted to them were too short. The author of the original novel, the late Anthony Burgess, attended the premiere at London's Barbican Theatre in February 1990, and was curt in his appraisal of the score.

"We heard he was a bit disdainful," The Edge admits, "but it was hard to take it seriously because I don't think he understood anything about what we do or anything about popular music. I've a feeling that it was just a reaction against the fact that it wasn't Beethoven, so I wasn't too upset."

A few of the snatches prepared for *A Clockwork*

Orange were combined to create 'Alex Descends into Hell for a Bottle of Milk', a B-side for 'The Fly'. The title has nothing to do with the Lypton Village character who was affectionately known as the Bottle of Milk. As far as we know...

lady with the spinning head

Achtung Baby had been such a difficult album to grind out that it was a surprise that the band had any energy left to do B-sides at all. 'Lady with the Spinning Head' was the original demo backing track that later spawned both 'The Fly' and 'Light My Way'. It's got a good groove courtesy of Larry's apparently carefree drum part and The Edge throws in a guitar-keyboard solo. The tracks that aren't laboured over tend to sound more like someone else, and Primal Scream and Happy Mondays lurk in the shadows here.

where did it all go wrong?

Most people have heard the story. When George Best was at the height of his powers and his fame with Manchester United, he was staying in a suite at the Dorchester Hotel. He had three beautiful blondes up in the room with him (or was it just Miss World?) and as they got into the spirit of things, the great footballer had occasion to send down for more champagne. Best opened the door to room service in his dressing-gown. A grizzled old porter from Best's home town of Belfast brought the champagne in and plonked it down on the table. He took a look at the scantily clad women and, as Best unfurled a wad of bank notes from which to tip him, he said, "George, where did it all go wrong?"

"It's a brilliant story," The Edge says. "We just wrote the song around that quote."

salome

STS Studios in Dublin played a pivotal role in U2's development. "The band works very well together there," The Edge says. "It was always a great song-writing tool. A lot of great ideas started out for us in STS, and there's a couple of finished tracks we could never match the feel of elsewhere, like 'Desire'." 'Salome' was done in STS. It was another song that did a cell-division and, at first, this was the discarded part. It ended up having a dual existence of its own: a blistering R'n'B version on the cassette single of 'Even Better Than The Real Thing' and a Zooromancer dance remix on the 'Who's Gonna Ride Your Wild Horses?' single.

slow dancing

Bono originally intended 'Slow Dancing' for Willie Nelson. A love song, he heard it in his head first in Nelson's distinctive, beautiful voice. The Edge supplied a middle-eight and when the demo was done, they sent it off – and heard nothing. "I assumed he just wasn't interested, that he didn't like the song," Bono says. So they whacked a version together and put it on the 'Stay (Faraway So Close)' CD single.

It turned out that Willie had simply put it on the back-burner. Flying into Dublin for a concert, he made contact with the band. They arranged to have a shot at recording the song, with U2 providing the backing. On the first take, when Willie opened his mouth to sing, Bono's heart soared. What a voice! "The vocals are amazing," The Edge says. "The whole thing has a kind of broken quality which I like. It's our job now to finish it but it was a wonderful experience working with him."

The band pulled it together as an additional track, released on the single version of 'If God Will Send His Angels'. A song that would be comfortable amid the sprawling Americana of *Rattle and Hum*, it's U2's deepest excursion into country: not a place they visit too often, but the journey is more than worth it on this occasion.

bottoms

Yes, there is a U2 track that you hadn't heard of. Or perhaps that should read a Passengers' track. One of the most important changes in music over the past decade is the emergence of the art of the re-mix. If there's enough raw material there to play with, it's possible to produce an utterly different end-product from the same sonic raw material. 'Bottoms' was a case in point.

"That was one of Brian's crazy mixes of 'Zoo Station'," The Edge explains. "He did different prototype mixes which

helped us get to our final version. 'Bottoms' was done in Japan, and we just built on that mix. Sometimes you can end up with something completely distinctive." In the end, 'Bottoms' finished up as an extra track on the Japanese version of *Original Soundtracks 1*.

hold me, thrill me, kiss me, kill me

When the offer came in to do a song for the *Batman Forever* soundtrack, The Edge was away. At first Bono dismissed the idea as not being right – at the time, at least – for U2. But the thought had been lodged, and gradually he started to come around.

There was a piece Edge loved, that they hadn't been able to finish for *Zooropa*. Bono listened back to the demo, and decided they might give it a go. When Edge got back, Bono phoned him. "Look, I know it's kinda mad," he said, "but what do you feel about doing something for the *Batman* movie? I think this tune could really work in that context."

The Edge had a listen. "I figured that it'd be good for us to be involved in something that's so obviously not serious – something basically throwaway and light-hearted," he recalls. "And so we gave it a shot."

Bono's lyrics are humorous and self-deprecatory. *"Dressing like your sister,"* he sings, *"living like a tart/If they don't know what you're doing/Babe, it must be art/You're a headache in a suitcase/You're a star."* Clearly he had other targets in mind too but the cartoon video which accompanied the single

made it quite clear that he was using the opportunity to poke a few holes in the U2 myth. The video was nominated for Best Video From a Film at the MTV Awards but didn't win (Seal did!).

mission impossible

With the success of 'Hold Me, Thrill Me, Kiss Me, Kill Me' under their belts, it was inevitable U2 would become contenders to handle other high-profile soundtrack songs. At early *Mission Impossible* production meetings, their name came up.

When the request arrived, Bono and The Edge were under pressure to deliver material for the follow-up to *Zooropa* – the first thoroughly-planned U2 album since *Achtung Baby*. They were about to turn down the offer to become involved in the movie when Adam and Larry stepped in and volunteered their services.

Strictly speaking, it isn't a U2 track at all: it's Adam Clayton and Larry Mullen Jnr. in the cockpit for the first time, and in handling the craft so well, they underline something that's too often forgotten or ignored. Which is this: they make a great rhythm section, and one which has been absolutely central to the success of U2, the band.

A gold album, a worldwide hit single, and at the première of the movie, people were pushing past Sharon Stone to try and get a word with Larry Mullen Jnr. Mission Impossible? Mission accomplished.

Emmanuelle Beart and Tom Cruise in *Mission Impossible*.

north and south of the river

Written with Irish folk hero Christy Moore in 1995, U2's version appeared on the CD single of 'Staring at the Sun'. Drawing its central metaphor the River Liffey, which divides Dublin culturally as well as geographically into North and South, at heart it's a political song about the difficulties of reconciling Nationalist and Unionist traditions in the north of Ireland. The soundscape is akin to that explored in 'You Made Me the Thief of Your Heart' and 'In the Name of the Father' – songs written by Bono with Gavin Friday and Maurice Seezer for Jim Sheridan's film *In the Name of the Father* – emphasising the Irish-ness of the theme, the tribal rhythm of the bodhrán introducing the song's sense of foreboding. An impressive track, it's a companion piece to U2's other songs about the national question – from 'Sunday Bloody Sunday' through ' Please' *to All That You Can't Leave Behind*'s 'Peace on Earth'.

two shots of happy one shot of sad

Bono was proud of having written this. Amid the car crashes and the excavation and the happenstance of U2's work – songwriting by accident, Bono jokes – this one sounds as if it emerged almost fully formed, as if Bono could hear the finished product before he'd even written it. And guess who was singing in the U2 singer's head? Frank Sinatra! In fact he made a vain attempt to get ol' blue eyes to record a song that was written specifically with him in mind. It's a shame Sinatra didn't bite: by any standards this is a great songwriter's song; capturing the Sinatra persona superbly, it's peppered with sparkling nuggets that temper the braggadocio of 'My Way' to achieve a finer, more bittersweet sense of defiance. Sinatra might have swung it a little harder but U2's version, produced by Nellee Hooper and released on the single 'If God Will Send His Angels', recalls 'Love Is Blindness' and boasts a superb vocal performance from Bono over a Craig Armstrong string arrangement.

i'm not your baby

When U2 set about making *Pop*, they wanted to de-construct the idea of a rock'n'roll band. They threw themselves into a way of working that was more trip-hop(py) or hip-hop(py), a cut-up style that was less about live playing and more about sampling themselves, cutting things up, using loops and so on. It was the way things were going in music. By the time the album was nearly done, however, they realized that the baby was being thrown out with the bathwater and they went back to basics, recording as a unit, sticking stuff down on the hoof. "When you go down that sampling route, you don't actually carry the personality of the band through," Edge relates. "You might persuade yourself that you're doing that but there's something about the here and now, the actual performance of the musicians unadulterated, which is at the core of what a band is."

'I'm Not Your Baby', an instrumental piece that wouldn't be out of place on *Passengers*, is a case in point. Produced by Howie B and Flood, it's U2 gone trip hop. And while it's engaging in its combination of sonics and rhythm, essentially it's background music.

summer rain

During the recording of *All That You Can't Leave Behind*, the band took a trip to the south of France. Larry has a place there and the climate is congenial. Besides, it helps every now and then to get out of Dublin, and away from all the associated pressures and hassles. "The red light scenario where you're *on* all the time is hard sometimes," Edge says. "You've got to be able to ignore the clock ticking if you're going to get anywhere. And so, going to France was just a great way of achieving that, at a time when the clock actually *was* ticking and we were getting close to the deadline."

'Summer Rain' was written there. A B-side to 'Beautiful Day', it's a gentle acoustic track in a minor key, that resonates of the 1960s, Bono musing about how he lost himself to the summer rain: you can see the clouds rolling in over Provence. "I love that tune," Edge says. "It just didn't quite measure up against other tunes on the record. Sometimes, giving a song like that away as a B-side hurts, because you know it's got something. But it's great for our fans to have a tune like that as a B-side, and for us it's great to have it out there."

big girls are best

From the *Pop* sessions, 'Big Girls Are Best' didn't surface until the release of the 'Stuck In a Moment' single. It has the sound of a track-in-the-making – something that hasn't been afforded the time or attention necessary to get it finished to album standard.

It's understandable. The idea had been explored elsewhere on *Pop*, on 'Miami' and on 'Mofo', Bono's most open appeal to the spirit of his departed mother. He's at a related game here, referring lovingly to the motherlode, and collapsing into incoherent homage to mama, mama, mama ('She's got a baby at her breast').

The melody owes more than a bit to John Lennon, and the sentiment too. While the title hardly sounds politically correct and the familiar U2 image of the man on his knees is accompanied in this instance by the equally inviting prospect of the woman on her back, it's actually a reassuringly wholesome little number.

"I wouldn't be too much into the lyric but it's a great rock'n'roll vibe," Edge says. "I think when Bono talks about big girls, he means large girls – not big-breasted, or anything like that. He's talking about women who aren't stick insects. We managed to find 15 minutes in Los Angeles to finish it – and it came together. It's pretty tongue-in-cheek and throwaway."

always

'Always' is the original band jam that gave birth to 'Beautiful Day'. Daniel Lanois feels that it's inspirational. Edge is a little less convinced. "It was a tune that we thought had a pretty good title from day one," he says. "We thought it had potential. But it really wasn't that unique or special and so when we finished 'Beautiful Day', we went back and said 'that's a B-side'. It doesn't really stand up." But as a prism through which to view the metamorphoses are involved in going from the idea for a U2 song to the finished article, it's well worth hearing.

Passengers

Produced by **Brian Eno (with Howie B).**
Recorded at **Westside Studios, London and Dublin.** *Released* **November 1995.**

united colours of plutonium

This place feels like it's straight out of *Bladerunner*. Twenty-foot neon signs blazing in the night. Little noodle bars down at street level. And outside, the bullet-proof, black Rolls Royces that can spell only one thing: Mafia.

Bono is looking out of the window of his Tokyo hotel. What an extraordinary city. What an incredible place. He's been feeling like this for a few days. It seems appropriate, somehow, that the *Zoo TV* tour should have ended up here – in the fucking future. Or that's what it looks like anyway. That's how it felt too, on the bullet train the other day. It was a special rush, that, with its own drama, its own mystery, its own music. Like travelling into the future.

Later . . .

Going into West Side Studios in London, that crazed finale of the *Zoo TV* tour was still on

Mixmaster Howie B.

everyone's brain. If they had a location in mind when they started jamming, that was it. Tokyo. They watched some Japanese animated Manga movies with the sound turned down for inspiration. When they started to record 'United Colours of Plutonium', they were thinking of the bullet train.

"We wanted that sense of speed," Bono recalls. "We wanted it to sound like being aboard the bullet train." He's in the front room of his house overlooking Dublin Bay. The railway running south from Dublin travels along the bottom of the hill below Bono's house. "I love trains," Bono says and less than 30 seconds later you can hear one chugging past below, making for Rosslare Harbour, where it will deposit travellers heading onwards to Europe. The whistle sounds, one of the simplest and most evocative musical notes imaginable. "When we were discussing the release of *Passengers*, we were going to launch the record on the Eurostar," he laughs. "We were going to bring in PA equipment and take people from London to Paris and play it for them, which would have been really great. The whole record seems to sound better at a certain speed, when you're travelling."

Originally U2 and Eno recorded an extended piece, improvising for as long as it felt right and productive. Initially, it was cut down to seven minutes. Howie B, who had first encountered U2 when he worked on a remix of Bono's version of 'Hallelujah' for the Leonard Cohen album *I'm Your Fan*, took the West Side tapes into STS Studios in Dublin and got a fix on what was there.

"It's what he didn't put in rather than what he did," Bono says. "There were no overdubs, but that's the way he mixes. He takes one thing and runs with it for a while and then punctures it with another track. Basically he plays the studio console as an instrument, leaving lots of spaces and then having things come in out of nowhere. It works particularly well here because it's like the kind of feeling you catch on a high-speed train."

Eventually it was snipped down even further to just five-and-a-half minutes. "It was murder trying to cut it down," Bono reflects. "It's a helluva sound, as an opening track. But it's probably still a bit too long."

slug

There had been talk about making a night-time record and some of *Original Soundtracks 1* does enter that territory. But 'Slug' is an attempt to paint a picture of the lights coming on in a city like Tokyo. "Which is like a Christmas tree," Bono says, explaining the sweet musical tinkling with which the track opens.

The original working title had been 'Seibu', after a department store in Tokyo. It had been recorded and forgotten and almost didn't make it onto the album until The Edge discovered it lurking among the also-rans – and brought it back to Eno's attention. In fact he still calls it 'Seibu', as if he'll always remember it that way.

The lyrics are simple, written in five minutes, but there's a lot of Bono in them nonetheless. *"Don't want to lose my shirt,"* he sings, *"Don't want to dig the dirt/Don't want you to get hurt/Can't help that I'm a flirt."*

"It's a portrait, rather like 'Arms around the World'. It's a portrait of somebody a little the worse for wear," he smiles, "which we all were in Tokyo, because it was the end of the tour. So tired you can't sleep. Wanting to go out to see what's going on in the city and not being able to stop yourself, though you should be looking after yourself better."

In a way it's reminiscent of 'Numb' and its series of negative commands, and there's a similar kind of ironic, self-deprecatory humour involved when Bono admits, *"Don't want what I deserve"*.

But the song has a genuinely reflective quality and it underlines the fact that, some 15 years on since the release of their debut album *Boy*, U2 are still running. *"Don't want to stay the same,"* Bono concludes at the end of 'Slug' and you know that he's as restless as ever.

your blue room

For the most part, the idea was that Brian Eno would be captain of the ship. He'd call the creative shots and, like good musicians, the members of U2 would obey. "The only tracks we really dug in our heels and did more work on and tried to craft," The Edge explains, "were 'Miss Sarajevo', 'Seibu' and 'Your Blue Room'. And I think it paid off. I really love '...Blue Room'. It just seemed obvious to me that they could be great songs, and so I did some extra work and pushed them."

Bono conceived of it as a kind of an erotic hymn. He'd always wanted to make a blue record, an atmospheric record. Going into the Passengers' project, he was thinking after-midnight. He was thinking music that you can have sex to. 'Your Blue Room' invites the listener into that erogenous zone.

"I suppose the blue room is an image that people can understand," he says. "But the song is based on the idea that sex is a conversation of a different kind. On one level it's purely carnal, but on another it's a prayer."

Bono: blue for you.

Musically, the band were thinking of Serge Gainsbourg: they wanted to achieve the feeling of intimacy that they'd been introduced to by 'Je T'Aime' in discos in Dublin all those years ago. Bono's voice has that deep, reassuring quality adopted by Leonard Cohen on his songs of seduction. The whole thing, gently massaged by Larry's light brush-work, is languorous and evocative, the organ adding a consciously spiritual quality.

"That's my favourite song on the record," Bono says unequivocally. "If we weren't keeping a low profile – we have to, because people get sick of us if we're always putting stuff out – we would have really pushed it. It's an incredible thing to say to your lover or your maker, the line, *"Your instructions, whatever the direction."* It's also very casual. *"One day I'll be back/Your blue room/Hope I remember where it's at/Your blue room."* So it's not earnest at all."

It also features Adam Clayton's first lead vocal on a U2 record. It's his voice which comes in at the end, quietly chatting in the background, like a late-night conversation *après*-sex.

"Adam was talking about the song to me," Bono remembers, "and I just wrote down an approximation of what he said and then we decided it'd be best if Adam actually spoke it. *'A lens to see it all up close'* – we wanted to use concrete images to balance the headiness of it all. Perspective is an extraordinary thing. Everything depends on how you look at it. You get moments of clarity every now and then, when you see things for a second and they make sense. I think religious experiences are like that. You see things from a higher perspective and you feel reassured by that. You quickly forget why – but it *did* make sense.

"The astronauts had that kind of experience, and I think that's to do with perspective. When you see the Earth as this little blue marble, the perspective you have on yourself and on the planet is so dramatic."

The Edge plays some beautiful, deep, guitar lines before fading out on slip-sliding bent notes that look for their bearings over an almost churchy organ. The effect overall is nothing short of... haunting.

'Your Blue Room' actually does feature in a film, *Par-Dela Les Nuages* (*Beyond the Clouds*), by Michaelangelo Antonioni and Wim Wenders, a film about love, about meetings, about sexual fascination.

always forever now

It helps to know what your purpose is. During the making of *Achtung Baby*, U2 were aware of what they didn't want to be: *earnest, polite, sweet, righteous, rockist* and *linear*.

And so the buzzwords began to identify themselves: *trashy, throwaway, dark, sexy* and *industrial*. During the course of the album, these would become touchstones, criteria against which each new evolving piece could be checked and balanced. It's an imperfect science but the process is a helpful one. At least you feel as if you know where you're going.

For *Original Soundtracks 1*, the imperative was more direct. On a blackboard in the band's new studio in Dublin, someone had scrawled a slogan as a motto: MAKE THE MUSIC OF THE FUTURE YOU WANT TO LIVE IN. During the recording of *Zooropa*, U2 had concluded that they didn't want to get drawn into presenting an image of the future as a cosmic wasteland, and their mood hadn't changed: in essence, *Original Soundtracks* would reflect a positive vision of where planet Earth was heading.

'Always Forever Now' fits that kind of thinking. Built around an urgent, throbbing bass triggered on the DX7 by the kick drum and a powerful rhythm part by Larry Mullen Jnr., it was seen essentially as an instrumental piece.

"We felt that the music had a feeling of 'State of Independence', the Donna Summer song,"

Damien Hirst: portrait of the artist.

Bono recalls. "It was that feeling we were looking for. A lyric never really seemed to suit it. The constant repetition of a mantra seemed to make more sense." And so that's what they went for.

The title was based on a picture by artist Damien Hirst. "It's just an affirmation," Bono says. "The words are self-explanatory." Which of course is only half true. You might interpret it as a confirmation of vows previously entered into. Then again, you might not.

Either way, the piece is beautifully structured. In the final section, a careful melody on synth climbs triumphantly through almost two octaves before climaxing on a gorgeously propulsive high. In his droll sleeve-notes, Brian Eno imagined a film featuring a team of female body-sculptors who become embroiled in heavy manners in the back alleys of Hong Kong. In fact the track was featured in *Heat*, Michael

197

Mann's blistering *film noir* in which Al Pacino, as the good cop, pursues Robert de Niro's scarily brutal bank robber. Heavy manners indeed.

a different kind of blue

Some reviewers claimed that U2 were nowhere to be heard on 'A Different Kind Of Blue', but at best they were only partially right. Bono had come up with the title and the beginnings of a jazz song to go with it. The Edge went into the studio and did a version of it which almost stood up – but the collective still weren't fully convinced. And then Eno got to work . . .

Occasionally, it's best to give one person his (or her) head. Brian was flying the aeroplane and he had a clear idea of what he wanted. And so he sneaked into the studio overnight and did his own thing, working from the bones of what U2 had left for him. "In a sense it's a hybrid," Bono reveals. "He used the title and the chords belonging to the version The Edge and myself had been playing with. He wrote a new set of very simple lyrics and he put the vocoder on the voice. It's Brian's first vocal in 15 years or something, so that was a thrill."

The odd perspective – *"Those cars/All new/So small/Down there"* – and the spare language may be Eno's, but the notion of "twilight breaking through" had come from Bono and The Edge. "It's that moment again," Bono says. "I'd say the perfect hour to listen to the record is either at dawn or in the half-light of twilight, when the sun is going down. What it suggests to me – 'twilight breaking through' – is getting up out of bed for the night."

In a sense it takes the band – and Eno with them – back to 'Twilight', the second track on *Boy*. "I think you go back again and again to the images and themes that are in you, that are you in essence," Bono argues. "Everything we do is about that duality, when things are neither one thing nor the other. The chord is neither major nor minor. The mood is not quite night, not quite day. Always wanting to paint a picture as things are, but also – at the same time – as they might be. That always runs through our work and twilight is the best image of that."

"I swear it was this big." Pavarotti enthuses about the rather nice piece of Dover sole he had for lunch.

beach sequence

Hey! Dig that funky piano player. The sensitivity. The finesse. That boy sure knows how to play. He's probably sick to his teeth of grinding out piano concertos to beat the band – so this is him in minimalist mode. Am I right?

"That's me," says Bono. "I'm playing one-finger piano. In fact it was called 'One Finger Piano' at one point, 'cos the first take was just me, fiddling around."

Which only goes to show that it doesn't take an instrumental genius to produce beautiful notes. 'Beach Sequence' is a whimsical, spacious ambient piece which was – like 'Your Blue Room' – used in the Michelangelo Antonioni and Wim Wenders' collaboration *Par-Dela Les Nuages (Beyond the Clouds)*. Edge strums some luxuriant, big, open chords and Bono's piano part evokes the "ice notes" that The Edge had trademarked on *October*.

The more some things change, the more others stay the same.

miss sarajevo

It all started to go wrong when MacPhisto phoned Pavarotti live from the stage in Bologna, during the Italian leg of the *Zooropa* tour. From that moment on, it became clear that the great Mr Pavarotti believed that U2 owed him a favour.

Coincidentally, that was the first night that

U2 made a satellite connection to Sarajevo, where the war was raging between the advancing Serbs and the beleaguered Bosnians of the city. The band had been alerted to what was happening there by an American journalist, Bill Carter, who came to Bono with the idea for a documentary on the underground resistance movement in Sarajevo. Bono provided the funds and produced the film, which chronicles one of the strangest events of the war in former Yugoslavia. "The camera follows the organizers through the tunnels and cellars of the city," the sleevenotes to *Original Soundtracks 1* tell us, "giving an unique insight into life during a modern war, where civilians are the targets. The film captures the dark humour of the besieged Sarajevans, their stubborn refusal to be demoralized and suggests that surrealism and dadaism are the appropriate responses to fanaticism."

But that was only one half of the equation that led to the recording of the track. The other half came in the very ample – and extremely persistent – form of one Luciano Pavarotti, who'd apparently decided that it'd be cool to play with U2.

"I was staggered by him," Bono says, whistling through his teeth. "He's quite the arm wrestler. He used to ring the house here all the time and he had this ongoing relationship with Teresa if I wasn't there. He'd ask if I had finished the song for him yet and she would say I was away and he would say, 'Tell *God* to give me a phonecall' and he'd put down the phone with a big laugh. He's just a great patriarch. You couldn't but give in to him."

Bono was giving the rest of the band a bit of a pain in the ass. He'd keep telling them that Pavarotti had been on again. That they'd have to write this song for him. Adam would laugh at Bono, tell him he must be out of his mind. Then at one o'clock in the morning Bono would listen to a piece and say 'maybe this would work with him'. No one knew if he was really serious but he seemed to have got stuck in a groove on it.

"We were in the middle of doing the Passengers' album," he recalls, "and we really didn't have time to do anything. Because it was such an honour to be asked, that if we were going to do something, we wanted to do it right." In the end they found a piece that had been intended for the Passengers' album, and worked out a deal to include it anyway. "It came together so well," Bono remarks. "We came up with that libretto, or the melody for it, by impersonating my father singing in the bath, impersonating Pavarotti!"

The Italian lyrics were written with Anna Coleman, wife of Marc Coleman, who works with the band. *"You say that like a river finds its way to the sea,"* Bono translates roughly, *"You will find your way back to me/You say that love will find a way/But love I'm not a praying man/And in love I can't believe anymore/And for love I can't wait anymore."*

"I think that's how a lot of people in Sarajevo felt at the time," Bono reflects. "Everywhere people had heard their call for help – but help never came. That was the feeling. I had tried before to tackle subjects like this head-on, but I'd learnt a lesson. You have to try and make the same points, in a different, less direct, more surrealist way."

'Miss Sarajevo' was premiered at the annual Pavarotti and Friends concert in Modena, Italy on 12 September 1995. Bono wore a cloth cap for the occasion, which also marked the first time that The Edge had appeared on stage *sans* headgear in many, many years.

"He's much more of a bohemian than you'd think," Bono says of the Italian tenor. "He's extraordinary, and big, in every way – big voice, big heart, girth, appetite. He would sing for 20 minutes and then he'd say, 'Now, we eat'. And we'd go and eat and then we'd come back and then we'd eat again.

"He picked us up at the airport. He's on the runway in his white Mercedes and we all get in and he drives us 15 miles to his house, drives through these gates, up a hill, round a corner, round a bend, past the house and up to the table, gets out and says, 'Pasta'. There's this beautiful woman who's been with him 40 years. She walks out with the food – and we eat. It's at the table that friendships are really made."

The Modena performance was broadcast live on Italian Rai Uno TV. 'Miss Sarajevo' was released as a single in aid of the War Child charity, in which Brian Eno is very involved, on 20 November, 1995. It did not become Christmas No.1 as it should have. That honour was lifted, in the UK at least, by Michael Jackson's 'Earthsong'.

ito okashi

You want Japan? Why not use a Japanese singer? Eno had some sensitive atmospherics in mind, the sound of a thousand wind-chimes floating on the bed of a musical bass – the kind of thing that could work with a female voice. He had heard a singer called Holi, with whom he'd been impressed. She'd released six albums and 12 singles in Japan and developed a reputation as a vocalist and songwriter of distinction. Subsequently she moved to London, releasing her debut English-language album *Under The Monkey Puzzle Tree* – produced by Steve Jensen and Mick Karn, both former members of the group Japan – on the Resurgence label in 1994. The probability was that she'd be available.

Having begun her career as a hard rock singer, Holi had gone on to do jazz training. That background suited what Passengers had in mind.

They wanted her to improvise the way Bono might have, inventing both the lyrics and the melody on the mike. She was confident enough to give it a go.

"I didn't even know U2 were waiting for me," Holi told *Propaganda*, the official magazine of the U2 fan club. "I just thought Brian needed someone to sing some Japanese. I was gobsmacked. Suddenly I was in the studio singing with Bono, Larry, The Edge and Adam and I didn't have anything prepared at all, really."

Bono was impressed nonetheless. "She kept using this phrase over and over – *ito okashi*. To be honest I didn't know what she was talking about but I kind of felt it. She was brilliant."

Ito okashi means "something beautiful" and around that simple, enigmatic idea Holi created a short, evocative almost *haiku*-style lyric in Japanese. If 'United Colours of Plutonium' brought the bullet train to mind, this was a reflective piece, evoking the sun rising in the East.

one minute warning

A TV was set up in the studio and the band were watching Japanese animation movies and other films, and playing to them. They'd run the pictures with the sound down and imagine a possible soundtrack. One of the films that influenced them greatly was Jean Luc Goddard's *Alphaville*. "It's a

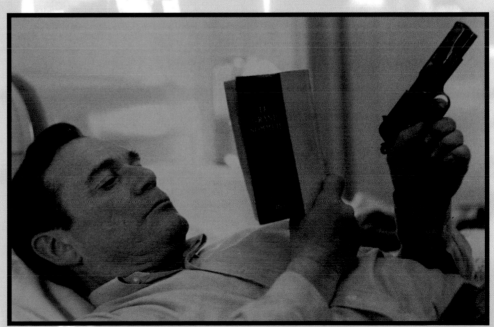

Happiness is a warm gun? The man in *Alphaville* relaxes.

look at modern architecture," Bono states. "One of the subtexts of that film was buildings. It was really helpful." It dovetailed with an interest of Eno's, inspired by Stewart Brand's book *How Buildings Learn – What Happens After They're Built*.

That was one source of inspiration for 'One Minute Warning'. Then they got a request in to provide a piece for *Ghost in the Shell*, an animation feature directed by Mamoru Oshia. The film was adapted from a graphic novel of the same name, written by Masamune Shirow. The improvisations which had been inspired by *Alphaville* seemed to fit. The track was transformed, however, when Howie B got to work on it.

"One of the contributions he made," Eno explained, "was the creation of space in the music. When you're in the studio, the tendency is to add things. It's automatically what you're inclined to do. You tend to fill up all the gaps.

"That is often not a good idea – part of the attraction of these things in the first place was that you could hear everyone. They were simple and clear in a certain way. When Howie came in, he left out huge elements that we had thought were very important. Just left them out. Suddenly that's very refreshing."

You hear it very well on 'One Minute Warning'. Eno's mix is dense and busy, and it's cut into an alternative mix by Howie which creates what Eno describes as a charged electric space, with very little going on but with a lot of tension.

"If you look at the record as a whole," Eno adds, "his mixes are quite important to the feeling of the record, because they have this tingling emptiness to them which I really appreciate a lot."

"When we're working, we take from all sorts of different sources," The Edge adds. "Everyone is open to suggestion. Eno'll pick up the microphone and try something. I'll play drums and Larry will play guitar. There's no demarcation."

When the time came, there was no better man than Howie B to play the desk.

corpse

On *Rattle and Hum*, U2 had got to grips with the blues, playing it straight just about as well as it can be played, on 'When Love Comes to Town'. The game from *Achtung Baby* onwards was a little bit more complex: if musical forms of this kind were going to be used, they'd have to be reinvented for the '90s. And so,

on *Zooropa*, 'Daddy's Gonna Pay For Your Crashed Car', which had been conceived with the voice of John Lee Hooker in Bono's head, was twisted and bent into the shape of what Bono called an industrial blues. It was still a kind of blues alright, but it was definitely a U2 kind of blues.

'Corpse (These Chains Are Way Too Long)' attempted a similar kind of transformation, only this time in the lyric department.

"I love the idea behind that," Bono laughs. "Most blues are about the chains that bind people but this is the opposite. This is a complaint that the chains are too long."

Thinking his way into the piece, The Edge adopted the perspective of a character on Death Row. But, inevitably, there's more than a bit of himself in there too. He'd been reflecting on how freedom has been the buzz word since the '50s, and U2 have more of it than 99 per cent of other people in the planet. "We have what Groucho Marx used to call 'fuck off' money," he says, "but it has struck me for a while that constraints, whatever form they take, are really important. I often feel that it's a sad and lonely place to be, when you see someone who's gone beyond constraints."

To capture that idea, he imagined someone on Death Row, or facing some prison sentence, who had allowed themselves to go all the way. Sung by The Edge, the song is a dirge-like acknowledgement of what can happen to someone who doesn't recognize any limits to human behaviour. It is, you could say, a different kind of blues.

elvis ate america

It began originally with an exhibition of artworks portraying Elvis Presley and Marilyn Monroe. The organizers, Geri de Paoli and Wendy McDavis, saw the potential in a book of the exhibition, and they gave it the same name – *2 x Immortal: Elvis + Marilyn*. Having rounded up works by, among others, Andy Warhol, Keith Haring, Jerry Kearns, Richard Hamilton and Rena La Cariz – who supplied an extraordinary image of Presley naked, seated on a throne, with his cock hanging free – they asked Bono to do the preface. He opted to write 'Elvis: American David' instead, a kind of beat poem that was also published as a poster in the band's fan magazine *Propaganda*.

"It's supposed to be a cross between Ferlinghetti, Kerouac, Ginsberg and all those," Bono explains. "It's just like a list. Some people don't get

Chuck D: loiters with intent on 'Elvis Ate America'.

that concept but the American David idea is interesting. I've always conceived of David in the Bible as the first blues singer. That sort of shouting-at-God aspect of the blues reflects what was going on in the Psalms, and Elvis had this dialogue where he was always torn between the sacred and the profane."

About two-thirds of the way through, the list becomes a rap. Bono knew that the last third would make a song: the question was how to do it. Howie B provided the answer. "Hip-hop is his thing," Bono says, "so he had a real feel for it. He's the guy who's chanting Elvis through it."

For the sleeve notes, Brian Eno conceived of an imaginary lost four-minute work, done on Super-8 by Jeff Koons when he was a teenager, entitled *Elvis Ate America*. He contacted Koons, who agreed to go along with the subterfuge.

As a portrait of the King, 'Elvis Ate America' is smart, humorous and potent – everything, lyrically, that 'Elvis Presley and America' on *Unforgettable Fire* wasn't. Bono's earlier stab at capturing the spirit of Elvis in a song had inspired a critical lashing from Dave Marsh. In contrast, Greil Marcus – the author of *Mystery Train* and a critic of similar calibre and influence to Marsh – was taken by 'Elvis: American David'.

"I got a beautiful note from him," Bono says. "I was very pleased that he had been taken with it." But then Greil Marcus is one of the two not-so-obvious characters mentioned in the song. Most students of popular culture will understand the allusions to Martin Luther King, Public Enemy,

Chuck D, Hitler, Nixon, Christ, and even Mishima (check the Paul Shroeder movie for reference). But is the mention of Jackson a reference to Jesse (unlikely), Michael (possible) or Joe (and I don't mean the singer)? Answers on a postcard please!

plot 180

What was the point of composing music for imaginary films? In *A Year With Swollen Appendices,* his diary of 1995, Eno unveils some of the rationale behind the *Original Soundtracks 1* concept.

The crucial assumption was that an awareness that music is being composed for a film stimulates the imagination to think pictorially and scenically. Eno refers on more than one occasion to David Lynch's use of Bobby Vinton's *Blue Velvet* in his film of the same name – and the way in which hearing the song in that context charged it with a new meaning, imbuing it "with more depth and ambiguity than it ever had before."

But the exercise also opened up opportunities for humour. Eno saw the possibility of inventing the films, writing synopses and placing the songs in that entirely artificial – and often wittily evoked – context.

As a title, 'Plot 180' sounds like a send-up of some standard stereotypical Hollywood piece of flim-flam. Equally it could be a reference to a graveyard. Or to something else entirely.

In *A Year With Swollen Appendices,* there is a story written by Eno entitled 'Sperm Auction'. It describes a scene sometime in the early-to-mid 21st century, at an auction at which couples bid for sperm from well-known characters from the past, with which the woman can be impregnated. The story is about Beryl and Robert and how at the auction they pay over $250,000 for sperm which (probably) belonged to Mikhail Gorbachev.

At the auction, it is Lot 180. Maybe it's a little oblique joke. Or might we be looking at a typographical error? (If you want an answer, try playing Plot 180 backwards).

theme from the swan

Brian's habit was to get up before anyone else. He'd head into the studio and dig around there and find a loop that would operate as the foundation

for a track: it could be anything, a moment from a chat show, a sequence of notes or the sound of someone tapping a bottle.

Once the foundation was established the rest of the band could come in and build on top of it again. Sometimes before the process was finished, the original starting point would be lost or obliterated; other times not.

The more U2 entered the mix, the more likely the former was to happen. But the point of the Passengers' album was that it should be a collaboration, and that Eno's signature should be clearly discernible.

It is in 'Theme from the Swan'. The imaginary film envisaged is slow and haunting and the piece fits. "It's mostly Brian," The Edge recalls. "He's playing the cello. The Passengers' record was our thank you to Brian, in a way, for him having to do it our way on so many other records. In this case it was 'OK Brian, we're gonna do it your way', which made it a far easier record for us to make."

theme from let's go native

There were times when U2 had sounded like Talking Heads. But there is, of course, a lot of Brian Eno in Talking Heads. Indeed it was Eno – a long-time fan of African music – who, as their producer, brought that crucial influence to bear on the band's music. 'Theme from Let's Go Native' therefore is somewhat of a return to familiar territory. With its heavy bass and powerful lolloping drums, it is first and foremost an impressive rhythm piece. "That's Brian's editing at its best," Bono says, "where he finds an 18- or 24-bar section in an improvisation and repeats it."

"He'd always talked about doing an experimental record with us, along the lines of *Bush of Ghosts* that he'd done with David Byrne," The Edge adds. With that background in mind, 'Let's Go Native' was a fitting wrap-up.

Brian Eno: more than just a Passenger on the U2 express.

In the vinyl era,

for every A-side there was just one B-side. It was a challenge to come up with consistently good stuff, but for the great bands it was a manageable one. In the CD era, there's no such thing as clearly definable 'sides' any more and with the plethora of formats – 7-inch and 12-inch vinyl, cassette single, CD single, double CD single, and so on – the demand on bands to produce additional non-album tracks has grown enormously.

For the most part, U2 have tended to use the available space to release more experimental cuts, live versions and interesting remixes. However, the self-styled worst covers band in the world had made the odd interesting stab in that direction during the latter part of the '80s, and gradually they began to apply that experience to their singles requirements.

The Self-Aid gig in Dublin in 1986 saw them whoop it up with Eddie Cochran's **'C'mon Everybody'** before hammering into a cathartic version of Bob Dylan's **'Maggie's Farm'**, which was immortalised on the live album of the event. Then they were invited to contribute to Jimmy Iovine's 1987 charity project *A Very Special Christmas,* and turned in an impressively faithful rendition of Phil Spector's **'Christmas (Baby Please Come Home)'**, apparently recorded at a soundcheck. And that was followed by a wonderfully spunky version of Woody Guthrie's **'Jesus Christ'** that appeared on *A Vision Shared,* a compilation that was dedicated to the songs of Guthrie and Leadbelly. It sounded like The Pogues, in rollicking form. "I guess so," Bono acknowledges. "I think it's in the nature of the song to come out like that."

However, *Rattle and Hum* saw the band stretching out musically, and experimenting with collaborations and cover versions to an even greater extent, working with Dylan, BB King, The Memphis Horns and the New Voices of Freedom, and performing songs by Dylan and The Beatles, among others.

The added confidence which that experience generated encouraged them further down an avenue that offers its own particular appeal for any band. In the post-*Rattle and Hum* phase, it occurred to U2 that, rather than feeling obliged to put sometimes weaker original ideas into the public domain, they might have more fun going down the covers route. In theory, they could then rely, at least, on the songs being strong.

"Every single, we were doing two B-sides," The Edge recalls, "and so

we thought we'd double up. Rather than having to do two original songs, we felt that including one original cover version would be more interesting." And so it proved, although the versions were often shambolic, with the fun factor clearly to the fore.

Patti Smith's **'Dancing Barefoot'** – the companion to 'When Love Comes to Town' in 1989 – was The Edge's choice and they played it fairly straight and grungy, in an unaffected tribute to a woman whose stream-of-consciousness poetry and intense, cathartic rock'n'roll had been a huge influence on the band during the late '70s.

Recorded in STS Studios in Dublin, **'Unchained Melody'** was Bono's idea, but U2 add nothing to a classic song, in a version that's perversely ordinary. Their cover of The Love Affair's **'Everlasting Love'**, which accompanied 'Unchained Melody' on the back of 'All I Want Is You', is scarcely better. You get the distinct impression that it was more fun to play than it is to listen to, harking back as it must to someone's childhood memories of pop heaven.

The *Red Hot and Blue* album of Cole Porter covers, for AIDS charities, offered the opportunity to don another kind of apparel. The album was being co-ordinated by Steve Lillywhite, and he chose **'Night and Day'** for U2, with Bono cast in the role of uneasy cabaret artiste; with the vital assistance of Paul Barrett from STS, they recorded a smouldering version in The Edge's basement in June of 1990. It was light years ahead of their previous attempts at this kind of material.

'Night And Day' was notable also for The Edge's use of infinite guitar, an invention of the composer Michael Brook that never got past the prototype stage. "Everyone knows what feedback is," The Edge explains. "But instead of acoustic feedback, with the infinite guitar, it's like kinetic feedback. As soon as you depress the string on the front it starts to vibrate and you get the note. Any note you press will just start to sing and will sustain at an even level for as long as you hold your finger down. So it turns the guitar into a kind of organ." (There are only three infinite guitars in existence and they're owned by Michael Brook, The Edge and Daniel Lanois.)

Achtung Baby was released in 1991. The band had been throwing the idea of the massive *Zoo TV* live production around for a while before the album hit the streets, and The Edge thought that **'Satellite of Love'** might have some special relevance in that context. They got a compelling version down pretty fast; it was their kind of noise. "I just thought it was a great song," Edge says, "but we also saw the possibility of making

a visual feature of it in the show. Pete Williams came up with the idea that the car – the Trabant – would be like the satellite and we would perform it under the car for the indoor shows." Live it worked remarkably well as a duet, with Reed's performance pre-recorded and shown on the television screen, giving it an eerie futuristic quality.

Their other *Achtung Baby*-era covers were less successful. An unremarkable version of the Rolling Stones' **'Paint It Black'** appeared as the B-side of the 'Who's Gonna Ride Your Wild Horses?' 7-inch, though it came alive on stage when a snatch of it was slipped into 'Bad'. And the 12-inch carried a cover of Creedence Clearwater Revival's **'Fortunate Son'**. "It was a great lyric, that, and a great song," The Edge says diplomatically. "But it was difficult for us. Some styles work and some don't."

You never know until you do 'em either. Certainly it would have been a brave pundit who'd have forecast that Bono banging away on a rhythm machine and Paul Barrett on keyboards could combine to provide such a bizarrely effective backing to Bono's hugely idiosyncratic and strangely moving take on the Presley classic **'Can't Help Falling in Love'.** It appeared on another CD version of 'Who's Gonna Ride Your Wild Horses?'.

And then there was Bono's collaboration with Frank Sinatra on **'I've Got You Under My Skin'**, which appeared first on Sinatra's *Duets* album. "That was sent over as a finished track for Bono to work on," The Edge says. "I didn't like the album, but that was one of the best things on it." In the U2 canon, it was included on the reverse of the 'Stay (Faraway So Close)' single, released in November 1993.

U2 had already signalled their respect for John Lennon by recording 'God Part II' on *Rattle and Hum.* **'Happiness Is a Warm Gun'** appearing on the 'Last Night On Earth' CD single is another slab of a version that grunges along in murky terrain. A curiosity, it never gets to a pitch where you can really see the point of the exercise.

'Pop Muzik' which follows it on the same single is a different matter entirely. The backing track with which the U2 show opened throughout the Popmart tour, it's a propulsive monster of a groove, that's undoubtedly one of U2's best dance moments. A hit for M – the alias for writer Robin Scott – in 1979, U2 bring a far bigger and weightier feel to what had originally been a clever and catchy little tune. An essential part of the canon.

1960

MARCH 13: Adam Clayton born in Chinnor, Oxfordshire.
MAY 6: American U2 spy plane shot down in the Soviet Union.
MAY 10: Paul Hewson born in the Rotunda Hospital, Dublin.

1961

AUGUST 8: Dave Evans born in Barking Maternity Hospital, east London.
OCTOBER 31: Larry Mullen Jr. born in Artane, Dublin.

1972

JANUARY 30: British paratroopers shoot dead 13 Catholic demonstrators at a civil rights march in Derry, Northern Ireland ('Bloody Sunday').

1974

SEPTEMBER: Iris Hewson dies of a brain haemorrhage four days after collapsing at her own father's funeral.

1976

AUTUMN: As Feedback, Paul Hewson, Dik and Dave Evans, Larry Mullen Jr and Adam Clayton play their debut gig at Dublin's Mount Temple Comprehensive School. The highlight of their messy 10-minute set is a cover of Peter Frampton's 'Show Me the Way'. They later become The Hype.

1978

MARCH 17: On St. Patrick's Day The Hype win £500 and some studio time at a Limerick talent contest sponsored by Harp Lager, Evening Press and CBS Records. Jackie Hayden of CBS Ireland, and later of Hot Press, is among the judges.
MARCH 20: At the suggestion of Steve Averill, lead singer with seminal Irish band The Radiators From Space, The Hype change their name to U2. Dik Evans leaves the band following a farewell gig at Howth Community Centre.
APRIL 28: Bill Graham writes first ever U2 interview in Hot Press under the heading "Yep! It's U2!"
MAY 25: At Bill Graham's suggestion, Paul McGuinness sees U2 live for the first time at a gig in Dublin's Project Arts Centre and decides to become their manager.
SEPTEMBER 9: U2 support The Stranglers at a gig in the Top Hat ballroom. Playing to 2,500 people, it is their biggest gig to date. They receive a fee of £50.
SEPTEMBER 18: U2 share the bill with The Virgin Prunes at a gig in the Project Arts Centre, then managed by the future filmmaker Jim Sheridan.
NOVEMBER: Larry's mother, Maureen Mullen, is killed in a car crash.
DECEMBER: U2 support The Greedy Bastards, a band made up of members of the Sex Pistols and Thin Lizzy, at the Stardust nightclub in Dublin. Soon afterwards
The Stardust burns down, with the loss of more than
20 lives.

1979

FEBRUARY: Bono borrows some money and travels to London to plug U2 at the offices of various record companies and music magazines.
MAY: U2 play the first of six now legendary afternoon gigs at the Dandelion Market in Dublin.

Organised in a disused car park next to what was known then as the Gaiety Green (beside Stephen's Green), these gigs are intended to expand the band's young fan base, enabling them to reach a crowd often prohibited from other U2 gigs because of Ireland's strict licensing laws.
SEPTEMBER: Their debut record, an EP entitled U2-3, is released in Ireland only, on CBS Records.
OCTOBER 5: U2 make their small-screen debut on RTE at a televised concert in the Opera House in Cork.
OCTOBER 26: U2 feature on the cover of Dublin's Hot Press magazine.
NOVEMBER 1: Chris Westwood writes U2's first cover story outside of Ireland in Record Mirror, a British music paper.
DECEMBER 1: Having borrowed £3,000 from family and friends to finance a short English tour, U2 play their debut London gig as support for The Dolly Mixtures in the Moonlight Club in West Hampstead. In a Sounds magazine review, Dave McCullough writes: "U2 are about four people. Their music has minimum distortion and their songs reflect the strength of the four individuals. There's a kind of naive, rushing feeling about their music."

1980

JANUARY 15: The band perform 'Stories for Boys' live on The Late Late Show. The following week, U2 win five awards in the Hot Press readers' poll, beating both The Boomtown Rats and Thin Lizzy in most categories.
FEBRUARY 26: Their second single 'Another Day' is released in Ireland on CBS and U2 play a sold-out show in Dublin's National Stadium at the end of a tour to promote it. The gig is recorded by RTE for broadcast later in the year.
MARCH 19: U2 share the bill with Berlin and The Virgin Prunes on the third night of the Sense of Ireland festival in the Acklam Hall in London. Many record company executives are present at the gig and four days later U2 sign a major international recording deal with Island Records.
MAY 23: U2's first release for Island, a Martin Hannett-produced single called '11 O'Clock Tick Tock', is released in Ireland and   the UK.
JULY 27: U2 play their debut open-air festival in front of a 15,000 strong audience at Leixlip Castle in Kildare. The Police top a bill which also includes Squeeze and   Q-Tips.
SEPTEMBER 6: Having finished recording their debut album with Steve Lillywhite in Dublin's Windmill Lane Studios, U2 kick off a lengthy British tour, with a gig in the General Woolfe in Coventry.
SEPTEMBER 7: U2 support Echo & The Bunnymen in London's Lyceum Ballroom.
OCTOBER 14: The band's first performance in mainland Europe happens before a small audience in the KRO Studios in Hilversum, Holland. The show is broadcast on Dutch radio the following day, to coincide with a gig in The Milkyway in Amsterdam.
OCTOBER 20: U2's debut album, Boy, is released in Ireland and the UK. It eventually peaks at No. 52 in the British charts.
DECEMBER 3: U2 play the last of three support gigs with Talking Heads at the Baltard Pavilion in Paris.
DECEMBER 6: U2 play their debut American gig at The Ritz in New York. The head of Premier Talent, Frank Barsalona, is in the audience and later he signs the band to his agency's roster.
DECEMBER 8: John Lennon is shot dead outside his apartment building in New York.
DECEMBER 9: U2 play at the El Mocambo in Toronto. The gig receives ecstatic reviews in the Canadian press.

1981

JANUARY: U2 and Stiff Little Fingers perform together in Belfast's Queen's University for a BBC Northern Ireland TV special. Four songs from their set are eventually broadcast on August 12. Towards the end of the month they embark on a short UK tour, with Altered Images supporting.
FEBRUARY 9: U2 perform two songs live on Swedish TV's Mandagsborsen show.
FEBRUARY 28: The band perform three songs on BBC's longest-running rock show, The Old Grey Whistle Test.
MARCH 3: Boy is released in America and U2 begin a support tour over there with a gig in the Bayou Club in Washington. In his review for The Washington Post Harry Sumrall writes: "U2, like The Police and The Clash, are taking New Wave to the next, higher, musical level. Their music is still simple, but never simplistic – and simply marvellous."
AUGUST 16: U2 play their only Irish gig of the year alongside Thin Lizzy and Hazel O'Connor at Slane Castle in Co. Meath.
OCTOBER 12: U2's second album October is released. It enters the British charts at No. 11.

1982

MARCH 3: U2 play the first of 14 support dates with the J. Geils Band in the Lee County Arena at Fort Meyers in Florida.
JULY 18: Members of U2 play alongside Rory Gallagher, Philip Lynott, Paul Brady and other leading Irish rock 'n' rollers at a festival in Punchestown Racecourse, Dublin, organised by Hot Press to celebrate its fifth anniversary.
AUGUST 8: U2 begin working with Steve Lillywhite on their third album in Windmill Lane Studios, Dublin.
AUGUST 21: Bono marries childhood sweetheart Alison Stewart at a ceremony in Raheny, Dublin.
DECEMBER 1: Having finished recording, the band break a long silence on the live front with a sold-out gig in Tiffany's, Glasgow.

1983

FEBRUARY 26: The War tour kicks off with a sold-out gig at the Caird Hall in Dundee, Scotland.
FEBRUARY 28: U2's third album, War, is released and goes to No. 1 in the UK.
MARCH 31: U2 perform 'Two Hearts Beat as One' on Top of the Pops.
APRIL 23: U2 kick off an American tour in Kenan Stadium, Chapel Hill, North Carolina.
JUNE 5: U2 play the Red Rocks amphitheatre in Denver. Despite adverse weather conditions, more than 9,000 fans show up. The gig is recorded and later released on video. Some tracks also appear on the live mini-album Under a Blood Red Sky, released later in 1983.
JULY: The Edge marries Aislinn O'Sullivan.
AUGUST 14: Bono's father, Robert Hewson, makes his first appearance on a U2 stage when he gets pulled up in front of 20,000 people at a gig in the Phoenix Park Racecourse in Dublin.
NOVEMBER: The mini-album Under a Blood Red Sky is released.
NOVEMBER 22: U2 play their debut Japanese gig at the Festival Hall in Osaka.
DECEMBER: U2 are voted 'Band Of The Year' in the Rolling Stone writers' poll.

1984

MAY 7: U2 hole up in Slane Castle, Co. Meath, to record with new producers Brian Eno and Daniel Lanois. Four weeks later they move back to Windmill Lane Studios to complete work on their fourth studio album.
AUGUST 1: Mother Records is established by the band as an outlet for new Irish talent.
AUGUST 5: U2 finish work on the album.
JULY 8: Bono joins Bob Dylan on stage at an open-air concert in the grounds of Slane Castle. He sings along on 'Leopard Skin Pillbox Hat' and 'Blowing in the Wind' (despite not knowing the lyrics). He also interviews Dylan and Van Morrison for   Hot Press.
AUGUST 29: U2 play the first of four gigs in New Zealand at the Christchurch Town Hall.
OCTOBER 1: The Unforgettable Fire is released worldwide.
DECEMBER 1: U2 begin the American leg of The Unforgettable Fire tour at the Tower Theatre in Philadelphia. Support is provided by The Waterboys.

1985

JANUARY 5: Bono joins Jim Kerr and Simple Minds onstage at the Barrowlands in Glasgow. They duet on Al Green's 'Take Me to the River' and The Doors' 'Light My Fire'
FEBRUARY: Sales of The Unforgettable Fire pass the million mark.
APRIL 1: U2 sell out Madison Square Garden in New York. A large Irish press contingent is present and the band use the opportunity to announce that they will play their most ambitious stadium gig yet in Croke Park, Dublin, on June 29.
MAY: Wide Awake in America is released.
JULY 13: Following an introduction by Jack Nicholson, U2 steal the show at Live Aid in Wembley Stadium, London, with a set that includes a stunning ten-minute version of 'Bad'. Their album and concert ticket sales treble over the next few months.

1986

JANUARY 30: Larry and Bono give the band's first major interview in several months to RTE's TV Gaga.
MAY 17: U2 play their only European date of 1986 at the Self Aid festival in the RDS Showgrounds, Dublin. Much controversy is generated when In Dublin magazine runs a highly critical story entitled 'The Great Self Aid Farce – Rock Against The People', using a shot of Bono on the cover.
JUNE 4: U2 join Peter Gabriel, Sting, The Neville Brothers, Joan Baez, Bryan Adams, Lou Reed and Jackson Brown at the Cow Palace, California, for the first date of the Conspiracy of Hope tour in aid of Amnesty International.
JULY 3: U2 crew member Greg Carroll is killed in a motorcycle accident in Dublin.
JULY 8: Carroll is buried at Kai-lwi Marae in New Zealand. Bono and Larry attend the funeral with Ali and Ann Acherson. U2 crew members Joe O'Herlihy and Steve Iredale are also present. Bono reads a poem during the service and later, at the traditional 'last supper', 'Knocking on Heaven's Door' and 'Let It Be'. When he returns to Dublin he writes the song 'One Tree Hill' for Carroll.
AUGUST 1: Recording sessions for The Joshua Tree begin in Dublin.
AUGUST 26: Robbie Robertson

203

chronology

arrives in Dublin to record two tracks with U2 for his debut solo album.

AUTUMN: Bono visits El Salvador and Nicaragua on the invitation of Rene Castro. His experiences there will form the basis of many of the songs on U2's forthcoming album ('Bullet the Blue Sky' etc.)

1987

MARCH: U2 perform the Peggy Seeger song 'Springhill Mining Disaster' on *The Late Late Show*'s 25th Anniversary tribute to The Dubliners.

MARCH 9: *The Joshua Tree* is released and quickly goes to No. 1 worldwide.

MARCH 27: U2 perform an impromptu gig on the roof of a liquor store in downtown Los Angeles to film a video for 'Where the Streets Have No Name'.

APRIL 2: *The Joshua Tree* tour begins with a gig at the State University Activity Centre in Tempe, Arizona.

APRIL 27: U2 become the third rock band to appear on the cover of *Time* magazine. Only The Beatles and The Who had been there before them.

MAY: Sales of *The Joshua Tree* pass seven million.

JUNE 27: Irish DJ Dave Fanning introduces U2 to a capacity crowd for U2's homecoming gig at Croke Park Stadium, Dublin.

NOVEMBER 8: An IRA bomb explodes in Enniskillen, Northern Ireland, killing 13 people. Onstage at the McNichols Arena in Denver, Bono launches an emotional attack on paramilitaries in Northern Ireland before the band perform a highly-charged version of 'Sunday Bloody Sunday'. The scene winds up in the *Rattle and Hum* movie.

NOVEMBER 11: U2 play an impromptu free gig to 'Save the Yuppie' in front of 20,000 people at the Justin Herman Plaza in San Francisco. During the show Bono spray-paints 'ROCK & ROLL STOPS THE TRAFFIC' on the nearby Vaillancourt Fountain, an act which outrages mayor Diane Feinstein. Bono is summoned to appear in San Francisco Municipal Court on December 16. A week later all charges are dropped. Feinstein loses the next election.

NOVEMBER 24: B.B. King supports U2 at a gig in the Tarrant County Convention Centre in Fort Worth, Texas.

1988

FEBRUARY: U2 move to Los Angeles to begin working with young director Phil Joanou on the *Rattle and Hum* movie. More than 160 hours of concert and documentary footage are studied, before being edited down to a 90-minute movie. While there, U2 also records some new songs at A&M Studios and STS Studios.

MARCH 2: U2 win 'Best Vocal of the Year' for 'I Still Haven't Found What I'm Looking For' and 'Album of the Year' for *The Joshua Tree* at the Grammy Awards.

MAY: U2 record some extra material for the movie in Dublin's Point Depot.

JUNE 7: Roy Orbison, for whom Bono and The Edge had recently written 'She's a Mystery to Me', dies in the US, before the release of his *Mystery Girl* album.

OCTOBER 10: The *Rattle and Hum* album is released.

OCTOBER 27: World premier of the *Rattle and Hum* movie at the Savoy Cinema on Dublin's O'Connell Street. More than 5,000 people gather outside the cinema to hear the band perform a short four-song set.

NOVEMBER: The Edge joins Bryan Ferry onstage for a surprise appearance in the RDS, Simmonscourt in Dublin.

1989

APRIL 27: Ex-Virgin Prune Gavin Friday launches his debut solo album *Each Man Kills The Thing He Loves* in Dublin's Pink Elephant nightclub. Bono joins him on stage for a version of Queen's 'We Are the Champions'.

APRIL 30: Bono makes his first live solo appearance at a fundraising event in the Abbey Theatre in Dublin, singing his own musical adaptations of two poems by William Butler Yeats.

JUNE 4: Bono joins Bob Dylan on stage for a version of 'Maggie's Farm' in the RDS, Simmonscourt.

AUGUST 6: Adam Clayton is arrested in Dublin on minor drug charges. He is later ordered to pay £25,000 to The Women's Aid Refuge Centre by a District Judge.

SEPTEMBER 21: The *Lovetown* tour kicks off in Australia, with the first of three sold-out gigs in the Perth Entertainment Centre. The Australian band Weddings Parties Anything and B.B. King support.

DECEMBER 31: After months of non-stop touring, U2 play the last of four packed nights in Dublin's Point Depot. At the end of the gig Bono announces their intention to go away and "dream it all up again". The show is broadcast, on radio, to upwards of 300 million people all over the world.

1990

JUNE 20: Bono joins David Bowie on stage at a gig in the Richfield Coliseum in Cleveland, Ohio.

NOVEMBER: U2 begin recording their new album with Daniel Lanois producing in Berlin's Hansa Studios. Brian Eno later joins them to help with the production.

1991

MARCH: U2 return to Dublin for further recording at STS and Windmill Lane Studios.

NOVEMBER 18: U2's seventh album *Achtung Baby* is released to widespread critical acclaim.

1992

JANUARY 15: The Edge joins Keith Richards, Neil Young and Jimmy Page for a version of 'Big River' at the New York Waldorf-Astoria. He had been invited there to induct The Yardbirds into the Rock & Roll Hall of Fame.

FEBRUARY 27: U2 record a live version of 'One' from a soundcheck in Florida for broadcast on *Top of the Pops*.

FEBRUARY 29: The *Zoo TV* tour kicks off with a gig at the Lakeland Arena in Florida. Support is by The Pixies.

MARCH 27: Bono orders 10,000 pizzas for the audience at a gig in Detroit. Speedy Pizzas eventually manage to deliver 100.

MAY 7: The European leg of the *Zoo TV* tour opens with a gig in the Palais Omnisports De Bercy Centre in Paris. Support is by Fatima Mansions.

JUNE 19: U2 play alongside Kraftwerk, Public Enemy and Big Audio Dynamite II at the 'Stop Sellafield' show in the G-Mex Centre in Manchester.

AUGUST 1: The Outside Broadcast leg of the *Zoo TV* tour opens with a gig in the Hersheypark Stadium in Hershey, Pennsylvania.

AUGUST 28: During a New York interview with Dave Herman for *Rockline* (a syndicated radio broadcast on some 300 local stations across America), US Presidential candidate Bill Clinton contacts U2 live on air.

DECEMBER: Adam Clayton participates in a tribute

on RTE's *The Late Late Show* for Sharon Shannon, an Irish traditional musician.

1993

JANUARY 20: Larry and Adam team up with REM's Michael Stipe and Mike Mills in Washington for a performance of 'One' at the MTV 1993 Rock & Roll Inaugural Ball for newly elected American President Bill Clinton.

FEBRUARY: U2 begin to record new material in Dublin.

MAY 10: Bono celebrates his 33rd birthday onstage at a sold-out gig in the Feyenoord Stadium in Rotterdam. Galway theatre group Macnas perform an anti-Fascist play before U2 take the stage.

JULY 5: The *Zooropa* album is released worldwide.

AUGUST 11: Controversial author Salman Rushdie joins U2 on stage in front of 70,000 people in London's Wembley Stadium.

SEPTEMBER 3: The Edge makes his first ever solo appearance at the MTV Awards in Los Angeles, where he performs 'Numb' in front of a mini-version of the *Zoo TV* set.

OCTOBER 1: U2 play a version of Thin Lizzy's 'The Boys Are Back in Town' at Gavin Friday's wedding reception in the Clarence Hotel in Dublin (which they'd recently purchased).

NOVEMBER: Bono records the vocal for his duet with Frank Sinatra 'I've Got You Under My Skin' in a Dublin studio.

NOVEMBER 12: The final leg of the tour – dubbed Zoomerang – opens with a gig in the Melbourne Cricket Ground.

DECEMBER 10: U2 play the final gig of the *Zoo TV* tour at the Tokyo Dome in Japan. Support is by Big Audio Dynamite II.

1994

JANUARY 19: Bono inducts Rita Marley into The Rock & Roll Hall of Fame in New York's Waldorf Astoria Hotel.

FEBRUARY: U2 issue a writ challenging the Performing Rights Society on their exclusive right to collect songwriting royalties for performances of songs.

MARCH: Author Charles Bukowski dies of leukaemia in Los Angeles.

MARCH: *Zooropa* wins the 'Best Alternative Album' award at the Grammys.

APRIL: Larry Mullen and Adam Clayton record four tracks with Nanci Griffith for her *Flyer* album.

APRIL 5: The *Live In Sydney* video is released in Europe.

NOVEMBER: U2 and Brian Eno spend two weeks recording new material in a West London recording studio.

1995

FEBRUARY: Bono and The Edge team up with veteran Irish songwriter Christy Moore to record 'North and South of the River' in Dublin's Windmill Lane Studios. Produced by Steve Lillywhite, the track is available in Ireland only.

MARCH 30: Bono joins Prince for some parts of 'The Cross' at his after-show performance in Dublin's PoD nightclub.

APRIL: Bono introduces a reading by Beat poet Allen Ginsberg at the Cúirt Festival Of Literature in Galway.

SUMMER: U2, Eno, Howie B. and other Passengers spend five weeks recording in Dublin.

JUNE 1: U2 release their first single of the year, 'Hold Me, Thrill Me, Kiss Me, Kill Me', a track that features in the *Batman Forever* soundtrack. It goes to No. 2 in the UK, No. 16 in America and No. 1 in Australia and Ireland.

JUNE 18: U2 give their first major interview in two years to Liam Mackey of *The X-Press*, a rebel organ launched by journalists who had found themselves unemployed when The Irish Press Group closed down. It is later reprinted in *Hot Press*.

SEPTEMBER 12: Bono, The Edge and Brian Eno premier 'Miss Sarajevo' at the annual Pavarotti And Friends concert in Modena, Italy.

NOVEMBER 6: Passengers' *Original Soundtracks 1* is released worldwide. On the same day, Tina Turner releases 'Goldeneye' – the theme to the new 007 movie, written by Bono and The Edge – on Capitol Records.

1996

JANUARY: U2 begin working on a new album in Dublin.

APRIL: The band relocate to Miami for further work on the album.

MAY 1: Adam and Larry release their version of the *Mission Impossible* theme track. It goes Top 10 in the US, the UK and numerous other territories.

MAY 11: *Hot Press* journalist Bill Graham dies suddenly at his home in Howth. The band fly back to Dublin from America to attend the funeral, where Bono performs a moving version of Leonard Cohen's 'Tower of Song'. Gavin Friday, Simon Carmody, Liam O'Maonlaí, Maire Brennan and Martin Hayes are among the many artists who play at the service.

JULY: The first deadline to finish *Pop* is missed. Release date put back.

SEPTEMBER: Second deadline missed. The decision not to release album till 1997 follows soon afterwards.

1997

JANUARY: Early snippets from *Pop* are made available via the internet. No-one is sure who is responsible.

FEBRUARY: 'Discothèque' single is finally released and goes straight to No. 1 in 13 countries. Later on in the month, on Ash Wednesday, U2 launch the *Pop* album and the Pop-Mart tour in the salubrious surrounding of the K-Mart supermarket in Manhattan. *Pop* is widely acclaimed as their finest album to date.

MAY: U2's PopMart tour opens in Las Vegas.

AUGUST: Following objections from residents in the area, Ireland's Supreme Court finally clears the way for U2 to play back-to-back concerts at Lansdowne Road in Dublin.

OCTOBER: Bono makes good his 1995 promise to the people of the city as U2 play to 45,000 in Sarajevo.

1998

APRIL: The band bring the final leg of PopMart to a close with a 67,000 sell-out show at the Johannesburg Stadium in South Africa.

MAY: U2 receive the ultimate accolade: an appearance in *The Simpsons*, during which Homer interrupts their concert in Springfield to tell the crowd – via the giant screen – that he should be the town's next sanitation commissioner.

OCTOBER: U2, along with Ash, The Divine Comedy, Van Morrison, Boyzone, The Corrs, Sinead O' Connor, The Cranberries and others, are featured on a new album that will benefit victims of the Omagh bomb in Northern Ireland.

NOVEMBER: The newly released compilation *The Best of U2 1980–1990* yields a smash hit single in the form of the reworked 'Sweetest Thing'.

1999

JANUARY: U2 begin work on new studio album in Dublin.
JULY: Bono adds verses and vocals to 'Slide Away', a track Michael Hutchence of INXS left unfinished before his death.
SEPTEMBER: Bono, Bob Geldof and Quincy Jones meet the The Pope on behalf of Jubilee 2000.
OCTOBER: Following the MTV Europe Awards show in Dublin, Bono joins Marilyn Manson and Iggy Pop onstage at the latter's gig across town in HQ.
The Bono/Wyclef Jean collaboration 'New Day' closes the NetAid gigs in New York, London and Geneva.

2000

FEBRUARY: Recording of the band's new album is put on hold as Bono travels to the Berlin Film Festival for the world premiere of *Million Dollar Hotel*, a movie written by the singer, directed by Wim Wenders and starring Mel Gibson.
MARCH: Soundtrack to *Million Dollar Hotel* released. U2 are granted the Freedom of the City of Dublin in a ceremony in the city's new Smithfield Plaza. The band mark the occasion with a short, open-air unplugged set for an audience of thousands of their hometown fans.
AUGUST: *Propaganda*, the official U2 fanzine, gives away 50,000 copies of *Hasta La Vista*, a live album recorded in Mexico on the *Popmart* tour.
SEPTEMBER: As part of his on-going Jubilee 2000 campaign in support of Third World countries, Bono delivers a 'Drop the Debt' petition to UN Secretary General Kofi Annan in New York.
OCTOBER: U2 take to the roof of the Clarence Hotel in Dublin to play their new 'Beautiful Day' single for *Top of the Pops*. U2 release their new album *All That You Can't Leave Behind*. 'Beautiful Day' debuts at Number One in the UK Singles chart.
DECEMBER: *All That You Can't Leave Behind* is banned by the Burmese Government. The album contains a track, 'Walk On', which is dedicated to the imprisoned opposition leader Aung San Suu Kyi.

2001

FEBRUARY: The band pick up an Outstanding Contribution to Music gong at the Brit Awards in London. Past recipients include David Bowie, Van Morrison, Queen, Eurythmics, Spice Girls, Rod Stewart and The Who.
MARCH: U2 open their 'Elevation' tour in Miami, Florida. The band win three awards at the 43rd Grammy Awards in Los Angeles. 80,000 tickets for U2's August Slane Castle show in Ireland – the 20th anniversary of their first appearance at the festival as a support act – are snapped up in 45 minutes. A second show is mooted.

SEPTEMBER: U2 and other big names in music and film took part in a show that raised $150 million for victims of the terrorist attacks in New York and Washington.

2002

FEBRUARY: Befitting U2's status as global megastars, they are the chosen act to perform live during the half time interval at Super Bowl XXXVI – traditionally the biggest TV event of the American calendar, with 130 million watching in the US, and 800 million globally.
MARCH: Wearing his trademark shades throughout, Bono has an audience with George Bush at the White House to discuss his campaign to fight against world poverty.
NOVEMBER: A new greatest hits compilation is released: *U2 – The Best Of 1990 – 2000*.

2003

JANUARY: U2 declare that they have started work on their next album.
JUNE: U2 win a Golden Globe for their contribution to Martin Scorsese's *The Gangs of New York*, 'The Hands That Built America'. Bono causes outrage in some quarters by describing the gong, on air, as 'really, really fucking brilliant'.

2004

JUNE: Bono takes more time out from the studio, and is back on the world stage addressing a summit of EU leaders in Dublin to present his views on aid development in Africa.
SEPTEMBER: Bono tells the UK government to 'get real' at the Labour Party Conference in Brighton.
NOVEMBER: U2 are inducted into the UK Rock and Roll Hall of Fame. The band's long-awaited 11th studio album, *How to Dismantle an Atomic Bomb*, hits the shelves and goes straight to No. 1 in the UK album chart.

2005

FEBRUARY: U2 win three Grammies for 'Vertigo', bringing the grand total up to 16 during their career.
MARCH: U2 are inducted into the Rock and Roll Hall of Fame in New York. The first leg of their world tour kicks off in San Diego.

discography

ALBUMS

boy

Release date: October 1980
Catalogue number: ILPS 9646
Producer: Steve Lillywhite
Track listing: I Will Follow/Twilight/ Into the Heart/Out of Control/ Stories for Boys/The Ocean/A Day Without Me/Another Time, Another Place/The Electric Co./ Shadows and Tall Trees.
Highest Chart Position: No. 52

october

Release date: October 1981
Catalogue number: ILPS 9680
Producer: Steve Lillywhite
Track listing: Gloria/I Fall Down/I Threw a Brick Through a Window/ Rejoice/Fire/Tomorrow/October/ With a Shout/Stranger in a Strange Land/Scarlet/Is That All?
Highest Chart Position: No. 11

war

Release date: March 1983
Catalogue number: ILPS 9733
Producer: Steve Lillywhite
Track listing: Sunday Bloody Sunday/ Seconds/New Year's Day/Like a Song/Drowning Man/The Refugee/Two Hearts Beat as One/ Red Light/Surrender/40.
Highest Chart Position: No. 1

the unforgettable fire

Release date: October 1984
Catalogue number: U25
Producer: Brian Eno/Daniel Lanois
Track listing: A Sort of Homecoming/ Pride/Wire/The Unforgettable Fire/Promenade/4th of July/Bad/Indian Summer Sky/ Elvis Presley and America/MLK.
Highest Chart Position: No. 1

the joshua tree

Release date: March 1987
Catalogue number: U26
Producer: Daniel Lanois/Brian Eno
Track listing: Where the Streets Have No Name/I Still Haven't Found What I'm Looking For/With or Without You/Bullet the Blue Sky/ Running to Stand Still/Red Hill Mining Town/In God's Country/ Trip Through Your Wires/One Tree Hill/ Exit/Mothers of the Disappeared.
Highest Chart Position: No. 1

rattle and hum

Release date: October 1988
Catalogue number: U27
Producer: Jimmy Iovine
Track listing: Helter Skelter/Van Diemen's Land/Desire/Hawkmoon 269/All Along the Watchtower/ I Still Haven't Found What I'm Looking For/Freedom for My People/Silver and Gold/Pride (In the Name of Love/Angel of Harlem/Love Rescue Me/When Love Comes to Town/Heartland/ God Part II/The Star Spangled Banner/Bullet the Blue Sky/All I Want Is You.

achtung baby

Release date: November 1991
Catalogue number: U28
Producer: Daniel Lanois, with special thanks to Brian Eno
Track listing: Zoo Station/Even Better than the Real Thing/One/ Until the End of the World/Who's Gonna Ride Your Wild Horses?/ So Cruel/The Fly/Mysterious Ways/Tryin' To Throw Your Arms Around The World/Ultraviolet (Light My Way)/Acrobat/Love Is Blindness.
Highest Chart Position: No. 1

zooropa

Release date: July 1993
Catalogue number: U29
Producer: Flood, Brian Eno & The Edge
Track listing: Zooropa/Babyface/ Numb/Lemon/Stay (Faraway, So Close)/Daddy's Gonna Pay for Your Crashed Car/Some Days Are Better than Others/The First Time/Dirty Day/ The Wanderer.
Highest Chart Position: No. 1

melon

Release date: Spring 1995
Catalogue number: MELONCD1
Producer: Various
Track listing: Lemon (The Perfecto Mix)/Salome (Zooromancer Mix)/ Numb (Gimme Some More Dignity Mix)/ Mysterious Ways (The Perfecto Mix)/ Stay (Underdog Mix)/Numb (The Soul Assassins Mix)/Mysterious Ways (remixed by Massive Attack)/ Even Better than the Real Thing (The Perfecto Mix)/Lemon (Bad Yard Club Mix).
Not a commercial release, Melon is a compilation of remixes only available to members of Propaganda fan club.

pop

Release date: 3rd March 1997.
Catalogue number: CIDU210/524334-2
Producer: Flood.
Additional Production: Steve Osborne, Howie B.
Track listing: Discothèque/Do You Feel Loved/Mofo/If God Will Send His Angels/Staring At The Sun/Last Night On Earth/Gone/Miami/The Playboy Mansion/If You Wear That Velvet Dress/Please/Wake Up Dead Man.

U2: the best of 1980-1990

Release date: November 1998
Catalogue number: U211
Producer: Flood
Additional production: Howie B, Steve Osborne
Track listing: Pride (In The Name of Love)/ New Year's Day/With or Without You/I Still Haven't Found What I'm Looking For/Sunday Bloody Sunday/Bad/Where the Streets Have No Name/I Will Follow/The Unforgettable Fire/Sweetest Thing/Desire/When Love Comes to Town/Angel of Harlem/All I Want Is You
Highest Chart Pos: No.1

hasta la vista baby!
U2 live from mexico

Release date: Summer 2000
Catalogue number: HASTACD1
Sound Engineer: Joe O'Herlihy
Sound Supervisors: Flood and Howie B
Track listing: Pop Muzik/MoFo/I Will Follow/Gone/New Year's Day/Staring at the Sun/Bullet the Blue Sky/Please/Where the Streets Have No Name/Lemon (Perfecto Mix)/Discotheque/With or Without You/Hold Me, Thrill Me, Kiss Me, Kill Me/ One
Not a commercial release, Hasta La Vista Baby is a live recording from Foro Sol Autodromo, Mexico City on 3 December 1997 during the PopMart Tour. It is only available to members of OEPropaganda fan club.

all that you can't leave behind

Release date: October 2000
Catalogue number: U212
Producers: Daniel Lanois and Brian Eno
Additional production: Steve Lillywhite, Mike Hedges, Richard Stannard and Julian Gallagher
Track listing: Beautiful Day/Stuck in a Moment You Can't Get Out Of/Elevation/Walk On/Kite/In a Little While/Wild Honey/Peace on Earth/When I Look at the World/New York/Grace/The Ground Beneath Her Feet
Highest Chart Position: No.1

U2: the best of 1990-2000

Release date: November 2002
Catalogue number: CIDU213
Track listing: Even Better Than The Real Thing/Mysterious Ways/Beautiful Day/Electrical Storm/One/Miss Sarajevo/Stay (Faraway, So Close!)/ Stuck In A Moment You Can't Get Out Of/Gone/Until The End Of The World/The Hands That Build America/ Discothèque/ Hold Me, Thrill Me, Kiss Me, Kill Me/Staring At The Sun/ Numb/ The First Time.
Highest Chart Position: No.2

discography

how to diamantle an atomic bomb

Release date: November 2004
Catalogue number: CIDU214
Producer: Steve Lillywhite
Track listing: Vertigo/ Miracle Drug /Sometimes You Can't Make it On Your Own /Love And Peace Or Else /City Of Blinding Lights /All Because Of You /A Man and A Woman/Crumbs From Your Table /One Step Closer /Original Of The Species /Yahweh.
Highest Chart Position: No.1

MINI-ALBUMS

under a blood red sky

Release date: November 1983
Catalogue number: IMA 3
Producer: Jimmy Iovine
Mixed by: Shelly Yakus
Track listing: Gloria/11 O'Clock Tick Tock/I Will Follow/Party Girl/ Sunday Bloody Sunday/The Electric Co./New Year's Day/40.
Highest Chart Position: No. 1

wide awake in america

Release date: US May 1985
UK (CD only) October 1987
Catalogue number: US 90279 UK CIDU22
Producers: U2, Brian Eno/Daniel Lanois, Tony Visconti
Track listing: Bad (live)/A Sort of Homecoming (live)/The Three Sunrises/Love Comes Tumbling.

SINGLES

U23

Release date: September 1979 (Ireland only)
Catalogue number: CBS 7951
Producer: Chas deWhalley/U2
Tracks: Out of Control/Stories for Boys/Boy-Girl

another day

Release date: February 1980 (Ireland only)
Catalogue number: CBS 8306
Producer: Chas deWhalley
Tracks: Another Day/Twilight

11 o'clock tick tock

Release date: May 1980
Catalogue number: Island WIP 6601
Producer: Martin Hannett
Tracks: 11 O'Clock Tick Tock/Touch

a day without me

Release date: August 1980
Catalogue number: WIP 6630
Producer: Steve Lillywhite
Tracks: A Day Without Me/Things to Make and Do

i will follow

Release date: October 1980
Catalogue number: WIP 6656
Producer: Steve Lillywhite

fire

Release date: June 1981
Catalogue number: WIP 6679
Producer: Steve Lillywhite
Tracks: Fire/J. Swallow;
12-inch: 11 O'Clock Tick Tock/ The Ocean (live) 7-inch double pack: Cry/The Electric Co./11 O'Clock Tick Tock (live)/The Ocean (live)
Highest Chart Position: No. 35

gloria

Release date: October 1981
Catalogue number: WIP 6733
Producer: Steve Lillywhite
Tracks: Gloria/I Will Follow (live)
Highest Chart Position: No. 55

a celebration

Release date: October 1982
Catalogue number: WIP 6770
Producer: Steve Lillywhite
Tracks: A Celebration/Trash Trampoline and the Party Girl
Highest Chart Position: No. 47

new year's day

Release date: January 1983
Catalogue number: WIP 6848
Producer: Steve Lillywhite
Tracks: New Year's Day/Treasure (Whatever Happened to Pete the Chop?); 12-inch & double pack: Fire /I Threw a Brick Through a Window/A Day Without Me (all live)
Highest Chart Position: No. 10

two hearts beat as one

Release date: March 1983
Catalogue number: IS 109
Producer: Steve Lillywhite
Tracks: Two Hearts Beat as One/Endless Deep; 12-inch & double pack: New Year's Day/Two Hearts Beat as One (US remixes)
Highest Chart Position: No. 18

pride (in the name of love)

Release date: September 1984
Catalogue number: IS 202
Producer: Brian Eno/Daniel Lanois
Tracks: Pride/Boomerang; 12-inch:

Boomerang II/4th of July
Highest Chart Position: No. 3

the unforgettable fire

Release date: April 1985
Catalogue number: IS 220
Producer: Brian Eno/Daniel Lanois/ Tony Visconti
Tracks: The Unforgettable Fire/A Sort of Homecoming (live); 12-inch: The Three Sunrises/Bass Trap/Love Comes Tumbling; 7-inch double pack: Love Comes Tumbling/ Sixty Seconds in Kingdom Come
Highest Chart Position: No. 6

with or without you

Release date: March 1987
Catalogue number: IS 319
Producer: Daniel Lanois/Brian Eno
A-side mixed by: Steve Lillywhite
Tracks: With or Without You/ Luminous Times (Hold on to Love); Cass & CD: Walk to the Water
Highest Chart Position: No. 4

i still haven't found what i'm looking for

Release date: May 1987
Catalogue number: IS 340
Producer: Daniel Lanois/Brian Eno
Tracks: I Still Haven't Found What I'm Looking For/Spanish Eyes/ Deep in the Heart
Highest Chart Position: No. 6

where the streets have no name

Release date: August 1987
Catalogue number: IS 340
Producer: Daniel Lanois/Brian Eno
A-side mixed by: Steve Lillywhite
Tracks: Where the Streets Have No Name/Silver and Gold; 12-inch, Cass & CD: Race Against Time
Highest Chart Position: No. 4

in god's country

Release date: November 1987 (US release only)
Catalogue number: 7-99385
Producer: Daniel Lanois/Brian Eno
Tracks: In God's Country/Bullet the Blue Sky; 12-inch & CD: Running to Stand Still
Highest Chart Position: No. 48 (on import)

desire

Release date: September 1988
Catalogue number: IS 400
Producer: Jimmy Iovine
Tracks: Desire/Hallelujah (Here She Comes); 12-inch: Desire (Hollywood Mix); Cass: Love Comes to Town/All I Want Is You

angel of harlem

Release date: December 1988
Catalogue number: IS 402
Producer: Jimmy Iovine
Tracks: Angel of Harlem/A Room at the Heartbreak Hotel; 12-inch & CD: Love Rescue Me (live) featuring Keith Richards and Ziggy Marley & The Melody Makers
Highest Chart Position: No. 9

when love comes to town

Release date: April 1989
Catalogue number: IS 411
Producer: Jimmy Iovine
Tracks: When Love Comes to Town/ Dancing Barefoot; 12-inch: When Love Comes to Town (Live From The Kingdom mix)/God Part II (Hard Metal Dance Mix)
Highest Chart Position: No. 6

all i want is you

Release date: June 1989
Catalogue number: IS 422
Producer: Jimmy Iovine
Tracks: All I Want Is You/ Unchained Melody; 12-inch & CD: Everlasting Love
Highest Chart Position: No. 4

night and day

Release date: December 1990. 12" promo issue only, limited edition. Taken from the Cole Porter tribute album, *Red Hot & Blue*, to benefit AIDS research and relief.
Catalogue number: RHB 1
Producer: The Edge/Paul Barrett.
Remixed by: Youth
Tracks: Night and Day (Twilight Remix)/Night and Day (Steel String Mix)

the fly

Release date: October 1991
Catalogue number: IS 500
Producer: Daniel Lanois
Tracks: The Fly/Alex Descends into Hell for a Bottle of Milk: Korova 1; 12-inch & CD: The Lounge Fly Mix
Highest Chart Position: No. 1

mysterious ways

Release date: December 1991
Catalogue number: IS 509
Producer: Daniel Lanois with Brian Eno
Tracks: Mysterious Ways/Mysterious Ways (Solar Plexus Magic Hour Remix); 12-inch & CD: (Solar Plexus Extended Club Mix)/ (Apollo 440 Magic Hour Remix)/ (Tabla Motown Remix)/(Solar Plexus Club Mix)
Highest Chart Position: No. 13

one

Release date: February 1992
Catalogue number: IS 515

Producer: Daniel Lanois with Brian Eno
Tracks: One/Lady with the Spinning Head (UV1); 12-inch & CD: Satellite Of Love
Highest Chart Position: No. 7

even better than the real thing

Release date: June 1992
Catalogue number: IS 525
Producer: Steve Lillywhite with Brian Eno & Daniel Lanois
Tracks: Even Better than the Real Thing/Salomé; 12-inch & CD: Where Did It All Go Wrong?/Lady with the Spinning Head (Extended Dance Mix)
Highest Chart Position: No. 12

even better than the real thing

Release date: June 1992
Catalogue number: REAL U2
Producer: Steve Lillywhite with Brian Eno & Daniel Lanois
Tracks: 12-inch & CD: Even Better than the Real Thing (The Perfecto Mix)/(Sexy Dub Mix)/(Apollo 440 Stealth Sonic Remix)/(V16 Exit Wound Remix)/(A44 vs U2 Instrumental Remix)
Remixed by: Tracks 1 & 2: Paul Oakenfold & Steve Osborne; tracks 3-5: Apollo 440
Highest Chart Position: No. 8

who's gonna ride your wild horses

Release date: November 1992
Catalogue number: IS 550
Producer: U2/Paul Barrett
Tracks: Who's Gonna Ride Your Wild Horses? (Temple Bar Edit)/Paint It Black; 12-inch & CD: Fortunate Son/Who's Gonna Ride Your Wild Horses? (Temple Bar Remix)
Highest Chart Position: No. 14

numb

Release date: August 1993
Catalogue number: 088 162 3
Producer: Various
Tracks: EP released only on video: *Numb*, directed by Kevin Godley; *Numb (Video Remix)*, directed by Emergency Broadcast Network; *Love Is Blindness*, directed by Matt Mahurin.

lemon

Release date: October 1993. Promo release only.
Catalogue number: 12LEMDJ1
Producer: Flood, Brian Eno, The Edge
Remix and additional production by: David Morales
Tracks: 12-inch: (Bad Yard Club)/ (Momo Beats)/(Version Dub)/ (Serious Def Dub)

stay (faraway so close!)/i've got you under my skin

Release date: November 1993.
Catalogue number: IS 578
Producer: Flood, Brian Eno & The Edge/Phil Ramone
Tracks: 7-inch & Cass: Double A side: Stay (Faraway So Close!)/I've Got You Under My Skin (by Frank Sinatra and Bono); CD: Lemon remixes by Dave Morales and Paul Oakenfold.
Highest Chart Position: No. 4

hold me, thrill me, kiss me, kill me

Release date: June 1995
Catalogue number: A7131CD
Producer: Nellee Hooper, Bono & The Edge
Tracks: 7-inch & Cass: Hold Me, Thrill Me, Kiss Me, Kill Me/Theme from *Batman Forever* by Eliot Goldenthal; CD: Hold Me, Thrill Me, Kiss Me, Kill Me/Theme from *Batman Forever* by Eliot Goldenthal/ Tell Me Now by Mazzy Star
Highest Chart Position: No. 3

discothèque

Release date: 3rd February 1997.
Catalogue number: CID649/854775-2 (CD)
CIDX649/854877-1 (Vinyl)
Producer: Flood.
Tracks: 'Discothèque'/'Holy Joe' Garage Mix/Holy Joe Guilty Mix.
'Second CD: Discothèque' DM Deep Club Mix/Howie B, Hairy B Mix/Hexidecimal Mix/DMTEC Radio Mix

staring at the sun

Release date: 14th April 1997.
Catalogue number: CID658/854975-2 (CD Single) CIDX658/854973-2 (CD Maxi)
Producers: Flood
Additional Production: Steve Osborne.
Tracks: 'Staring At The Sun'/'North And South Of The River'/'Your Blue Room'

last night on earth

Release date: July 1997
Catalogue number: CID 664/572 051-2
Producer: Flood
Tracks CD1: Last Night on Earth (single mix)/ Pop Muzik (PopMart Mix/ Happiness is a Warm Gun (The Gun Mix)
CD2: Last Night on Earth (First Night In Hell Mix)/ Numb (The Soul Assassins Mix)/ Happiness is a Warm Gun (The Danny Saber Mix)/ Pop Muzik (Pop Mart Mix)
Cassette: Last Night on Earth (single mix)/ Pop Muzik (PopMart Mix)
Highest chart position: No.10

please

Release date: September 1997
Catalogue number: CID 673/572129-2
Producer: Howie B
Tracks CD1: Please (single version) / Dirty Day (Junk Day Mix) / Dirty Day (Bitter Kiss Mix) / I'm Not Your Baby (Skysplitter Dub Mix)
CD2 (PopHeart EP): Please (live from Rotterdam) / Where the Streets Have No Name (live from Rotterdam) / With or Without You (live from Edmonton) / Staring at the Sun (live from Rotterdam)
Cassette: Please (single version) / Dirty Day (Junk Day Mix)
Highest chart position: No. 7

if god will send his angels

Release date: December 1997
Catalogue number: CID 684/572189-2
Producer: Flood, Howie B, Steve Osbourne
Tracks CD1: If God Will Send His Angels (single version)/Slow Dancing/Two Shots of Happy, One Shot Of Sad/ Sunday Bloody Sunday(live from Sarajevo)
CD2: MoFo (Phunk Phorce Mix)/MoFo (Mother's Mix)/If God Will Send His Angels (Big Yam Mix)
Cassette: If God Will Send His Angels (single version)/MoFo (Romin Remix)
Highest chart position: No.12

sweetest thing

Release date: November 2 1998
Catalogue number: CID 727 572 466-2
Producer: Steve Lillywhite with Daniel Lanois and Brian Eno
Tracks CD1: Sweetest Thing/Twilight (live from Red Rocks, 1983)/An Cat Dubh(live from Red Rocks, 1983)
CD2: Sweetest Thing/Stories For Boys (live from Boston 1981)/Out Of Control (live from Boston, 1981)
Cassette: Sweetest Thing/Out Of Control (live from Boston, 1981)
Highest chart position: No.3

the ground beneath her feet

Release date: October 1999
Catalogue number: GROUNDCD1
Producers: Daniel Lanois and Brian Eno
Lyrics by Salman Rushdie
Tracks CD: Promo release only. The Ground Beneath Her Feet/Million Dollar Hotel Movie Trailer

beautiful day

Release date: October 2000
Catalogue number: CID766/562 945-2
Producers: Daniel Lanois and Brian Eno
Tracks CD1: Beautiful Day/Summer Rain/Always
CD2: Beautiful Day/Discothèque (Live from Mexico City)/If You Wear That Velvet Dress (Live from Mexico City)
Cassette: Beautiful Day/Summer Rain
Highest chart position: No.1

stuck in a moment you can't get out of

Release date: January 29 2001
Catalogue number: CIDX770/572779-2
Producers: Daniel Lanois and Brian Eno
Tracks CD1: Stuck in a Moment You Can't Get Out Of/ Beautiful Day (live at Farmclub)/New York (live at Farmclub)
CD2: Stuck in a Moment You Can't

Get Out Of/ Big Girls are Best/ Beautiful Day (remix by Quincy & Sonance)
Highest chart position: No.2

electrical storm

Release date: October 2002
Catalogue number: 0639092
Producer: William Orbit
Tracks: Electrical Storm/New York (Nice Mix)/New York (Nasty Mix) / Live medley of Bad, 40 and Streets (Recorded live at the Elevation tour in Boston) / Electrical Storm (William Orbit Mix)
Highest chart position: No. 5

vertigo

Release date: November 2004
Catalogue number: CID878
Producer: Steve Lillywhite
Tracks: Vertigo/Are You Gonna Wait Forever/ Vertigo /Jacknife Lee /Neon Lights
Highest chart position: No.1

sometimes you can't make it on your own

Release date: February 2005
Catalogue number: CID886
Producer: Chris Thomas
Tracks: Sometimes You Can't Make It On Your Own/Fast Cars - Jacknife Lee Vertigo - Redanka Remix/Ave Maria - Jacknife Lee Mix / Vertigo - Trent Reznor Remix
Highest chart position: No.1

index

ACKNOWLEDGEMENTS

The publishers would like to thank the following sources for their kind permission to reproduce the pictures in this book:

All Action/Tony Kelly, Jim Steele; **Camera Press**; Photography by Anton Corbijn ©U2 Limited; **Corbis-Bettmann**, Everett, Reuter, UPI; **Greg Evans International**; **Mary Evans Picture Library**; **Caroline Forbes**; **Getty Images**/Carlo Allegri, Dave Hogan, Dave Hogan/distributed by Getty Images on behalf of the Band Aid Charitable Trust; **Amy Garvey**/Hugo McGuinness; Photography by **Anja Grabert** ©U2 Limited; **Colm Henry**; **Hot Press**; **Hulton Getty**; **London Features International**/Adrian Boot, Andy Catlin, Kevin Cummins, Nick Elgar, Steve Granitz, Gie Knaeps, Colin Mason, Kevin Mazur, Andy Phillips, Derek Ridgers, Tom Sheehan, Van Tine; **Mansell Collection**; **Pacemaker Press**; **Pictorial Press**/Patrick Lyttle, Jeffrey Mayer, William Rutten; **Barry Plummer**; **Popperfoto**; **Redferns**/GEMS, Fin Costello, Bob King, Hayley Madden, David Redfern, Kerstin Rodgers, Ebet Roberts, Barbara Steinwehe, Bob Willoughby; **Retna Pictures**/Stephen L Davis, Steve Double, Photofest, Clements Rikken, Paul Slattery, David Tonge, Theodore Wood; **Rex Features**/P Bertini, Andre Csillag, Kamenko Pajic, PF/Keystone USA, Simon Roberts, SIPA, Jacques Witt; **S.I.N**/Peter Anderson, David Corio, Hayley Madden, Kieron Murphy,Illpo Musto, Katia Natola, Ian Tilton, Virginia Turbett; Photography by **Stephane Sednaoui** ©Stephane Sednaoui.

Special thanks are due to Colm Henry.

Every effort has been made to acknowledge correctly and contact the source and/or copyright holder of each picture, and Carlton Books Limited apologises for any unintentional errors or omissions which will be corrected in future editions of this book.